1983.

Daddy,

a very happy Ch

Lots of Love

Julia x .

THE AMERICA'S CUP
1851~1983

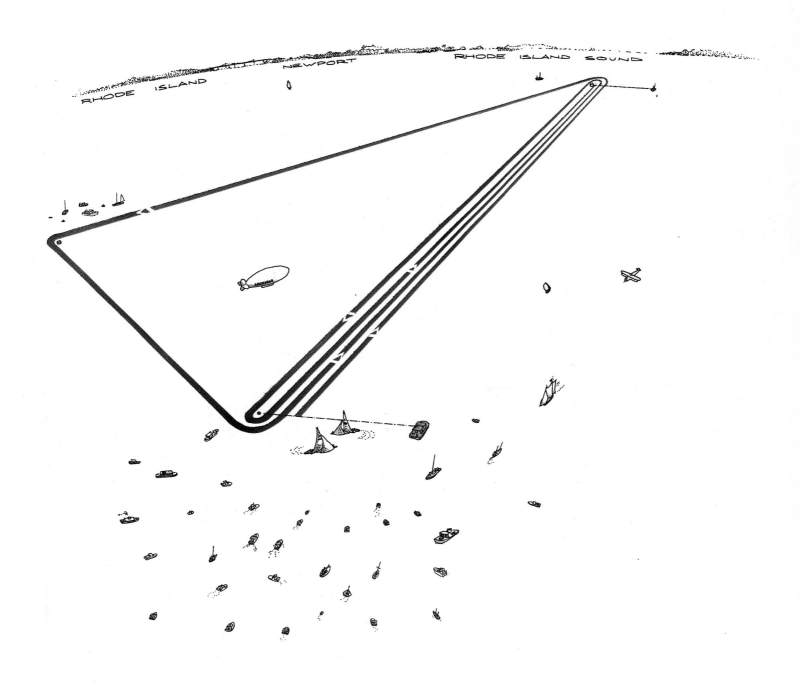

First published in Great Britain by
Pelham Books Ltd
44 Bedford Square
London WC1B 3DU
1983
© 1983 by Overseas s.r.l.
via Moscova 27
20121 Milano (Italy)

Historical section
Copyright © 1983
John Rousmaniere

Written by John Rousmaniere
Articles for the 1983 challenges were written by: Jonathan
Eastland (Great Britain), Thierry Rannou (France), Bob Ross
(Australia), Jack A. Somer (United States of America), Richard
Holmes (Canada), Fabio Ratti-Riccardo Villarosa (Italy). The
article on the rating rules was written by Nicola Sironi while that
covering the elimination trials is by Jack A. Somer and the 1983
challenge is by Jonathan Eastland.
Art direction: Giorgio d'Andrea
Associate designer: Carlotta Maderna
Editor: Clive Foster

British Library Cataloguing in Publication Data

Rousmaniere, John
America's Cup 1851-1983
1. America's Cup races - History
I. Title
797.1'4 GV829

ISBN 0-7207-1503-2

Printed by Grafiche Editoriali Padane, Cremona, Italy.
Color Separations by Cooperativa San Patrignano, Rimini, Italy.

THE AMERICA'S CUP 1851-1983

John Rousmaniere

PELHAM
BOOKS

Contents

The Rating Rules

	L.O.A.	L.W.L.	S.A.	
America	101'9''	96'6''	5263	sq. ft.
Reliance	143'8''	89'8''	16,159	sq. ft.
Ranger	135'2''	87'	7546	sq. ft.
Columbia	69'5''	45'5''	1846	sq. ft.

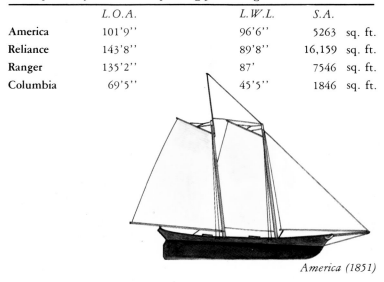

America (1851)

Even though a handicap system to allow boats of different dimensions to race together on equal terms was looked into as far back as 1826, the Hundred Guinea Cup won by the schooner *America* was run on elapsed time. Only with the first challenge of 1870 was a rule, known as the waterline area, introduced. In practice, the waterline section area was measured and, using the data obtained, a correction of a certain number of seconds/mile was attributed to be added to the elapsed time taken to complete the course.

The following year the rules were modified and a formula was adopted which took into account the displacement when assigning the correction in seconds/mile. *Columbia*, the American defender chosen to race against *Livonia*, was lighter and had therefore a handicap in her favor. With the lack of wind in the first races she met with no problems and won both on elapsed time and on handicap. The English, however, won the third race and the Americans immediately opted for a heavier boat, *Sappho*, which won the last two races.

In the following challenge, five years later, the rating rules were once again modified. The displacement measurement was changed to the gross tonnage measure, which is used still today to determine the capacity of merchant vessels. Measurements were made in cubic feet of the capacity inside the boat, from the waterline to the interior of the keel, in three sections: one at midships (A1) and the other two (A2, A3) at one quarter and at three-quarters of the length from the stern (L). The corrected time calculated in seconds/mile was derived from the formula:

$$\sqrt[3]{\frac{(A1 + A2 + A3) \times L}{4}}$$

The false-keel of the boat was not included in the sum and, for this reason, boats with a relatively flat bottom with an external fin keel were at an advantage. This formula was applied in the challenges of 1876 and 1881.

In 1882 the deed of gift was slightly modified: it required that the challenger be built in the challenging nation and that the measurements had to be communicated to the New York Yacht Club at the moment of the challenge being made; they could be modified at a later stage, but only if made smaller. This allowed the Americans to build a larger boat than the challengers. The rules were modernized with the introduction of the sail area (S): $\dfrac{L \times S}{4000}$ = rating in sailing tons.

The sum obtained was then used to determine the handicap according to the regular seconds/mile tables. The rules worked well and were kept for nine challenges of the America's Cup, over a period of almost twenty years. Moreover, this did prove somewhat indulgent since no consideration was made of overhangs, nor of draft, nor of displacement and this allowed designers of the period to study the possibilities of some very interesting boats. In particular Nat Herreshoff produced very pure forms of keel, with an extremely reduced waterline length and enormous tapered overhangs which considerably increased the potential speed of the boat. A classic example of this type of boat was *Reliance*, the greatest of all those built for the America's Cup. Her waterline length was near the limit imposed by the deed of gift, but full length out of water was almost double.

After the challenge of 1903, in which *Reliance* beat Sir Thomas Lipton's third *Shamrock*, it was decided to take steps to stop this unbridled growth which proved extremely dangerous for the crew.

In the early years of this century a New York committee, which included Nat Herreshoff, devised a more perfected formula which took overhangs and displacement into account, and which was adopted as the Universal Rule. With the new rules the length taken into consideration was no longer the waterline but a length measured at a quarter of the maximum beam amidships and at a tenth of the width above the waterline. In this way overhangs and the shape of the hull were taken into account a little above the waterline to measure the effective dynamic length when the boat was sailing and not

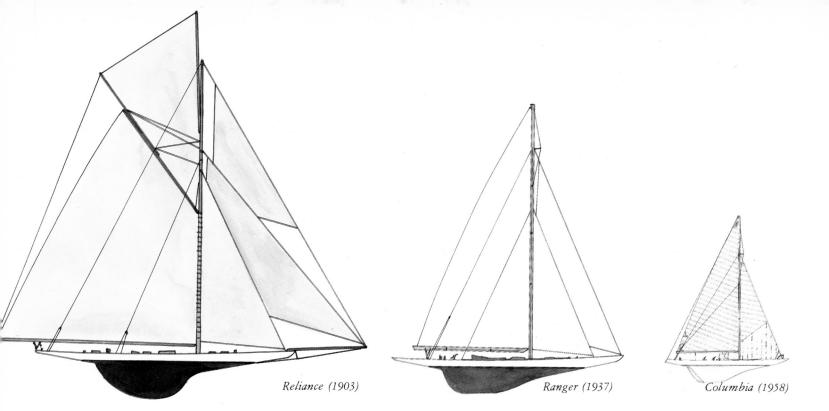

Reliance (1903) *Ranger (1937)* *Columbia (1958)*

only when static. The length measured in this way was multiplied by the square root of the sail surface area and divided by the cube root of the displacement:

$$L \times \sqrt{\frac{S}{\sqrt[3]{D}}}$$

The result gave the rating used to calculate the handicap from the tables. In the 1920 challenge the new rules were used and Lipton managed to win two races, the only ones in thirty years of challenging. During the series the boats could be ballasted or lightened, thus changing their rating according to weather conditions.

Ten years later, in 1930, the handicap rule was abandoned and the J class of Universal Rule was adopted for the America's Cup races. The rating was of 76 feet calculated by the formula already introduced in 1920; a displacement limit was also brought in.

After the war, the New York Yacht Club decided to modify the deed of gift so as to give the cup breathing space. It was decided to adopt the 12-Meter International Rule. This type of rule had been developed in the first years of the century by the Royal Yachting Association in England and William Froude, one of the greatest hydrodynamic theorists, had taken part in the studies. The International Rule, effective since 1906, had given good results in the period between the two wars, above all in the smaller classes, 6 and 8-Meters, which were also Olympic classes. The formula took into account the length (L), the sail area (S) and a girth measurement difference (2d) which measures how much the maximum beam section differs from a certain standard.

The formula was: $\dfrac{L + \sqrt{S} + 2d - F}{2.37}$

As opposed to the Universal Rule, displacement was not controlled completely but there was a limit under which it could not go. The same went for the length and draft, which were measured only to control whether they went above or below a certain limit. The formula of the International Rule is therefore very simple but at the same time demands millimetric precision in that it is necessary to remain within the limits without juggling the various measurements by combining them in a different way, above all in connection to displacement. Thanks to this strictness the formula has stood up well to the assaults of designers in search of loopholes.

The most substantial modification came about in 1974. In that year both the 12-Meters had a number of openings on deck for weight reduction purposes, and this made them somewhat unsafe in a rough sea. For this reason rules were introduced as regards the number and maximum dimensions of the openings on deck.

In 1980 further modifications were introduced: the first dealt with the "bendy" masts used first by the English and then by the Australians in the previous challenge. This type of mast allows a larger mainsail area which is not "taxed" for rule purposes. For this reason the width of the mainsail at various heights was limited and in this way "bendy" masts disappeared. The second modification concerned the height of the freeboard. *Freedom*, the 1980 defender, rode very low on the water offering less resistance to the wind and lowering the boat's center of gravity. To eliminate this advantage, which was to the detriment of safety, the penalty for low freeboards was increased.

This year the Australians under Alan Bond appeared with a very special keel fitted with two foils, hidden well out of sight. The boat has proved very fast and it is therefore probable that the question will be discussed at the November meetings of the IYRU, either to prohibit or penalize the system in some way or other.

FROM SCHOONERS TO J-CLASS

Large crews race under clouds of canvas.
Throughout the "Belle Epoque", the Great War, the Wall Street
crash and prohibition the America's Cup was firmly
held by the New York Yacht Club. It all
began with a race in the United Kingdom under the eyes
of a still young Queen Victoria.

1851
The Hundred Guinea Cup

The men who won the cup called America's were sons of the Industrial Revolution, and their slippery schooner was as much a product of that fantastic era of invention as the steamboats and locomotives whose profits created the pastime of yachting. Without the smoking factories and slag heaps of the early nineteenth century, without the competition for new markets, without the sensitivity to forces and power and how things worked that grew from generation to generation, such modern concepts as leisure and sport might never have been born. And without money, free time, and competition, there would be no America's Cup sailing as we know it.

On both sides of the Atlantic, tough, cunning men with engineering insight and an intuition for new ideas made their fortunes and, exhausted, died and left them to their more relaxed sons. Besides the money, the heirs inherited their fathers' distaste for losing, but with the confidence that comes with second generation wealth they spread their competitiveness around. The result was the invention of modern sports. Football, baseball, tennis, and golf all became popular in the first half of the nineteenth century, as did the "blood sports" of boxing and hunting that, as William Cobbett proclaimed, "tend to make the people bold, they produce a communication of notions of hardihood." Yacht racing lay somewhere in between. After an intentional collision and the resulting brawl confused the finishing order of a race in 1829, the Royal Yacht Squadron committee awarded the trophy to one boat on the grounds that "the use of axes in the cutting away of rigging was unjustifiable". The same intensity surfaced in wagers. These men would bet small fortunes on yacht races, horse races, on who would next walk through a door. In the 1830's, some £50,000 (perhaps more than $1 million today) changed hands after a 224 mile race in the English Channel.

The heroes of the new aristocracy were rich amateur athletes who could wager, sail, shoot, and ride with equal skill. The sportsman-soldier Marquis of Anglesey has been described as "typical of his generation: hard-living, hard-riding, and hard-swearing, and yet kind-hearted and extremely hospitable". The same might be said of many in the America's Cup history, especially the man who started all the commotion in 1851, John Cox Stevens, principal owner of *America*.

Stevens was a grandson of a member of the Continental Congress and son of a Revolutionary War colonel turned entrepreneur. Colonel John Stevens, of Hoboken, New Jersey, and his sons were responsible for a number of inventive firsts that created the fortune that built the schooner. The colonel owned the first steam ferry that crossed the Hudson and developed the first ferry service to Philadelphia. Son Robert invented a bomb that could be shot from a cannon and the T-shaped railroad track. Son John Cox steered the first propeller-driven boat in 1804, when he was nineteen, and later with his brothers developed steam gunboats and ran a highly profitable steamship line up the Hudson River. In addition, their father owned all of Hoboken, New Jersey, where they developed a town, an amusement park, and a seaport. In modern terms, the Stevens family was a bloodline conglomerate.

As the brothers prospered, they learned how to enjoy their wealth. In 1823, before an intersectional match race for stakes of $20,000 between their horse Eclipse and the Southern champion Sir Henry, they bet all their cash and then threw their pocket watches and diamond stick pins onto the pile. Eclipse won by a nose, and John Cox later became president of the prestigious Jockey Club.

Moreover, of course, the Stevens brothers sailed, especially John Cox, who built a succession of ever larger boats to race on New York's then pristine harbor. He was fascinated by the mechanics of sailing and, at one time or another, experimented with a catamaran (called *Double Trouble*), with moveable ballast, and with centerboards and leeboards. He spent an estimated $100,000 on modifications to his 110 foot centerboard sloop *Maria*, which his brother Robert originally designed. She may have been one of the first boats to carry outside lead ballast, smeared like paint over her bottom. Her main boom was almost as long as her hull. *Maria* was called an "out-and-outer" — a racing machine in our parlance — because she was an out-and-out speed demon of a boat not fit for the open sea. Periodically, Stevens would race her against a yacht sailed down from Boston, for high stakes and in a blizzard of publicity. More often than not, *Maria* would break down and lose, leaving Stevens to try to justify her design in long, emotional letters to Boston and New York newspapers.

A reproduction of the schooner America, *destroyed in the collapse of a shed in 1943,*
built in 1966 by Rudolph Schaefer, the American beer magnate. She now belongs to an Argentinian.

The old New York Yacht Club, which was once at Hoboken in New Jersey. After various "moves" the wooden building now stands in the Mystic Seaport Museum in Connecticut.

It was all very challenging, and before too long enough people shared his passion to join him in a club that, like the Jockey Club, would soon come to dominate its sport. At 5 p.m. on Tuesday, July 30, 1844, Stevens and eight friends assembled in his 51 foot schooner *Gimcrack* and formed the New York Yacht Club — the third organization of its type in the United States and the fifth in the world. The first commodore was Stevens himself, "that prince of good fellows" his friend Philip Hone called him in his diary. Three days later, the fleet sailed East on the first New York Yacht Club cruise and off Newport, Rhode Island, ("a tolerably dull place of sojournment" according to Hone) they raced with some boats that had come down from Boston, one of them owned by a shipping tycoon named Forbes (a name we shall read again).

Always in the air in those early days of yachting were interregional and international challenges like the one that had matched Eclipse and Sir Henry on the track. Boston and New York were natural sources of these bluffs and threats, as Bostonians struggled to balance the loss of religious and economic hegemony over the United States to the rapidly rising seaport to its South by gaining some leverage in other areas, such as culture and yachting. Meanwhile, an English yachtsman would sometimes float a challenge that would receive considerable publicity and no takers. In 1835, the Marquis of Waterford — a sportsman who practiced for the hunt by shooting out the eyes of the family portraits hanging in his castle — appeared in New York in his schooner *Gem*. No races resulted, but there was a wild dinner that was broken up by the police. Two years later, Joseph Weld, like Waterford a member of the Royal Yacht Squadron, bet the world at large that his big cutter *Alarm* would win a two out of three match against

any yacht. Although there was talk of sending Stevens' out-and-outer *Wave* across, nothing came of it. English and American yachts finally knocked heads in 1849 in Bermuda, the American *Brenda* nipping the English *Pearl* by 55 seconds. The rest of the time, logistics and interminable haggling about whether the Americans could or could not use their centerboards got in the way.

By 1850, certain forces were at work that made such a trans-Atlantic challenge inevitable. First, American nationalism had reached an apex of intensity. The United States had just taken Texas, New Mexico, and California from Mexico in a short war, and there was talk of building an interoceanic canal through Nicaragua — talk that was increasing tensions with Great Britain. Americans seemed capable of accomplishing anything: American clippers were dominating the tea trade between China and Britain; American inventors had produced the telegraph, the sewing machine, the rotary printing press, and the safety pin; and American railroad mileage (over Robert Stevens' tracks) had increased by seven thousand miles since 1840. Soon, American manufactured goods would be worth more than agricultural products — an idea as startling to most people in 1850 as the reverse would seem to us today. Moreover, New York had become the nation's financial capital, thanks greatly to the work of the Stevens family. Its population of half a million was nine times what it had been at the turn of the century, two and a half times that of 1830. The economy was booming and Commodore John Cox Stevens, wealthier than ever, rode high. In 1849, he built a Greek Revival town house that he called a palace. "The house is, indeed, a palace", Philip Hone reported in his diary. "The Palais Bourbon in Paris, Buckingham Palace in London, and Sans-Souci at Berlin are little grander than this residence of a simple citizen of our republican city, a steamboat builder and proprietor; but a mighty good fellow and a most hospitable host, as all who know him will testify".

Sometime in 1850, this simple citizen and mighty good fellow decided to build a yacht and sail her to England to show off American shipbuilding at the time of the Great Exhibition of 1851. Although he certainly could have afforded to do it alone, Stevens gathered a small syndicate of five friends around him, no doubt to minimize his risk should the boat be unsuccessful, but also because he was an affable man who enjoyed company.

Not surprisingly, he asked one of his brothers to join him. This was Edwin A. Stevens, yet another inventor and steamship promoter, who later would be the yacht club's third commodore and found the Stevens Institute of Technology in Hoboken, where, a century or so later, a sophisticated model towing tank would become an important tool in designing America's Cup defenders. Another syndicate member was Vice-Commodore Hamilton Wilkes, son of a president of the Bank of New York and, like John Cox Stevens, both a horseman and a

The schooner America *close-hauled; note her characteristic round cockpit.*
This boat beat the English thanks also to her cotton sails, which were cut better than the
flax ones of her opponents.

yachtsman. John K. Beekman Finlay joined the syndicate out of friendship for the others and patriotic fever; he lived in upstate New York and knew little about sailing.

The remaining members of the syndicate were in some ways the most interesting of the six. James Hamilton was the third son of Alexander Hamilton, the remarkable West Indies born politician who more than any other of the Founding Fathers was responsible for the strong federal government that gradually united the former colonies after the American Revolution. His controversial, productive life ended in 1804 when Aaron Burr, the Vice-President of the United States, killed him in a duel. Young Hamilton was also a politician — ''facile, smooth tongued, and ambitious'', according to one biographer. He first opposed his father's pro-business policies and helped get Andrew Jackson elected President. Later he served briefly as Secretary of State before leaving the Democratic Party and sliding over to

the Whigs, who were usually more loyal to Federalist principles. The remaining member, George L. Schuyler, was thrice related to James Hamilton, whose mother was a Schuyler and whose daughters married George — the first one when he was a bachelor, the second when he was a widower. Grandson of a famous Revolutionary War general and heir to one of the great colonial fortunes, George Schuyler developed steamship lines and wrote history. Only 39, he was the youngest member of the syndicate. He outlived all the others and, as we shall see, had a lot to do with getting Cup matches off on a sound footing.

It was Schuyler who dealt with the builder, William H. Brown, who promised that for the steep price of $30,000 he would build ''in the best manner'' a yacht ''faster than any vessel in the United States brought to compete with her'' on penalty of her being handed back if she failed a trial. While Brown's credentials were noteworthy, the syndicate went to him primarily

13

because his house designer, George Steers, was responsible for the fastest pilot boats in New York. He had designed some boats for the Stevens brothers, including *Gimcrack*, and now at the ripe age of thirty was handed the best job an ambitious young naval architect could hope for: to design the fastest possible yacht for the richest and best possible sailors. As the new schooner rose in her stocks on the Manhattan bank of the East River, at 12th Street, during the bitterly cold winter of 1851, all who visited could see that Steers had taken a step or two beyond even his most radical pilot boats. For years he had worked away from the traditional "cod's head and mackerel tail" bluff-bowed and sharp-sterned shape inherited from England, and his most recent pilot boat, the *Mary Taylor*, had shown a long, sharp bow and a broad stern. *America* (as the yacht was inevitably named) went further. From above, her forward sections seemed to form a huge arrowhead, its sides slightly hollowed out and culminating in a clipper bow. Her widest beam was well aft, and the lines from there back to her sharply-raked transom were smooth and powerful. Instead of the centerboard often found in New York yachts, she had a deep, sharply raked keel. From the side, she was dainty forward and massive aft, as though she were two boats oddly mated. Mounting the hull were two steeply raked masts that would carry sails made of Colt's Cotton Duck, woven across the Hudson in Paterson, New Jersey, and much less stretchy than traditional English flax. Her dimensions probably were 102 feet length overall, 89 feet length waterline, 22 feet 6 inches beam, 11 feet draft, 170 tons displacement, and 5,263 square feet sail area (jib, foresail, and mainsail). Sources disagree slightly on these dimensions, possibly because each measured her in different trim.

Like most boats, *America* was launched late. In her trials against *Maria*, she impressed many observers as being at least as fast as that out-and-outer, which carried half again her sail area on a 95 foot boom and immense bowsprit and was nowhere near as fit for going to sea. But John Cox Stevens argued strenuously in letters to newspapers that *Maria* had suffered from poor handling and damage, and *America* was the inferior yacht — a claim that, calculated or not, earned a thirty-three percent discount from the builder, so the syndicate got *America* for only $20,000. On June 21 she was towed out into New York Harbor and got under sail under the command of Captain Dick Brown, a respected pilot-boat skipper. None of her owners was aboard.

Twenty days later, she dropped anchor in Le Havre, France, after averaging 6.6 knots — perfectly respectable considering that she was under short canvas and not pushed hard. There she was spruced up and painted and her racing sails were bent on, and there, too, the Stevens brothers and James Hamilton came aboard, their ears still red from lectures imposed on them by Americans in Paris. Horace Greeley, the editor of the *New York Tribune* (and, twenty years later, an unsuccessful can-

Above: John Cox Stevens, founder of the New York Yacht Club, an expert sailor and promoter of the syndicate which financed the building of America.
On the opposite page: the 53 mile long course of the historical race held on August 22 1851 around the Isle of Wight, beginning and ending at Cowes.

didate for the Presidency), warned Hamilton, "The eyes of the world are on you. You will be beaten, and the country will be abused". He told Hamilton not to return to the United States if *America* lost.

Now fully aware their voyage had major international implications, *America*'s crew set sail for Cowes, on England's Isle of Wight, and headquarters of the Royal Yacht Squadron. Back in February the Squadron's commodore, the Earl of Wilton, had written to offer the squadron's facilities, and though the letter had said nothing about racing, Stevens knew that if *America* was to find competition it would lie in the roadstead of Cowes. And as commodore of the infant New York Yacht Club, he was drawn to the great 36-year-old Squadron like an iron filing to a magnet. After crossing the Channel, *America* became befogged in a calm and anchored for the night.

As they got under way the next morning, July 30, a racing cutter, *Lavrock*, sailed out to them from Cowes,

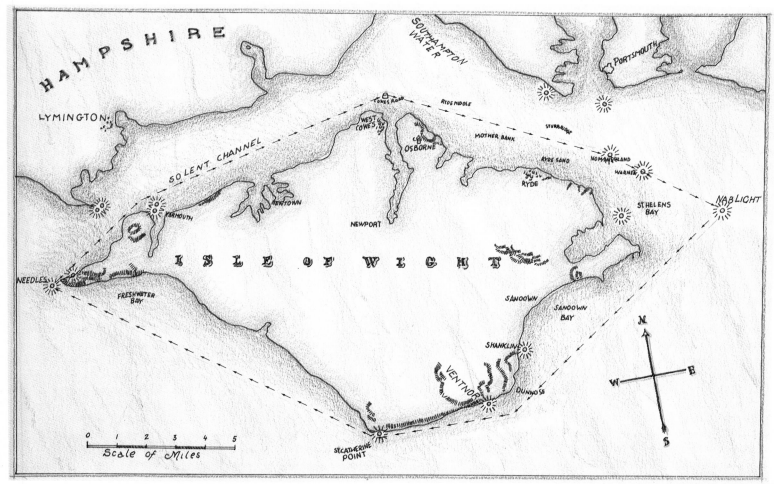

towing a dinghy. *Lavrock* jogged around as *America* gathered speed in the light wind, and then turned to lead her to the harbor. Stevens interpreted this as a challenge; so, too, did hundreds of curious Englishmen gathering on the shore. "After waiting until we were ashamed to wait longer", Stevens later wrote, "we let her go about two hundred yards ahead, and then started in her wake". As Dick Brown hunched in *America*'s round cockpit, her long tiller under his arm, Stevens' heart pounded with a dread greater than what he had felt when he bet his fortune on *Eclipse* in the race with Sir Henry thirty years earlier. The schooner slowly edged to windward of the cutter's wake, slipped by her, and beat her to Cowes by one-third of a mile after five miles of sailing. "The crisis was past", Stevens would remember, "and some dozen of deep-drawn sighs proved that the agony was over".

Minutes after the jubilant crew dropped anchor and doused sails, a welcoming party led by the Earl of Wilton came aboard to make good on the promise of hospitality. In this group was the crusty 83-year-old Marquis of Anglesey (who was also the Earl of Uxbridge), that paragon of sportsmen praised earlier. He had lost a leg at the battle of Waterloo and had clumped around on deck with a wooden leg for four decades. He was soon stretched out on the bowsprit gazing at *America*'s sharp bow and muttering, "If she is right, then all of us are wrong".

Perhaps shy, but more likely intimidated by her performance against *Lavrock* and her piratical looks ("a suspicious-looking craft", warned one newspaper), every yachtsman refused to challenge *America* to a race. The nearby Royal Victoria Yacht Club would not allow her to enter its annual regatta because she was owned not by a single gentleman but by a business-like syndicate. Flustered by the prospect of finding no action after going to all that trouble to build his yacht and sail her over, Stevens shocked everybody by offering to sail against any Squadron yacht over a twenty-to-seventy mile course for the astronomical stakes of £10,000 — at $50,000 more than double the cost of *America* and maybe half a million dollars in today's currency. Nobody picked up that pricey gauntlet, but Stevens did succeed in winning the support of the English newspapers. The dignified *Times* compared English yachtsmen to a flock of pigeons paralyzed by fear at the sight of a hawk, and questioned their "pith and courage" and their dedication to "our national naval spirit".

All this touched a tender nerve at the Squadron, whose members were the only yachtsmen privileged to fly the white naval ensign. *America* was invited to sail in their annual race around the Isle of Wight, the prize to be an "ordinary" silver bottomless ewer that was 27 inches in height and weighed 134 ounces. It was called the Hundred Guinea Cup because that is what the London

15

firm of R. and S. Gerard charged for it. (The fiction that it was presented by Queen Victoria was created, probably accidentally, by John Cox Stevens.) Stevens would have preferred a match for prize money, but by the time one was finally arranged with an old family friend and fellow railroad tycoon, Robert Stephenson, it was too late to back out of the other contest, scheduled for August 22.

However, before then, *America*'s confidence was rent by disharmony. Feeling left out of things in Cowes, whose rigid class-consciousness had been embraced by Stevens, George Steers, her designer, and his brother and a nephew packed up and left on the 18th. Besides the social tensions, the Steers brothers were irked by Stevens' nagging about all the rum that had somehow disappeared during the trans-Atlantic passage. Fortunately, James' other son, fifteen-year-old Henry Steers, decided to stay, so *America*'s brilliant designer was represented at least symbolically in the famous race for the Hundred Guinea Cup.

The English may have been slow to take up Stevens' challenge, but they did what they could to aid the visitors. A local shipbuilder, George Ratsey, built a jib boom to help her speed off the wind.

The Squadron graciously exempted *America* from meeting three of its rules: her crew could use poles to ''boom out'' her sails on a run before the wind, since her steeply raked masts kept the sails from swinging out naturally when the wind was light; she could be entered by her syndicate and not, as was customary, by an individual owner; and she could withdraw from the race if the wind dropped below 6 knots — even by English standards her sail area seemed much too small for calm weather.

Meanwhile, the American consul at nearby Portsmouth had hired a local pilot to navigate *America* around the Isle of Wight's dangerous shoals.

Above: George Steers, the designer of English origin, who designed America, *which was built at the yard of William H. Brown in New York.*
Below: A picture from the end of last century at Cowes on the Isle of Wight. On the left can be seen the Gloster Hotel which was the headquarters of the Royal Yacht Squadron before it moved to Cowes Castle, at the end of the promenade.

When the starting gun fired at 10 a.m., *America's* crew was slow weighing anchor and getting under way from the standing start, perhaps intentionally so she would start clear of her fourteen English competitors. In any case, she was soon running fast with boomed out sails in the light West wind, dodging a large steamer packed with spectators, and working her way up through the fleet, which while not exactly clearing a thoroughfare for the overtaking Yankee did not unfairly obstruct her, either. She took the lead after an hour and a half and never lost it thereafter. At 3:30 p.m., half-way around the fifty-three-mile course, she had a lead of two and a half miles. Two hours later she stretched it to seven miles after a beat to windward in fresh wind. She finally finished off Cowes at 8:30 in a dying breeze. Although myth has it that Queen Victoria, who was watching from the royal yacht *Victoria and Albert*, was told, "Madam, there is no second", there was a runner-up — and a close one at that. The cutter *Aurora*, smallest boat in the fleet, finished somewhere between eight and twenty-four minutes later (the squadron committee was, understandably, distracted by *America's* marvelous performance and did not time *Aurora's* finish reliably) and might have won the race if it had been sailed on handicap.

How did *America* do it? First of all, she was not unlucky. One set of race instructions required the fleet to round the Nab Light Vessel; another said nothing about it. *America* was given the second set of instructions and saved a couple of miles — but so, too, did some English competitors. And three of the English boats dropped out of the race due to a series of mishaps: one lost her bowsprit in a collision with another boat; another ran aground; and Joseph Weld's great *Alarm* went to the aid of the stranded boat. But *America* had also lost a quarter of an hour when the brand-new jib boom broke about half-way around the island.

But good luck (or the absence of extreme bad luck) is only part of the explanation. She was well-sailed by Dick Brown and his eighteen-man crew, and safely piloted by the Englishman, Robert Underwood, who aimed her away from both shoals and strong head currents. Most important, *America* was *fast* even in the light airs that John Cox Stevens so greatly feared. As an Englishman put it to an American spectator, "That boat of yours is a wonderful creature — she beats us going large or to windward, and when the breeze died out the other day, she actually *out-drifted* us". Her carefully-cut duck sails held their shape better than the hosts' flax sails, which had to be wetted down with buckets of water to reduce stretch, and her long, fine bow carved through the choppy Channel waters like a hot knife through soft cheese. So astonished was he by *America's* speed that the Marquis of Anglesey came back aboard, hoisted his aged body over the transom, and squinted in search of a propeller. Only a quick tackle of his good leg by Stevens kept him from getting a closer, wetter look at the

Commodore Stevens receiving Queen Victoria on board America. *She regularly spent her summer holidays at Osborne Castle at Cowes and watched part of the famous race in 1851.*

schooner's underbody. Finally conceding that the Yankees had not cheated, he sighed, "I've learned one thing: I've been sailing my yacht stern foremost for the last twenty years". Others were not so easily convinced that she was not a steam-driven, unseaworthy out-and-outer until they saw her hauled out or took a tour of her extremely comfortable interior.

One delightful visitor was Queen Victoria, who was less concerned about rule-beating than about cleanliness. She ran her handkerchief over a galley shelf and, when it came up dustless, had a gold sovereign issued to each crewmember and gave Dick Brown a gold watch. One of the unprovable myths about *America's* voyage of conquest is that Dick Brown asked Prince Albert to wipe off his feet before going below and, when the consort seemed not to obey orders, said, "I know who you are, but you'll have to wipe your feet".

Yet the race had considerably more significance than these anecdotes suggest. In the year of her glorious

Great Exhibition, England had been humbled in her natural element, the sea. ''We have had 'Britannia rules the waves' over our door for a long time'', admitted one Englishman, ''but I think we must now take down the sign''. Over in the former colonies, which needed every possible distraction from the looming issue of slavery, the news was greeted triumphantly. ''Like Jupiter among the Gods, America is first and there is no second'', proclaimed the golden-voiced orator and statesman Daniel Webster in a speech to the Massachusetts House of Representatives. Down in New York, the lawyer George Templeton Strong complained in his diary, ''Newspapers crowing over the victory of Stevens' yacht, which has beaten everything in the British seas. Quite creditable to Yankee ship-building, certainly, but not worth the intolerable, vainglorious vaporings that make every newspaper I take up now ridiculous. One would think yacht-building were the end of man's existence on earth''.

Like almost every defender of her cup, *America* won because she was technologically superior to her competition, because she was a little lucky, and because she was managed efficiently by a wealthy, ambitious syndicate uninterested in anything but winning. Just how unsentimental John Cox Stevens and his friends were is shown in *America*'s brief subsequent history under their ownership. On August 28, she beat Robert Stephenson's *Titania* by an hour in a forty-mile race sailed in a gale and won $500. Then, on September 1, only a month after her cautious arrival in Cowes and ten days after her glorious victory, Stevens & Co. sold her for £5,000, or $25,000, to Lord John de Blaquière, an Irish peer. They returned to New York with the bottomless silver pitcher in their arms and a $1,750 profit, after reckoning expenses, on their books. A fabulous welcoming dinner followed, with fabulous toasts: ''Our Modern Argonauts: They have brought home, not the Golden Fleece, but that which gold cannot buy, National Renown''. George Steers was not invited to the dinner, but Stevens ended the ensuing scandal by giving him full credit for *America*'s design. Steers became an extremely successful naval architect before being killed in a horse carriage accident in 1856, at the age of thirty-six. The syndicate's alumni were reduced to five when Hamilton Wilkes died in 1852 of consumption brought on, it was said, by too many visits to William Brown's uncovered shipyard while *America* was under construction. As New York raced into ever greater prosperity and the United States tumbled toward civil war, the five survivors passed the Hundred Guinea Cup from town house to town house and talked of perhaps melting it down into souvenir medals to pass out to their grandchildren. Soon the great race around the Isle of Wight settled into legends told in memoirs and around bottles of spirits in men's clubs, where romance and adventure always outlive unpleasant practicality.

Yacht	Class	Rating (tons)	Elapsed time	Owner
America	Schooner	170	10.37.00	Mr. J.C. Stevens, et al
Aurora	Cutter	47	10.45.00	Mr. Le Marchant
Bacchante	Cutter	80	12.07.00	Mr. B.H. Jones
Eclipse	Cutter	50	12.22.00	Mr. H.S. Feron
Brilliant	Schooner	392	15.57.00	Mr. G. Ackers
Beatrice	Schooner	161	Not timed	Sir W.P. Carew
Wyvern	Schooner	205	Not timed	The Duke of Marlborough
Ione	Schooner	75	Not timed	Mr. A. Hill
Constance	Schooner	218	Not timed	The Marquis of Conyngham
Gipsy Queen	Schooner	160	Not timed	Sir H.B. Hoghton
Mona	Cutter	82	Not timed	Lord A. Paget
Freak	Cutter	60	Not timed	Mr. W. Curling
Fernande	Schooner	127	Not timed	Major Martyn
Alarm	Cutter	193	Did not finish	Mr. J. Weld
Volante	Cutter	48	Did not finish	Mr. J.L. Cragie
Arrow	Cutter	84	Did not finish	Mr. T. Chamberlayne

Above: America *at Charleston in 1863. Below:* America *under sail photographed twenty years after her historic victory in 1851.*

19

1870
Magic-Cambria

Cambria was the first British challenger. James Ashbury, the owner, son of a mechanic, had made a fortune through the invention of a railway carriage.

Even as they considered melting the Hundred Guinea Cup down to make medallions, the men of *America* had something else in mind, a legacy more permanent and splendid. John Cox Stevens, who had resigned as commodore in 1855, died on June 10, 1857, and on July 8 the cup was turned over to the New York Yacht Club with a letter containing a two hundred and thirty-nine word deed of gift. We know that the deed was drafted at least five years earlier because it is signed by Hamilton Wilkes, who died in 1852, but we can only hazard a guess as to why the transaction was delayed. Very likely, the syndicate did not wish to give up the one object that symbolized their fellowship until they lost their leader and father figure.

The deed of gift established the trophy as "perpetually a Challenge Cup for friendly competition between foreign countries" and drew three firm guidelines. First, "matches" (the word is important) would be held officially between yacht clubs, not individuals or govern-

ments, and the winning club would take possession of the cup. Second, if the challenging and defending clubs could not come to mutual consent about the conditions for the match, it would be sailed over the course used in the defender's annual regatta. And third, the challenging club would give six months' notice and declare the size and rig of its yacht (presumably so the defender would be similar and the match would be close).

Having accepted the cup and deed of gift, the yacht club promised "a liberal, hearty welcome and the strictest fair play" in letters to eighteen British yacht clubs and other clubs in Canada, Belgium, the Netherlands, and Russia (where the St. Petersburg Yacht Club was attracting the richest young men in the country). No challenges were forthcoming for more than ten years. The main reason was the American Civil War, whose internecine battles (the casualty rate was thirteen times that of World War II) all but ended pleasure sailing in New York and had major international repercussions. Under different leadership, and without the calming influence of Prince Albert, Britain might well have entered the war and fought with the Confederacy, which supplied much of the cotton for her textile mills and food for her tables. As it was, British-built warships sank considerable Northern shipping, and the Union responded with criticism and out-and-out retaliation, at one stage seizing two Confederate officials from a British steamer, the *Trent*.

Representative of British pro-rebel activity was the sale of *America* to the Confederate States Navy by Henry E. Decie, of Plymouth. Her decade in Britain since the race for the Hundred Guinea Cup was anything but triumphant. She had raced a few times, once beating a Swedish near-copy named *Sverige* (in 1977, another *Sverige* was to appear in Newport to race for her Cup), had cruised to the Mediterranean, and, changing hands several times, ended up rotting at a mooring. On March 14, 1862, some Union sailors found her partly scuttled in Dunn's Creek, off Florida's St. John's River, her short life as a Confederate blockade runner ended. She became a Union dispatch vessel, was transferred to the United States Naval Academy as a training ship, and, in the late nineteenth century, had a colorful career as a racing schooner and symbol of national pride. She finally fell to pieces in 1942 when the snow-covered roof of the shed that protected her aging frames collapsed. Her long tiller now hangs in the front lobby of the New York Yacht Club, and shreds of her shattered planking are handed around and treasured like splinters of the cross. She will appear a few more times before this account ends, a floating memorial to the audacity and engineering skill of a handful of mid-nineteenth century Americans, a monument to nationalism, a celebration of fast sailing.

Peace, prosperity, and grand yachting returned after the war ended in 1865. The next year, three rich, young Americans bet $30,000 each on a race between their schooners to England — in December. In absolutely horrible conditions, six sailors were killed, but this first true ocean race re-established reasonably friendly communications between the American and English yachting establishments, even if the two governments were at each other's throats over reparations. A challenge for the Hundred Guinea Cup — also called the *America* Cup and the Queen's Cup — appeared imminent, but somehow, no English gentleman seemed interested.

A challenge finally surfaced, but it was not from the Royal Yacht Squadron. As would happen many times again in the Cup's history, the challenger was not a man of secure privilege but one of hungry ambition — some might call him a social climber. This eager outsider was one James Ashbury. Like Stevens, he had inherited and increased a fortune derived from transportation. His father had built an early railway carriage, and now as he expanded upon the resulting windfall profits young

Magic *in drydock. Born as a centerboard sloop in 1857 she was rigged as a schooner in 1869. Captain Comstock was the skipper in 1870.*

Ashbury hoped to leap the class boundaries prejudicial to the unschooled sons of wheelwrights. He desired particularly to be elected to Parliament. Following the example of many men on the other side of the wall, Ashbury commissioned a big schooner from the Ratseys of Cowes. Launched in 1868, *Cambria* soon whipped a visiting American yacht, *Sappho*, in a race around the Isle of Wight, and this encouraged Ashbury to write off to the New York Yacht Club offering to race one of its schooners to New York and then for the cup in a best of three series. He also announced that he would not race against a centerboarder because the Royal Yacht Squadron banned the type thinking it unfairly fast and unseaworthy.

The club turned him down because he had not challenged through a yacht club, as the deed of gift specified. There followed a year's thick, convoluted correspondence in which both sides gradually worked out the ground rules for a match, although the yacht club never did tell Ashbury their curious definition of the word: *Cambria* would race against not one yacht but the club's entire fleet of schooners, all thirty of them. Perhaps Ashbury was aware of this deception; if so, he had become so much a prisoner of his ambitions that he did not care. In the middle of this prolonged negotiation, he sailed to Egypt for the royalty-studded grand opening of the Suez Canal, through which *Cambria* was the first non-royal yacht to sail.

Only Commodore Henry G. Stebbins, a stock-broker and railroad official, voted against the defensive all-against-one format. The prevailing feeling in New York was that *Cambria* would have to take the cup just as *America* did, even though it meant a great deal more now than it had in 1851. Unfounded rumors about

English cheating during the Isle of Wight race further encouraged a spirit of vengeance. All this seemed justified when *Cambria* arrived in New York on July 27 the narrow winner of a close trans-Atlantic match race against Vice-Commodore James Gordon Bennett Jr.'s *Dauntless*.

The "match" was sailed on August 8, *Cambria* and seventeen New York Yacht Club schooners. Most were smaller than she, which in a large fleet in narrow New York Harbor was to their advantage. The course was packed with spectator boats; one newspaperman counted fifty-eight steamers, some carrying as many as three thousand passengers — all too many of them drunk to the gills and brawling over bets. Representing the Royal Thames Yacht Club, *Cambria* was assigned the favored position at the windward end of the line, but by the time the starting gun fired and the anchors were aweigh a wind shift had put her far to leeward. With her 12 feet of draft and huge sails, she was at a disadvantage anyway since she could not sail in shallow water or change tacks as well as the small centerboarders, one of which, *Magic* (at 84 feet some 20 feet shorter than *Cambria*), leapt to a quick lead that she never lost. As the yachts beat to windward through the Narrows off the club's new headquarters on Staten Island, they were followed by the immense spectator fleet. "New York emptied itself through the Narrows", a reporter wrote, "until the offing was like a crowded port with pillars of steam and glimmer of sails, and the shores of Staten Island were like swarming cities". The spectators were

especially attentive to *America*, racing under U.S. Navy command, which had become a symbol of indomitable patriotism. Yet when *Cambria* rounded the outer mark, the Sandy Hook light vessel, she was greeted by cheers and "God Save the Queen" played by a brass band on a spectator boat.

Never in contention, the English challenger finished a distant tenth after handicaps were computed, forty-two minutes behind *Magic* and fourteen behind fourth-place *America*. On the all-important first leg, she had been put about half a dozen times while on starboard tack by boats on port tack, and a collision damaged her topmast shrouds. Her foretopmast eventually broke and hit Ashbury a glancing blow. He did not protest, but Commodore Stebbins soon had a summary of the racing rules printed up and distributed to his squadron, many of whom barely knew starboard from port, much less that starboard tack had right of way. Owners then knew little about the rules, and their professional skippers did not care.

Ashbury took his defeat with surprisingly good grace. He sailed with some success on the New York Yacht Club Cruise (despite its name, a series of races between New England ports) and was rewarded for his good sportsmanship by being joined for breakfast aboard *Cambria* by President Ulysses S. Grant. Sometime during this brief honeymoon he commissioned a new schooner from the Ratseys and commenced his next campaign to win the cup, a campaign that would be a trial by battle for all concerned.

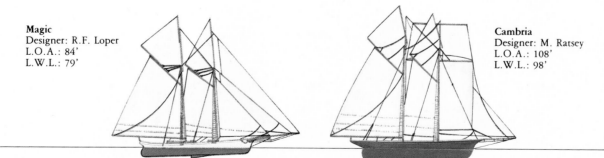

Magic
Designer: R.F. Loper
L.O.A.: 84'
L.W.L.: 79'

Cambria
Designer: M. Ratsey
L.O.A.: 108'
L.W.L.: 98'

	date	course	allowance	elapsed time	corrected time	wins by
Magic	8/8	N.Y.Y.C. course. 35.1 miles	12'14''	h. 04.07.54	h. 03.58.21	39'17''
Cambria				h. 04.34.57	h. 04.37.38	(tenth)

Cambria *managed a mere tenth position against seventeen American yachts, here led by* Magic *which won by almost forty minutes over the British challenger.*

1871
Columbia-Livonia

If James Ashbury had learned anything during his unsuccessful 1870 campaign, it was that the New York Yacht Club owned the cup and would do just about anything to keep from losing it. Early in 1871 he told some friends that he no longer regarded the deed of gift as a document to be given "an equitable, sportsmanlike interpretation"; he was prepared, he stated, to give it "a purely legal construction". Consulting lawyers, he first decided to attack the yacht club's distinctive definition of the word "match". Over in New York, the club asked the opinion of George Schuyler, the only survivor of the original *America* syndicate, who rather testily sided with Ashbury, saying that a contest like the one in 1870 "renders the *America*'s trophy useless as a challenge cup".

So the club announced that the races would be sailed one-on-one, adding that it reserved the right to choose its defender on the morning of each race. Ashbury and a great many other people quickly saw through this claim of equity. The club could select the boat best able to win in the day's wind conditions while the challenger would have to sail in *all* conditions, light and heavy. He responded with a charade of his own: not only was he challenging on behalf of the Royal Harwich Yacht Club, of which he was commodore, but Ashbury was the certified representative of eleven other British clubs, most of them under royal patronage. One race each, he argued, seven out of twelve to win the cup. He also proposed sailing in the open ocean off Newport, Rhode Island, and, once again, the elimination of centerboard yachts.

The yacht club did not respond to Ashbury's ingenious twelve-challenge declaration until he arrived in early October, and this answer was so critical — "sharp practice" was mentioned — that the Englishman angrily withdrew it and replaced it with one even more radical: twelve races would be scheduled, one for each of his clubs, "and the first race *Livonia* won I should in that case formally and officially claim the cup on behalf of whose flag I sailed under".

On through early October this wordy battle raged until Ashbury finally gave in, declaring that it was getting too cold to sail. He accepted a proposal of a four out of seven-race series, three to be sailed on the inside New York Harbor course, three on the ocean off Sandy Hook,

Livonia took part in as many as five races but met with no better success than Cambria. *At the end of this series of elimination trials her owner, James Ashbury, got carried away in controversial comments.*

and the last, if needed, to be held on a course to be agreed upon. Clearly, if he had not gone along with this proposal, which was the exasperated yacht club's last offer, he would have suffered the even greater embarrassment of returning home to the voters without having raced at all.

Named after a Russian province where Ashbury's railroad enterprises had thrived, *Livonia* was as exotic as her inspiration. Twenty feet longer than *Cambria*, she carried more than twice her predecessor's sail area — more than 18,000 square feet of American-made cotton duck, the greatest spread of working sail ever flown by a cup yacht.

However, she was not much faster than *Cambria*, and no American knees quaked at the sight of her. Still, the yacht club assigned four of its best schooners to the team from which the daily selection would be made: Commodore Bennett's *Dauntless* (fifth in the 1870 race), the very successful *Palmer*, Ashbury's old antagonist *Sappho*,

Columbia, *the first American defender to be defeated in an America's Cup race. It all happened in the third race because of a crew change and some damage.*

and the spanking new *Columbia*, widely considered the best light-air boat around and the first of three boats of that name to be selected to defend the cup. *Columbia* and *Sappho* appeared at the line on October 16 and since the wind was light, *Columbia* was chosen to sail. She easily beat the much larger challenger, which owed her more than a minute on handicap, on both elapsed and corrected times. Emboldened by *Columbia*'s performance, the yacht club sent her out for the second race even though a moderate gale was blowing. For some reason, the race committee laid out a course that was ten miles short of the forty they had committed themselves to, but that error was obscured by a greater one that they made. The printed race instructions did not specify how the yachts were to pass the mark. When *Columbia*'s owner, Franklin Osgood, noticed the omission, he had himself rowed over to the committee boat where he was told to round the mark either way. Unfortunately, the committee did not see fit to pass the same advice on to

Ashbury, who decided to leave the mark on the starboard hand as was done in England when specific instructions were not given. Reaching the mark just ahead of *Columbia*, *Livonia* rounded it with a long, slow, and (considering the rough weather) dangerous jibe. *Columbia* merely tacked around, ended up to windward of the challenger, and easily sailed by her to win. *Livonia* might have won had it not been for the mark rounding.

Quite rightly, Ashbury protested the race. The committee first claimed that the instructions were clear, which was untrue, and then tried to defend itself in a long, self-justifying missive full of irrelevant citations to the controversy over whether *America* should have rounded the Nab Light Vessel twenty years earlier. The race results stood, but Ashbury kept his own scorecard and figured that the series was now even.

The next day it became 2-1 by anybody's reckoning. Much like the British fleet back in '51, the American team was in a shambles. *Columbia* had sprung, or

The deck of Livonia *photographed with her crew a quarter of a century after her races in American waters.*

strained, a mast, her crew was exhausted, and her skipper was injured. For some reason *Palmer* and *Dauntless* had been allowed to sail along and watch the second race, and both had suffered badly torn sails. *Sappho* was in dry dock.

The club chose *Dauntless*, but one of her stays broke during the tow out. After considering entering *Magic*, the 1870 winner, with Ashbury's approval, the club finally ended this comedy of errors by choosing *Columbia* and manning her with a mixed crew of amateurs and professionals from the other yachts. Though the wind was strong, *Columbia*'s sails were not reefed and she paid the price, broaching and nearly capsizing all over the course, blowing out sails and rigging, and scaring her crew half to death. Her steering gear finally broke and, as she lay rolling helplessly in the rough seas, the crew smashed the wheel box open with axes and rigged an emergency tiller. She later limped home nineteen minutes behind *Livonia*.

That was the series for *Columbia*. *Sappho* then whipped the challenger in two races held in more strong, late October winds to win the cup for the Americans, 4-1, and almost everybody prepared to go home for the winter.

But as far as James Ashbury was concerned, the score was only 3-2. On October 24, he sailed a challenge race against *Dauntless* that, though *Livonia* was beaten, he counted to his credit since *Dauntless* did not acknowledge it to be an actual cup race.

When Commodore Bennett's yacht did not appear at the starting line in miserable weather on the 25th, Ashbury claimed the race and the match, 4-3. By his logic, it was all very simple. He had won and he demanded the cup.

You should not be surprised to learn that the New York Yacht Club did not hold a grand banquet in Ashbury's honor and hand over the cup. Neither should you be shocked that Ashbury went home and wrote yet another long letter in which he accused the club of being "cute" — Victorian for "cunning" — and of having acted in "unfair and unsportsmanlike proceedings". The club immediately returned three cups that he had donated and informed the international yachting establishment that Mr. Ashbury had acted in an ungentlemanly fashion. "He seems", they wrote, "to look behind every action for an unworthy motive, and seek in every explanation evidences of concealment and want of candor". Which might have been true. For their own part, the New York Yacht Club's hierarchy might have eased an already tense situation by putting themselves in the shoes of an outsider working entirely independently far from home. American public opinion sided with the underdog. As one newspaper said after *Livonia*'s single triumph over *Columbia*, "It had been supposed that the New York Yacht Club had made their preparations so carefully as to leave Mr. Ashbury no chance whatsoever of winning a race. Accidents, however, can annul the most careful calculations". A challenger would not win another race until the 1920 match.

Following the defeat of Columbia *the New York Yacht Club decided to set* Sappho *against* Livonia; *the former is here seen to windward of the English yacht.*

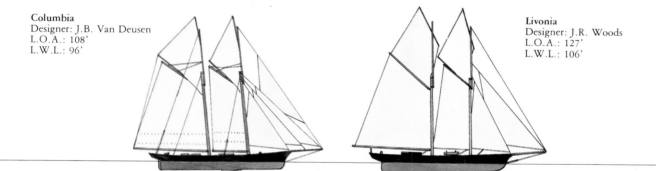

Columbia
Designer: J.B. Van Deusen
L.O.A.: 108'
L.W.L.: 96'

Livonia
Designer: J.R. Woods
L.O.A.: 127'
L.W.L.: 106'

	date	course	allowance	elapsed time	corrected time	wins by
Columbia Livonia	10/16	N.Y.Y.C. course. 35.1 miles	01'46''	h. 06.17.42 h. 06.43.00	h. 06.19.41 h. 06.46.45	27'04''
Columbia Livonia	10/18	20 miles to windward from Sandy Hook Lightship and return. 40 miles	05'17''	h. 03.01.33 h. 03.06.49	h. 03.07.41 h. 03.18.15	10'33''
Livonia Columbia (partially disabled)	10/19	N.Y.Y.C. course. 35.1 miles	04'23''	h. 03.53.05 h. 04.12.38	h. 04.02.25 h. 04.17.35	15'10''
Sappho Livonia	10/21	20 miles to windward from Sandy Hook Lightship and return. 40 miles	00'53''	h. 05.33.24 h. 06.04.38	h. 05.39.02 h. 06.09.23	30'21''
Sappho Livonia	10/23	N.Y.Y.C. course. 40 miles	01'09''	h. 04.38.05 h. 05.04.41	h. 04.46.17 h. 05.11.44	25'27''

1876
Madeleine-Countess of Dufferin

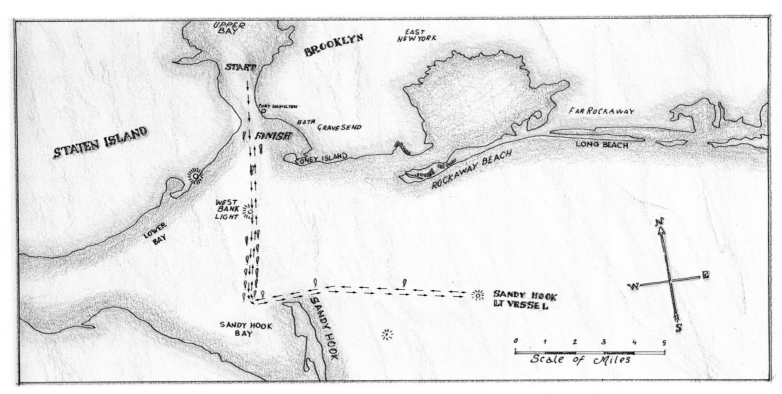

Before being transferred to Newport, part of the match was held practically in the port of New York.
The courses could be of two types: the first with start and finish in front of Staten Island,
while the second was from Sandy Hook Lightship to a windward mark about 20 miles away and back.

James Ashbury finally got himself elected to Parliament. He raced *Livonia* a while longer, though on one occasion a New York Yacht Club member refused to compete against him, and eventually emigrated to New Zealand where he became a sheep farmer. Passing through New York in 1885, he was as eager as everybody else to clamber aboard a spectator steamer and go out to watch the cup match between *Puritan* and *Genesta*.

The same indelible lure of the America's Cup colored the next two challenges, in 1876 and 1881. Though won in walkaways by crack American racing yachts over rather clumsy Canadian vessels, these two matches have a certain drama worth remembering. And, perhaps more important for the history of the America's Cup, they mark the maturation of the New York Yacht Club from an awkward adolescent ever eager for a bicker or a fight to an adult sensitive to large issues, such as fairness.

Mark Twain called this period "the Gilded Age", a time of attention to superficial value rather than to in-

herent worth. Another novelist writing a century after Twain, Gore Vidal, describes the United States then as "this vigorous, ugly, turbulent realm, devoted to moneymaking by any means". If the day had a motto it was "I seen my opportunities and I took 'em", which is how the New York political leader George Washington Plunkett justified taking bribes. Action, bigness, conflict, progress, and zealous devotion to each of those ideals — those were the signs of the times in Manhattan around 1880.

It was not too much different on the water, either. Speed was everything. Big boats sailed faster than little boats, so people built the biggest, fastest boats that they could afford (and at prices about the same as the cost of *America*, many new tycoons could afford them). When a young yacht designer named Nathanael G. Herreshoff showed up at the New York Yacht Club's centennial regatta in 1876 in a strange-looking boat with two hulls only 25 feet long and promptly walloped every big yacht

Countess of Dufferin, *to leeward of* Madeleine, *was
the first Canadian yacht to challenge.
She was designed and built by Alexander Cuthbert.*

in sight, the response was an instantaneous prohibition of catamarans, which set yacht design back one hundred years. She was too small and inexpensive to be so fast.

Likewise, the handicap rules of the day were, to say the least, *laissez-faire*. They imposed no regulations on sail area because, as the common wisdom put it, "a tax on sail is a tax on skill". A builder-designer's job now was to whittle out a model based on a successful boat, (*Columbia*, say), take measurements from the model and scale them up or down depending on whether the boat would be larger or smaller, build the tallest spars she could carry without tipping over at her mooring, build the hull, fill the bilge full of lead, rig her — and pray that luck was on his side. If everything went right, she would be fast and reasonably stiff, her wide beam more or less supporting her huge sails if she got caught in a small gale.

Almost all of these boats were centerboarders. Originally intended to allow a boat to sail in thin water over the sand shoals of New York Harbor and New Jersey, the centerboard also encouraged high speeds, especially in fresh wind. Many of the "out-and-outers" of the '70's were centerboarders, generally fast and unseaworthy, which is partly why the British handicap rules penalized them heavily or even prohibited them. But to tell an American to give up his centerboard would have been like ordering an Englishman to stop honoring Queen Victoria. And around the time of the first Canadian challenge, centennial fever created a rash of patriotism that took symbols like centerboards very seriously indeed.

But things could go wrong... The mania for huge centerboard schooners peaked in an ill-considered vessel called *Mohawk*. Built in 1875 for Vice-Commodore William T. Garner (who reportedly earned $2 million tax-free annually from his textile mills and once bet $75,000 on a yacht race), *Mohawk* was a monster: 141 feet long, 250 tons displacement, 32,000 square feet of

sail, yet with only 6 feet of draft when her 24 foot, 7 ton centerboard was raised. For stability, she depended almost entirely on her beam of 30 feet. The common wisdom was that she would be faster than and as safe as *Columbia*, after which she was modelled. The common wisdom conveniently forgot *Columbia*'s problems in the third race in the 1870 match. The only disagreement came from "Devoted Yachtsman", the anonymous columnist for the sporting weekly, *The Spirit of the Times*. "If they ever carry her lee rail under, with all sail set, there will be some danger", he warned. "It does not answer to get a wide flat boat too far over".

He was right. On July 20, 1876, while her crew was raising her anchor off the New York Yacht Club's Staten Island clubhouse, *Mohawk* capsized in a quick, relatively mild squall and Garner, his wife, and three others were drowned. The tragedy immediately caused a reaction against these extreme craft. By the early 1880's a whole new type of boat mid-way in shape between the beamy American schooners and the narrow English cutters had evolved. Seamanship had caught up with the Gilded Age.

Anchored near *Mohawk* at that moment of disaster that would bring such change was the 107 foot Canadian America's Cup challenger *Countess of Dufferin*, just arrived after a month-long passage from Toronto down the St. Lawrence River and around Nova Scotia. She looked much like any local centerboard schooner — in fact, it was rumored that her lines were borrowed from a New Jersey-built boat — except that she was finished very rough and her sails were quite baggy. Far from being a copy, she was designed and built by Alexander Cuthbert, an enthusiastic builder of fishing schooners.

Though she unofficially beat *America* in a race from Sandy Hook to Newport and return, she scared nobody. The yacht club had not committed itself to whether it would name one defender or, as in 1871, a pack to pick from; once its members had a look at *Countess of Dufferin*, they selected an older, much-modified centerboard schooner called *Madeleine*.

Besides handily licking the Canadian yacht in both races of the two out of three series, *Madeleine*'s greatest distinction lies in her name. In the entire history of the America's Cup, she is the sole defender to carry not the name of the country, of a famous warship, or of some grand ideal, like reliance or freedom. She was named after a woman.

In the second race, the challenger was helmed by an American, Captain Joe Elsworth, but he was unable to hold off either *Madeleine* or the twenty-five-year-old *America*, which started four and one-half minutes late but beat *Countess of Dufferin* to the finish by almost twenty minutes. *America* had been bought for only $5,000 by Benjamin F. Butler, a famous Civil War general and controversial Massachusetts politician who frequently cloaked himself in patriotism. If *America* helped his career, he more than paid her back over the twenty years that he owned her with meticulous care and periodic modernizations at the hands of people like the clipper shipbuilder Donald McKay and the yacht designer Edward Burgess.

Madeleine, *easily beat* Countess of Dufferin. *Here, the defender leads* America, *which was an informal entrant in the second race and easily beat the Canadian.*

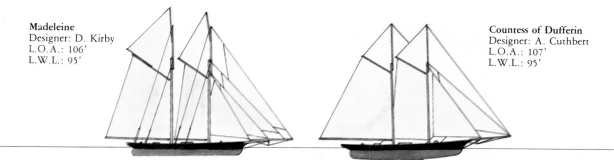

Madeleine
Designer: D. Kirby
L.O.A.: 106'
L.W.L.: 95'

Countess of Dufferin
Designer: A. Cuthbert
L.O.A.: 107'
L.W.L.: 95'

	date	course	allowance	elapsed time	corrected time	wins by
Madeleine **Countess of Dufferin**	8/11	N.Y.Y.C. course. 32.6 miles	01'01''	h. 05.24.55 6. 05.34.53	h. 05.23.54 h. 05.34.53	10'59''
Madeleine **Countess of Dufferin**	8/12	20 miles to windward from Sandy Hook Lightship and return. 40 miles	01'01''	h. 07.19.47 h. 07.46.00	h. 07.18.46 h. 07.46.00	27'14''

1881
Mischief-Atalanta

The most disappointed man in New York after *Madeleine*'s easy win in 1876 was Alexander Cuthbert, the losing boat's designer and builder. Like many yacht designers, he was sure that he had a cup winner's dimensions and shape stored in his brain and was haunted by the prospect that she would never take three-dimensional form. As *Countess of Dufferin* lay in the yacht basin at Staten Island, watched carefully by a crew of bill collectors, Cuthbert began to plan the changes that would surely make her a winner next year — move the masts, reshape the stern, perhaps lengthen the waterline. Then the creditors descended and were satisfied with one syndicate member's share. In September, now planning a new boat, Cuthbert and *Countess of Dufferin* headed North. Not for five years did the New York Yacht Club hear from him again, and then through the secretary of an obscure organization called the Bay of Quinte Yacht Club, in Belleville, Ontario, about one hundred miles East of Toronto. The boat named was Cuthbert's own *Atalanta*, at 70 feet the smallest challenger until 1958.

The letter was written in May and the match was scheduled for September, but the New York Yacht Club, as usual, waived the six months' notice required by the deed of gift. They did something else, too. A committee of flag officers recommended that a single defender be named for the entire series of races. "In this view", they wrote, "we sincerely trust that the interpretation of the deed of gift may be so liberal and sportsmanlike to be beyond cavil". The club as a whole agreed (although one newspaper looking for a controversy with which to fill its columns claimed this was "conceding advantages to which no challenging party is entitled").

Surprisingly, since nobody seemed especially worried about Cuthbert's new boat, the three flag officers formed a syndicate to build a boat especially for the cup match. Perhaps it was the gamble of trying something new that appealed to them, but whatever the reason was, the commissioning of *Pocahontas* brought the America's Cup to a higher level of seriousness.

As Cuthbert was personally putting *Atalanta* together up North, other club members — gratifyingly surprised by the relatively low cost of sailing mere 70-footers — prepared for the first set of defenders' trials. The fastest

George L. Schuyler, the sole member of the America syndicate to live till almost the end of last century.
On the following pages: Atalanta to leeward of Mischief.

boat around was owned by a non-member; not to worry, promised *Pocahontas*' designer, David Kirby, the new boat would be a vast improvement. Then there were *Gracie* and the iron *Mischief*, which, just to confuse matters, was owned by an Englishman who *was* a member. In the trials, *Pocahontas* proved to be both slow and prone to damage, *Gracie* won one race, and *Mischief* took the other two and was selected. *Gracie*'s people let out a terrible howl: she had won her race by almost four minutes and had been barely beaten by only fourteen seconds in the last one, but the selection committee stayed firm (as selection committees would in many such controversies in the future). One attraction of *Mischief* was that she was closer to the challenger's size and handicap, making it easier for her to cover *Atalanta* when ahead since they would be sailing in similar winds. Only the second metal yacht built in the United States, *Mischief* was also one of the first designed scientifically using drawings instead of the rule of thumb method of whittling models. Her designer was A. Cary Smith, the yacht club's measurer.

Ten days after the trials ended, on October 30, *Atalanta* made her long-delayed appearance. Short of funds, Cuthbert simply could not hire enough craftsmen to build her in time, and then her delivery down the Erie Canal had been very slow. Too wide for the canal, the hull was heeled sharply and, banging and scraping along the rough walls, she was towed on her side by a team of mules.

Accounts of her delivery trip sent up howls of laughter about unsophisticated Canadians, and the jokes did not end until after she was soundly beaten in two windy, cold races held on November 9 and 10. For the first time in cup history, the boats set the ballooning sails that had been developed on the English yacht *Sphinx* in 1865. Spinnakers, as they were called, had been illegal in New York Yacht Club events until 1881.

Over-rigged and badly prepared, *Atalanta* was also poorly handled by her mostly amateur crew — the first and last in cup races until the 1950's. Designer-builder-skipper-owner Cuthbert seemed unfazed by her problems and by cynical newspaper comments such as, "a procession with a first-class chance for a capsize by the Canadians", and, "The race Wednesday — if race it can be called — amounts to this: *Mischief*, a tried and proven sloop, confessedly one of the fastest in the world, thoroughly fitted out and equipped, fully manned, and magnificently handled, distanced the *Atalanta*, a new yacht, hastily built, totally untried, and miserably equipped, with sails that fitted like a Chatham Street suit of clothes, and bungled around the course by an alleged crew, who would have been overmatched in trying to handle a canal boat anchored in a fog".

Still game after all that, Cuthbert announced that he intended to leave *Atalanta* in New York and challenge once again in the spring of 1882. Embarrassed perhaps as much for him as for themselves, and worried that the cup had become nothing more than a regional prize, the yacht club thrust the trophy and the deed of gift back into George Schuyler's hands and asked him to make alterations that would take account of the problems that had appeared during the first four challenges. On February 2, 1882, Schuyler returned with the second deed of gift. Couched in more legalistic language, and, at five hundred and two words, two hundred and sixty-three words longer than the first deed, it required the defender to name only one representative and, in three quick slashes, decapitated Alexander Cuthbert's hopes: participating clubs must run their races on salt water; a losing boat may not challenge again within two years; and participating boats must sail to the event on their own bottoms. So Cuthbert shrugged his shoulders and headed North once more.

Belittling Alexander Cuthbert's two charges at the New York Yacht Club's windmill is all too easy. Rather than dismissing the Canadian challenges as jokes or as the nadir in the America's Cup's long history, as some writers have done, we prefer to regard them as two of its proudest moments. Eighty-nine years later, Charley Morgan, a designer-builder-skipper-owner-sailmaker from Florida, would make the same effort, with the same results. We toast them both with words that Winfield S. Thompson wrote in 1902: "Captain Cuthbert handled the straight-edge and the adze, and he was the only man who ever challenged for the cup who could and did himself create with brain and hand a vessel to sail under his challenge."

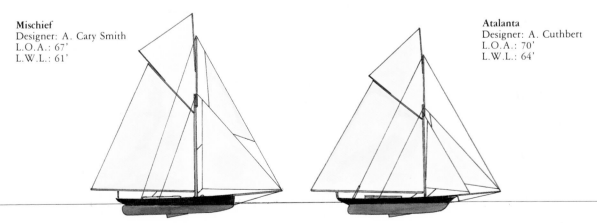

Mischief
Designer: A. Cary Smith
L.O.A.: 67'
L.W.L.: 61'

Atalanta
Designer: A. Cuthbert
L.O.A.: 70'
L.W.L.: 64'

	date	course	allowance	elapsed time	corrected time	wins by
Mischief	11/9	N.Y.Y.C. course. 32.6 miles		h. 04.17.09	h. 04.17.09	28'30''
Atalanta			02'45''	h. 04.48.24	h. 04.45.39	
Mischief	11/10	16 miles to leeward from Buoy 5		h. 04.54.53	h. 04.54.53	38'54''
Atalanta		off Sandy Hook and return. 32 miles	02'45''	h. 05.36.32	h. 05.33.47	

1885
Puritan-Genesta

Fishing for a new challenge, the New York Yacht Club dangled the second deed of gift in the still pools of several prestigious foreign yacht clubs. After three years of patient waiting, they came up with not one but two shining trout. A British yacht designer, J. Beavor-Webb, initiated a paired challenge on behalf of two of his clients, Sir Richard Sutton and Lt. William Henn, Royal Navy. Sir Richard's *Genesta*, representing the Royal Yacht Squadron, would race first in late August 1885; if she lost, Lt. Henn's *Galatea*, from Scotland's Royal Northern Yacht Club, would race two weeks later. The yacht club preferred to distribute this rich feast over two tables, and Henn soon agreed to postpone his challenge until 1886.

Though it has never taken even the most flagrantly incompetent challenger for granted, the New York Yacht Club was deeply concerned about these two. English yacht design had come a long way since the day when the Marquis of Anglesey looked at *America* with amazed incomprehension. The deep, narrow English cutters designed by Beavor-Webb and George L. Watson and built on the banks of Scotland's River Clyde were known to be fast and reliable — and not just because traveling American yachtsmen said so. A successful Watson-designed cutter called *Madge* had been shipped across the Atlantic in 1881 and had won seven out of eight races against American yachts. She was the first true cutter that most Yankees had ever seen, and they were impressed. 46 feet long, *Madge* had a beam of only 7 feet 9 inches and a keel that stretched 8 feet 3 inches below the water. A comparably-sized New York centerboard sloop had almost twice that beam and half that depth. Though less than dry on deck — Winfield Thompson wrote that she was "as wet as a half-tide ledge in a sea-way" — *Madge* was fast, and she had an arrowy, efficient beauty that converted many yachtsmen from the ancient American faith in the centerboard to the new creed of the keel. These men called themselves "cutter cranks". Today, it is hard to imagine how so many people could get so worked up about yacht design, but in those simpler days, when whole regions of America still depended on sailing ships for their commerce, when anything even slightly hinting of England touched the raw nerve of nationalism, and when engineering was still couched in a language that any

man could understand — back then, a foot or two of beam or draft could stimulate a whole winter's controversy. The *Mohawk* disaster and a few other catastrophes involving extreme centerboarders had defined the limits of wide, shoal-draft design. Now *Madge* showed the other extreme. Somewhere in between, it was thought (and argued even in newspaper editorials), lay the ideal: a fast, seaworthy hull. Of course, that ideal has been sought since the days of Noah and will continue to be tracked down until the seas are dry. Of course, too, everybody has his own definitions of "fast" and "seaworthy", which only makes the endless debate that much more interesting.

In any case, while the cutter cranks turned out narrow "plank on edge" cutters, and while other designers and builders continued to build beamy sloops, a few people took the greatest risk of all by daring to attempt a compromise between the two extremes. Few boats were as radically thin as *Madge* or as fat as *Mohawk;* most continued to carry centerboards, those most American fittings. There gradually developed in the 1880s a new hull shape that, if it could be compared with anything else, was a throwback to the wholesome, low-resistance underbody of *America*. The appearance of *Madge* transformed the shape of American yachts from that of the pumpkin seed to that of the almond. Ten years later, a more radical innovation — Nathanael Herreshoff's fin keel — would force another change that would be less healthy in the long run.

In the middle of this shift in design philosophy, people worried about the future of the America's Cup wondered whether an American yacht designer could produce a boat as fast as Beavor-Webb's *Genesta* and *Galatea*, which, by all accounts, were unbeatable. Whether "all accounts" were trustworthy or not was difficult to determine, assuming that anybody wanted to know the truth behind the stories of the boats' runaway speed. It is curious how the wide Atlantic ocean magnifies rather than diminishes rumors of bad news (the Pacific was to do the same when the Australians challenged ninety years later). Perhaps portents of defeat were functionally necessary to stir up interest and money for good defenders.

The New York Yacht Club appealed to other American clubs for potential defenders. The circular,

Men at work on the bowsprit of Puritan, *the boat of the*
Eastern Yacht Club of Marblehead designed by Edward Burgess.

Genesta, *the English cutter belonging to Sir Richard Sutton and designed by J. Beavor Webb, lost in two races.*

sent out in May 1885, said nothing about requiring that the defender be a club member, but that probably was understood. Obviously, the club did not have complete faith in *Priscilla*, the iron sloop that its own measurer, A. Cary Smith, had designed for its own flag officers, Commodore James Gordon Bennett and Vice-Commodore W.P. Douglas. Even before the S.O.S. was mailed, a few members of the Eastern Yacht Club, in Marblehead, Massachusetts, met to consider building a defense candidate.

"The Eastern", as New Englanders call it, was to Boston what the club that held the cup was to New York, and the competition between the two sailing centers was no less intense than it had been back in the 1840's, when John Cox Stevens was racing "out-and-outers" against New England invaders. Dominating the meeting was J. Malcolm Forbes, whose father had made a fortune in shipping and railroads, and who was rapidly building on it. The Forbeses and the other men around

the table were sportsmen-businessmen in the old Stevens mold, and not like many new tycoons of the Gilded Age who put wealth far before pleasure. Old John Murray Forbes, J. Malcolm's father, boasted of sometimes shrinking his business activities "so as to have time for farming, shooting, and other gentlemanlike occupations". The writer Ralph Waldo Emerson once said something of him that also would apply to his son: "It is of course that he should ride well, shoot well, sail well, keep horse well, administer affairs well, but he was the best talker, also, in the company...".

J. Malcolm Forbes agreed to pay most of the new boat's bills, his friend (and New York Yacht Club member) Charles J. Paine said he would manage her, and Edward Burgess, The Eastern's secretary, took on the responsibility of designing her. And so was launched the first modern America's Cup defense syndicate. The boat, *Puritan*, followed several months after. Every "expert'' on the Atlantic seaboard immediately criticized her as being either too much a sloop or too much a cutter, for Burgess had created a 94 foot compromise between the American and English traditions. She was moderately wide by New York standards, and had a moderately shallow keel by Cowes standards (with a moderately short centerboard dropping through it).

It took a great amount of courage to be such a compromiser in those days of extremes, but Edward Burgess knew what he was doing. He had sailed since his youth and had acquired an objective, scientific approach to yacht design through the study of entomology, which he had taught at Harvard before becoming a naval architect in 1883. A summer spent on the Isle of Wight had exposed his sharp eyes and analytical intellect to the English cutters, and intuition, his knowledge of how boats sail, and practicality led him to design the controversial *Puritan*.

She quickly silenced her critics by beating *Priscilla* in most of their races, but when *Genesta* appeared in mid-July and began to tune up for the cup match, nobody in the yacht club felt confident. A classic narrow and deep ''plank on edge'' cutter — her model in the New York Yacht Club seems perpetually to be teetering — she was the first challenger to be carefully prepared and managed. Beavor-Webb's assiduous attention to her sails alone was enough to frighten the defenders.

The first race, on September 7, was not finished before the time limit ran out, but *Puritan* ran up a 2 mile lead in light wind. At the running start the next day (starts from anchor having been dispensed with), *Puritan*, on port tack, was rammed while trying to squeeze across the bow of *Genesta*, on starboard. Although the race committee immediately disqualified

the defender — which was unable to continue, anyway, because her mainsail was badly torn — Sir Richard Sutton turned away the committee's advice to sail around the course. ''We want a race'', Sutton was quoted as saying; ''we don't want a walk-over''. He even refused Paine's offer to pay for repairs.

Such sportsmanship was rarely displayed in Gilded Age New York, and Sutton was wildly praised with rolling phrases like ''graceful magnanimity'' and ''most honorable and sportsmanlike spirit''. Whether similar accolades would have rewarded a *defender's* refusal of an easy win is an open question. The issue never arose again because the yacht club began to require a sail-over if the other yacht was damaged.

After two more unsuccessful attempts to get a race off in light winds, *Puritan* finally beat *Genesta* handily on the 14th before a big spectator fleet that included Nathanael Herreshoff in his catamaran *Stiletto*. Two days later, the Boston boat narrowly beat the challenger in one of those tight, nervy races that occur all too infrequently in cup competition. The lead changed hands twice on the long run in fresh wind, and *Genesta* led by two minutes at the outer mark. Sailing a little faster and pointing slightly closer to the wind, *Puritan* gradually caught her on the fifteen-mile beat to the finish in a gusty 30 knot wind, as both boats' leeward decks plunged deep into the ocean. *Puritan* gained four minutes to win by one and one-half minutes on corrected time.

It was the best racing in the history of the cup, in fact the best match of the five. It seemed as if this ''Challenge Cup for friendly competition between foreign countries'' was finally leaving the thicket of bitter haggling that had for so long entangled it.

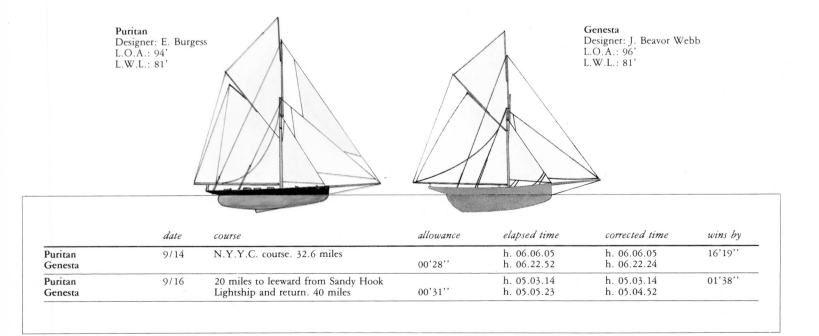

Puritan
Designer: E. Burgess
L.O.A.: 94'
L.W.L.: 81'

Genesta
Designer: J. Beavor Webb
L.O.A.: 96'
L.W.L.: 81'

	date	course	allowance	elapsed time	corrected time	wins by
Puritan	9/14	N.Y.Y.C. course. 32.6 miles		h. 06.06.05	h. 06.06.05	16'19''
Genesta			00'28''	h. 06.22.52	h. 06.22.24	
Puritan	9/16	20 miles to leeward from Sandy Hook Lightship and return. 40 miles		h. 05.03.14	h. 05.03.14	01'38''
Genesta			00'31''	h. 05.05.23	h. 05.04.52	

1886 Mayflower - Galatea

Lt. William Henn's challenge with the Beavor-Webb cutter *Galatea* was accepted a few months after the 1885 match, and because she was 6 feet longer than *Genesta*, Edward Burgess was commissioned to design a new defense candidate — this time solely for Charles J. Paine. J. Malcolm Forbes bought *Puritan* outright for a reported price of $13,500, perhaps one-third her original cost, and planned his own campaign. Sticking to colonial history, Paine named the new boat *Mayflower*. She was broken-in early in tune-up trials against *Puritan* and then easily won the trials against her, *Priscilla*, and a new boat, *Atlantic*, built by a syndicate from the Atlantic Yacht Club, in Brooklyn, before winning the match handily. The only controversy to appear all summer was so minor that it barely deserves mention. Before the second race, Lt. Henn requested that the course be shortened from 40 to 30 miles because he was ill. The race committee refused, the race was sailed, and not an angry word was ever breathed about it.

The 1886 match is fascinating not because the results were typical but because of the startlingly contrasting styles of the principals. William Henn was what we today would call a live-aboard cruising sailor. Born in Ireland, he joined the Royal Navy at the age of thirteen and performed long service off Africa — he was second-in-command of the 1872 mission sent to locate the explorer and missionary David Livingstone. Retiring from the Navy three years later at the age of twenty-eight, Henn decided to pursue pleasure sailing full-time. He married a lady who was willing both to endure cruising's frequent discomforts and to help with the expenses (it was Mrs. Henn, in fact, who paid for *Galatea*). For seven years they lived aboard a yawl in which they voyaged almost 50,000 miles, and when they decided to buy a larger boat they became interested in racing.

Galatea may have been potentially fast, but she was not a successful racing boat. This was partly because Lt. Henn approached the sport with the insouciance typical of a sailor who has spent years cruising for pleasure. Symptoms of his "what's the hurry?" attitude were his predilections for carrying only small working sails instead of acres of racing canvas and for towing the dinghy while on tuning-up exercises in New York Harbor. So consistent was his casualness that the newspapers interpreted it as a smoke screen for *Galatea*'s blazing speed, and the pre-match publicity brought out thousands of curious spectators who jammed the course. By then, the yacht's designer, J. Beavor-Webb, had taken over command and the helm in a last-ditch effort to make his

Mayflower *to windward of* Galatea, *which was a veritable "lead mine" with no less than eighty-one tons of ballast in the keel.*

creation look as good as the newspapers threatened, but he failed.

If even Beavor-Webb was unable to get *Galatea* moving in the predominantly light conditions, it was because the challenger — while she looked efficient if not racy on deck — was furnished like a Victorian mansion down below. The weight of all the layers of rugs, all the heavy tables, and all the mirrors and mementoes and paintings did not make her any faster. For the Henns had moved aboard directly from their old yawl,

many wealthy Bostonians, he volunteered for duty in the Civil War. He served on the staff of General Benjamin F. Butler (who later bought *America*) and commanded troops — including a division of black volunteers — before leaving the army as a temporary major general. All that before Paine's thirty-third birthday. He expanded his inheritance by running railroads in the Southwest states and Texas, staying as close to Boston as possible so he could continue the lifelong love affair with sailing, which may have been the only

Charles J. Paine from Boston must be given credit for having organized no less than three boats, including Mayflower, to have successfully defended the Cup last century.

Edward Burgess, an entomologist forced by necessity to devote himself to the profession of naval architect, was the forerunner of a dynasty of designers of America's Cup defenders.

and there they lived in comfort. Once New York knew that Mrs. Henn was on board, *Galatea* became packed with potted plants sent by admirers, which only added to the comfort — and detracted from the speed. Despite Mrs. Henn's presence and her husband's casual jauntiness (he carried with him a whale's tooth walking stick), the star of *Galatea* was Peggy. Peggy was the Henns' pet monkey, and she had been trained to help the professional sailors hoist and douse sails. Whether she helped clean up after the dogs that also sailed aboard, we do not know, but it was reported that she was given a first-class naval funeral after she died.

On the other hand, the only simian behavior that Charles Paine allowed aboard his yachts was Edward Burgess' celebratory double-somersault after each first place. Shy and unpretentious in public, Paine was a firm, brilliant leader when under sail. A great-grandson of a signer of the Declaration of Independence, he was born in Boston in 1833 and educated as a lawyer. Like

character trait that he shared with William Henn. Like his friend Burgess (who named one of his sons after Paine) he had developed through years of sailing an intuitive feel for boats. While Burgess directed that mastery toward creating the ideal shape for a hull from a sheet of drawing paper and some instruments, Paine took his genius on board. He was especially skillful at getting the best out of a boat by making a myriad of small improvements. In the 1880's, he bought an old, slow schooner called *Halcyon* and through hard work made her a champion. With *Puritan*, *Mayflower*, and their successor *Volunteer* he started with one big advantage: Edward Burgess designed them to be fast in the first place. But Paine's attention to detail never lapsed.

For example, before the 1885 match, he had *Puritan*'s white topsides "pot leaded" with a gray mixture of varnish and dry lead and then rubbed down until they were smooth as glass. At the same time, an emergency strap was installed on her bow to support the bobstay leading

to her huge bowsprit in case there was an accident. Paine was as attentive to sails as he was to the hull; to prevent the mainsail's leech area from becoming too flat, he developed a special type of batten composed of six or eight bamboo fishing rods lashed together. Once he was worried that his boat was too heavy, so he had the crew plane exactly one-fourth of an inch off her deck to lighten her by several hundred pounds.

Charles Paine was the manager, not the skipper, of these defenders. Helming big yachts was still considered to be a professional's job. A handful of especially skilled, aggressive skippers of fishing schooners found themselves called on summer after summer to take over millionaires' pleasure boats. Their jobs were well-paid, but not easy. On one hand they had to recruit and supervise twenty or thirty hard-handed (and usually hard-headed) Swedes, Scots, or Downeasters from Maine. They trained them in sharp sail-handling and, if they were good, made them mates. On the other hand, they were beholden to the owner or, if that gentleman so delegated, an amateur manager who may or may not have known as much about yacht racing as he made out. Some owners gave their professional captains complete charge, for which the skippers were eternally thankful. Some tried to advise and only got in the way. A few truly knew what they were talking about. Charles Paine, who had raced smaller boats successfully, was one of the latter. There were, too, some gentlemen who helmed their own yachts out at Oyster Bay, Long Island, where the Seawanhaka Corinthian Yacht Club was created in 1871 under the then radical theory that amateurs were competent to take charge. Other amateurs raced their own small boats against professionals and became exceptionally competent and ruthless as a result. One of these men was C. Oliver Iselin, who managed several America's Cup defenders between 1893 and 1903. As a young man, he won many rough and tumble races in

Above: the interior of Galatea *was furnished more as a cruising boat rather than a racer. Below:* Galatea *at a mark.*
As can be seen, the America's Cup races
were very keenly followed by the spectators even in those days.

some anything-goes competition in boats called sand-baggers. "There was no sentiment in the game of sand-bag racing", the yachting historian W.P. Stephens once wrote; "the first thing was to win, the second to get the prize after you had won it". Why the American defenders always won against foreign challengers is a question that everybody asks about the America's Cup. The answer, at least partially, is that the defenders were run by exceptionally competent, aggressive amateur sailors who, before 1920, were content just to oversee the professional skipper and crew. Rarely, if ever, were challengers managed by men of the caliber of Paine and Iselin. These complicated, expensive yachts demanded good organization, and there was something about the American system that provided it.

Paine's good judgement paid off in three happy, successful defenses. In 1885 he invited Joe Elsworth, who had sailed in *Countess of Dufferin* nine years earlier, to help his Bostonian captain Aub Crocker get around the tricky waters off New York, and some say that Elsworth made the difference. Elsworth was also the only man to sail in both a challenger and a defender.

The difference between Paine and Henn was in what they wanted to get out of racing. Paine wanted to win, and so he did. Henn, however, had other interests, as he indicated when asked if the Royal Yacht Squadron might challenge again: "The club hardly thinks the game is worth the hunting. It is a long trip over here in the first place, and then you miss a whole racing season abroad. Then the chances are that you come over here and have virtually no race, for the weather is so calm that it is no real racing". To Charles Paine and his successors there was no such thing as "no real racing".

William Henn, an ex-Royal Navy officer, had more the soul of a sportsman than a racer. In fact he lived permanently on Galatea together with his wife.

Mayflower
Designer: E. Burgess
L.O.A.: 100'
L.W.L.: 86'

Galatea
Designer: J. Beavor Webb
L.O.A.: 103'
L.W.L.: 87'

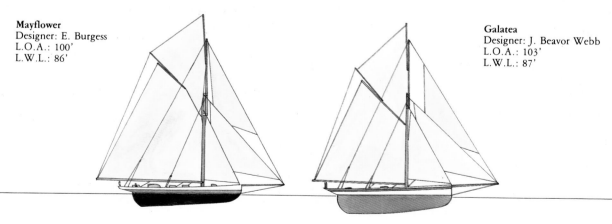

	date	course	allowance	elapsed time	corrected time	wins by
Mayflower	9/7	N.Y.Y.C. course. 32.6 miles		h. 05.26.41	h. 05.26.41	12'02''
Galatea			00'38''	h. 05.39.21	h. 05.38.43	
Mayflower	9/11	20 miles to leeward from Sandy Hook Lightship and return. 40 miles		h. 06.49.00	h. 06.49.00	29'09''
Galatea			00'39''	h. 07.18.48	h. 07.18.09	

1887
Volunteer-Thistle

For the third straight year, Edward Burgess went to work designing a cup contender for Charles Paine. This time, the challenge came from the Royal Clyde Yacht Club and named a new George Watson-designed cutter called *Thistle* whose waterline length, the New York Yacht Club was assured, would be 85 feet—about that of *Mayflower*. The Scots titillated everybody by building *Thistle* in secret, not revealing any dimensions not required by the deed of gift, and eventually launching her under a huge canvas bib. Of course, this hide and seek tactic succeeded in attracting immense publicity, which increased to an epidemic level when Watson began to plant the plans of other boats he had designed with gullible journalists, claiming they were those of *Thistle*.

Besides being shrewd and imaginative, George Watson was a superb yacht designer who created some of the most beautiful vessels ever built, among them *Thistle* and the royal racing cutter *Britannia*. He was also hardworking, and research he conducted on New York sailing conditions convinced him to pile clouds of sail on the new boat in anticipation of light winds. Obviously, he could not have made this commitment without the enthusiastic support of a rich syndicate that cared little for success in fresh British winds. The favorable chances of light winds also encouraged him to cut away the lateral profile of *Thistle*'s keel in order to reduce resistance. Whether Watson was right or wrong, Edward Burgess finally had met his match in creativity.

Meanwhile, Burgess designed his biggest, fastest yacht yet. Named *Volunteer* in honor of Paine's Civil War service, she was made of steel at a yard in Wilmington, Delaware, and then towed to Boston for finishing-off and rigging. She was built much more quickly than her wooden predecessors — and less well. Her finish, in particular, was very rough. Paine and other Americans came to believe that the challenger would have to give ten instead of six months' notice in order to allow a proper design and construction job. Once she was finally ready to race, however, *Volunteer* was clearly superior to *Mayflower*. She went on to dominate the summer's racing season and beat *Mayflower* in the only trial race by more than sixteen minutes. Across the Atlantic, *Thistle* had come out of wraps to win eleven of fifteen races and with her 9,000 square feet of sail — 1,500 feet greater than *Galatea*'s

rig — quickly won a reputation as a "big, sail-carrying brute".

When the two boats finally came together in the same water, observers were astonished that they were so similar. A change in British handicapping rules allowed greater beam, so *Thistle*, at 20 feet, was all of 5 feet wider than her predecessor *Galatea*, and only 3 feet narrower than *Volunteer*. Both boats had handsome clipper bows, though the American's was more pronounced than the Scotsman's; both designers had pared away the underbody, though Watson had taken more slices than Burgess. Of course, *Volunteer* had a centerboard and a steering wheel for her aggressive skipper, Hank Haff, a Long Island professional, and *Thistle* had a deep keel and a long tiller, at which her Scots captain, John Barr, tugged with tackles. But for the first time since Alexander Cuthbert ventured South with his versions of centerboard schooners, the challenging and defending yachts came from the same school of yacht design — albeit not from the same classroom.

Unfortunately, a scandal soon broke through the atmosphere of cordial reunion. When *Thistle* was measured, her waterline was found to be not the promised 85 feet but 86.46 feet (in their anguish, contemporary commentators made sure always to carry the decimal to the hundredth place). Perhaps if the Scots had been less blatantly secret about their boat, the yacht club would have reacted more calmly; after all, the time allowance system would easily compensate for the difference. But the issue seemed to be larger than mere measurements. Despite claims to the contrary, international sports competition has always been a lightning rod for nationalistic energies. That is probably no more true than in the America's Cup matches, where a veneer of gentlemanly civility can gild deep-seated cut-throat impulses on both sides. Add the normal suspicions between peoples who share a language and you have all the elements for an explosion, given the right bolt of controversy. Honor, trust, and, if we may be a little cynical, the New York Yacht Club's control over the America's Cup were at stake, and the British — especially George Watson — were allowed to feel the full chill of the club's cold fury. Some club members even suggested cancelling the match. For the third time George Schuyler was invited to mend a rift in the international

Volunteer *(above)* and Thistle *(below)*. Volunteer, *designed by George Watson, was captained by John Barr, brother of the more famous Charlie, skipper of numerous victorious defenders.*

cup community. Now seventy-six years old, he heard testimony from all parties and advised that despite the ''remarkably inaccurate information'' provided by Watson, there was no evidence of bad faith on the part of *Thistle*'s owners.

After all that build-up, the races were, sadly, a bleak disappointment. *Volunteer* won them by nineteen and eleven minutes, and *Thistle*'s crowd of supporters, who had arrived on their own steam yacht in a haze of Scotch whiskey and a flurry of bagpipes, drank one last toast to the unwinnable cup and went home. George Watson explained the loss by saying that he had cut *Thistle*'s underbody away excessively, allowing her to slide sideways too quickly under her immense sails. She was soon sold to Kaiser Wilhelm II of Germany, who renamed her *Meteor* and rerigged her as a schooner, but Watson would have the satisfaction of seeing his ideas copied and carried further in the next generation of cup yachts.

Thistle was an excellent boat, perhaps the best challenger in the cup's short history, but she was beaten by a superior, a great yacht that was better managed and better sailed. Charles Paine, who had been worried about the challenger, pulled out his bag of tricks well before the match started. While racing one day in an increasing wind, he noticed *Thistle* keeping pace off to the side of the course. Instead of having the crew douse the topsail in order to decrease the angle of heel, he lugged the sail through some strong gusts hoping to convince Watson that *Volunteer* was abnormally stable. Sure enough, Watson added several tons of unnecessary ballast to *Thistle* to make her as stiff as her competitor, with the end result that he only slowed her down.

A few days after the last race, the city of Boston honored Paine and Burgess in an extraordinary ceremony at Faneuil Hall, the Revolutionary War meeting place known as ''the cradle of liberty''. In

Above: challenger and defender during a race with a light wind.
Below: Thistle *in dry-dock. Note the clipper bow which contrasts with the vertical cutter bow of her predecessors.*

speech after speech, dignitaries embarrassed their two shy guests with elaborate praises for their achievement — winning three America's Cup matches in a row. It was an evening not without humor: Oliver Wendell Holmes sent a message claiming that Paine was the only general "I ever heard of who made himself illustrious by running away from all his competitors". Burgess modestly said of Paine that he "thought out the effect of every line, and every detail of construction and rig, and directed all so as to secure him the possession of the fastest yacht in the world..... I have been simply his executive officer".

And Paine predicted that while challengers would improve, "we may always feel hopeful of a happy result while my young friend Mr. Burgess is ready to bring forward a boat to meet them".

Down in Manhattan, members of the New York Yacht Club were singing:

The Cup! The Cup! Fill up! Fill up,
   o sirs, the night is young,
And faint the heart would care to part
   before the song is sung!

'Tis Neptune strikes the string
   till the grand traditions ring;
Oh, never yet have yachtsmen met
   a nobler theme to sing!

I pledge you, sirs, the Cup!
   May we never give it up!
A bumper, sirs: The Club! Hurrah!
   The Cup! The Cup! The Cup!

Yet tragedy and time-consuming controversy would interfere before the cup would be sailed for once again.

Just as in 1983, the challenger's keel was the subject of intense public debate enhanced by tight secrecy. Here a diver, hired by a newspaper, goes down to discover its shape. It turned out that the water was too muddy.

Volunteer
Designer: E. Burgess
L.O.A.: 107'
L.W.L.: 86'

Thistle
Designer: G.L. Watson
L.O.A.: 109'
L.W.L.: 87'

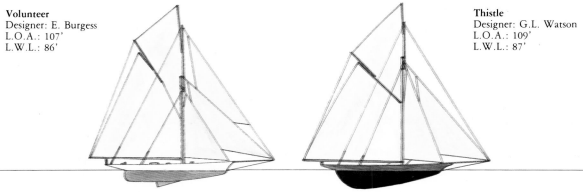

	date	course	allowance	elapsed time	corrected time	wins by
Volunteer	9/27	N.Y.Y.C. course. 32.6 miles		h. 04.53.18	h. 04.53.18	19'23''
Thistle			00'05''	h. 05.12.46	h. 05.12.41	
Volunteer	9/30	20 miles to windward from Sandy Hook		h. 05.42.56	h. 05.42.56	11'48''
Thistle		Lightship and return. 40 miles	00'06''	h. 05.54.51	h. 05.54.45	

1893
Vigilant-Valkyrie II

Having survived James Ashbury's litigiousness, Alexander Cuthbert's ineptitude, Lt. Henn's monkey, and *Thistle*'s stretched waterline, the New York Yacht Club decided that if the America's Cup was to survive God knows what other controversies and idiosyncrasies, the matches would have to be held in a more businesslike way. Rejecting an immediate challenge from a Scot who lived in New York, the club had a committee write up a new deed of gift to be signed by George Schuyler, and it was accepted only a month after the last *Volunteer-Thistle* race. While its two predecessors had been relatively informal letters of transmittal, this was an officious legal document overflowing with contractual terminology; at more than one thousand words, it was five times the length of the 1857 deed. Although much of it was a lawyer's rewriting of earlier provisions, the new deed included some new requirements. One satisfied old complaints about the New York Harbor course: from now on, all races would be held on the ocean over alternating triangle and windward-leeward, 30 mile courses. The committee (which included Charles Paine) also lengthened the time between the challenge and the first race to ten months.

There was also the matter of dimensions. Still sore about the *Thistle* dispute and no doubt unsure about the direction in which yacht design was headed, the committee specified that not just the waterline length but also the draft, waterline beam, and extreme beam be provided with the challenge so that American designers would know what kind of boat they were up against — and so challenging designers would be more careful with their calculations. Finally, the seriousness of the *Thistle* campaign led the committee to plan for the day when an American boat would be the challenger: centerboarders would always be eligible.

To the yacht club's obvious surprise, the third deed of gift was greeted by howls of protest directed mainly at the dimensions clause, which, some people cried, would require the challenging designer to give away his boat's shape. "The terms of the new Deed of Gift are such that foreign vessels are unable to challenge", proclaimed the Yacht Racing Association, which comprised many European yacht clubs. An Irish lord, the Earl of Dunraven, challenged through the Royal Yacht Squadron on the assumption that it would not have to enforce the deed if

Lord Dunraven, on the right, took up the controversial legacy of James Ashbury. His attitude did, however, prove useful in modifying certain stands of the New York Yacht Club.

Vigilant at a mark. *This boat, a centerboarder, was the first of a long series of defenders designed by Nat Herreshoff.*

he won. When the yacht club assured the Squadron that that was not the case, the challenge was withdrawn, and for several years the cup was held captive by controversy and rumors. An Australian yacht designer named Walter Reeks appeared in New York and London and claimed there was interest in a Sydney challenge. Lt. Henn alternated hints of making another go of it with demurrals (no Briton "even thinks about the America's Cup", he reported in 1891); and despite his aristocratic claim that the deed of gift was "altogether too complicated a document to govern a matter of sport such as yacht racing", Dunraven never entirely backed away.

Probably more objectionable than the dimensions clause was the New York Yacht Club's continued claim of absolute ownership of a trophy that only two generations earlier had been purchased and awarded by the Royal Yacht Squadron. That the Americans couched this apparent theft in that most American of institutions, a written document, must have been especially

galling to English aristocrats, with their long, proud heritage of unwritten laws guided by custom. To New York businessmen, there was no other way to establish the parameters of an event as complex and prestigious as an America's Cup match.

Thus they were astonished by Lord Dunraven's eagerness to make suggestions as to how the conditions for the matches should be set. Dunraven had no right to circumvent the new deed; in any case, some of his ideas betrayed not only a misreading of the situation but also complete naïveté. In one of his many magazine articles on the subject, Dunraven proposed that three Americans and three Englishmen meet "in New York or London, or in some other convenient place — Paris might be suitable — and sit down and discuss the matter thoroughly and draw up definite rules". That settled, they would draw lots to determine the race site.

Dunraven, like Ashbury before him, finally realized that the yacht club was not going to be swayed. He more

49

or less recognized the third deed of gift as authoritative, and the club in return accepted a challenge that included only the waterline length of his Watson-designed *Valkyrie II*. When asked by a journalist if after all the negotiation he expected to win, Dunraven answered simply, ''I have a wholesome regard for the genius of Herreshoff''.

We have already encountered Herreshoff in his experimental catamarans. With his blind brother John, he had made the Herreshoff Manufacturing Company, in Bristol, Rhode Island, the major builder of steam yachts, and now in the early Nineties he was turning out a whole new breed of sailboat.

Where *Puritan* and her breed had looked like shaped logs, *Gloriana*, *Wasp*, *Navahoe*, and the other Herreshoff ''out-and-outers'' were great canoes with narrow fin keels appended. Not surprisingly, he produced two new defense candidates in 1893 to sail against two Boston boats (one designed by Charles Paine's son, John, and managed by Paine). Managed by a wealthy, intense New York banker-yachtsman named C. Oliver Iselin, *Vigilant* was chosen to defend. ''The prototype'', Winfield Thompson wrote, ''of a vicious kind of yacht, whose existence has been more a curse than a blessing to the sport of yacht racing'', *Vigilant* cost over $100,000 to build and race (*Volunteer* cost about $40,000) and had a crew of seventy (*Volunteer* carried fewer than thirty) not so much because her rig required them but because their combined weight of 5 tons added to her stability and, by sinking her lower in the water, increased her sailing length and maximum speed. Only Herreshoff was able to steer this wild vessel with any skill, but he was sometimes required to leave the helm to supervise repairs to her complicated rigging.

After winning two races with surprising ease — *Valkyrie II* was considered to be quite fast — *Vigilant* and Herreshoff had the race of their lives. Damage to both boats caused a delay in the start, and then the Watson-designed challenger pulled away on the 15 mile beat to windward in 25 knots of easterly wind to lead by two minutes at the mark. Soon after rounding, Iselin and Herreshoff had a man hoisted onto the boom by a halyard, and this daredevil walked the length of the 90 foot spar cutting the reef points, suspended only feet above the rushing water. While shaking the reef out, *Vigilant*'s crew hauled the large topsail aloft to replace the small heavy-weather topsail, and under this cloud of heavy canvas and the huge balloon jib topsail and spinnaker twinned forward of the mast, she roared after *Valkyrie II*. More seaworthy and less hard-driven, the challenger's crew left her reef tied in and, unlucky as well, they watched two spinnakers rip to shreds.

Averaging 11.5 knots down the run, *Vigilant* won by a little more than two minutes on elapsed time and only forty seconds on corrected time, and as she charged across the line only her thundering bow wave kept Iselin and Herreshoff from hearing the cheers of the fifty thousand or so spectators in the huge steamer fleet. The closest and most exciting race so far, it not only ended the series but also allowed Lord Dunraven to go home with both excuses as to why he had no victories and well-founded hopes for future success against his reckless opponents.

But as it turned out, Dunraven himself was the one who behaved with heedless abandon.

On the following page: Valkyrie II passes to leeward of Navahoe, an American yacht, during a race held on the Solent before she left for the United States.

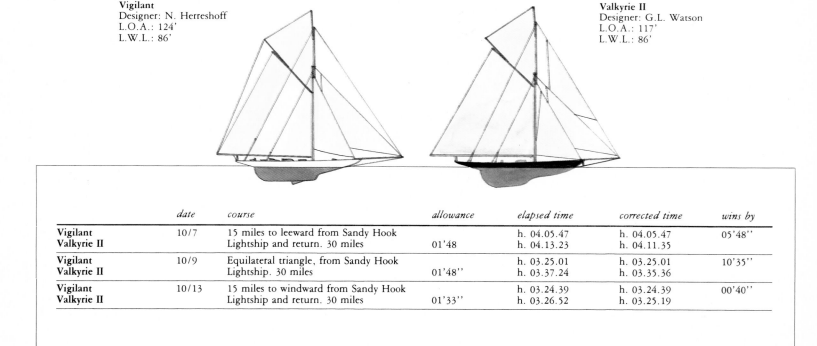

Vigilant
Designer: N. Herreshoff
L.O.A.: 124'
L.W.L.: 86'

Valkyrie II
Designer: G.L. Watson
L.O.A.: 117'
L.W.L.: 86'

	date	course	allowance	elapsed time	corrected time	wins by
Vigilant	10/7	15 miles to leeward from Sandy Hook		h. 04.05.47	h. 04.05.47	05'48''
Valkyrie II		Lightship and return. 30 miles	01'48	h. 04.13.23	h. 04.11.35	
Vigilant	10/9	Equilateral triangle, from Sandy Hook		h. 03.25.01	h. 03.25.01	10'35''
Valkyrie II		Lightship. 30 miles	01'48''	h. 03.37.24	h. 03.35.36	
Vigilant	10/13	15 miles to windward from Sandy Hook		h. 03.24.39	h. 03.24.39	00'40''
Valkyrie II		Lightship and return. 30 miles	01'33''	h. 03.26.52	h. 03.25.19	

1895
Defender-Valkyrie III

The chaos and interference caused by the excessive number of spectators' boats was one of the reasons for Dunraven's complaints.

Windham Thomas Wyndham-Quin, fourth Earl of Dunraven and second Baron Kenry of the United Kingdom, was born in County Limerick, Ireland, in 1841. Descended from the Hy-Ifearnean clan, he was heir to one of the few titles of Celtic origin in the Irish peerage. As a child, he was forbidden by his father, a convert to Catholicism, to be with his Protestant mother and was packed off to school in Rome. These events "produced an obstinate resistance" (as a biographer of the Earl puts it) that reverberated throughout his long life. In 1871, he went to America to hunt big game and, guided by the famous Indian scout Buffalo Bill Cody, shot elk in Nebraska. He returned several times and bought sixty thousand acres of land for a game preserve in the Colorado Territory. He wrote books about his hunting adventures and about spiritualism, in which he was more than a dabbler, and moved into politics with, as he wrote, an independent "cross-bench mind" that did not endear him to the leadership of his party, the

Liberals. Twice Under-Secretary for the Colonies (he resigned once on principle), he later chaired a committee in the House of Lords working for the reform of workhouses, those hell holes where children and old people were forced to labor fifteen hours a day. It was during this period when, with typical contrariness, Dunraven began to sail expensive racing cutters.

Not a lazy man, as we have seen, Dunraven studied yacht design after returning from his first Cup challenge and produced a small boat, *Audrey*. She beat an imported Herreshoff design, so Dunraven felt optimistic about the new challenge, and not simply because George L. Watson promised something special. When *Valkyrie III* and the Herreshoff-designed *Defender* (managed by C. Oliver Iselin) finally met in September 1895, observers were astonished to see that the challenger was a beamy sloop some three feet wider than the American boat. There had already been some cries of treason over the fact that *Defender* was the first

Defender, *built in bronze, steel and aluminum and soon to suffer the negative effects of galvanic corrosion, was captained by Hank Haff. Overleaf:* Valkyrie III *displays her impressive sail area.*   53

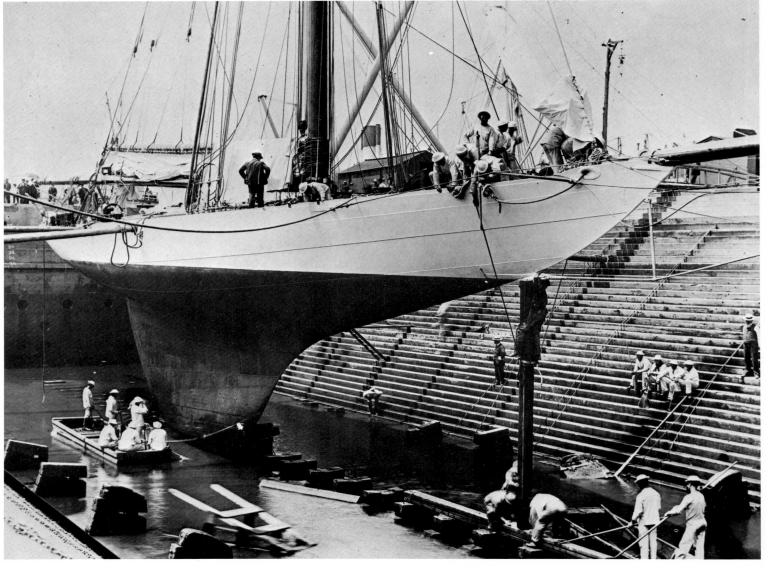

Defender, *which had a crew of 30, in drydock. She was the first*
American boat (other than America *herself) not to have a centerboard.*

American boat to sail for the cup (other than *America* herself) not to have a centerboard, but her relative narrowness was confounding. Her other mark of distinction was her part-aluminum, part-bronze hull, which began to corrode almost immediately due to galvanic action.

As far as the racing went, *Defender* won the only real contest in a light shifting wind. Three days later, after a break to remeasure requested by Dunraven — who thought *Defender* lower, hence longer, in the water since the pre-match measurement (the difference was only 1/8 inch) — his boat won but was disqualified for fouling *Defender* at the start. Separated by a blundering spectator boat as they approached the line, the two boats converged as the challenger bore down on the defender to avoid starting prematurely. *Valkyrie*'s helmsman, Edward Sycamore, headed up sharply when the rigs threatened to touch, but the end of his boat's long overhanging boom raked his opponent's deck and broke her windward topmast shroud. *Defender* limped

around the course (losing by only forty-seven seconds) and, using photographic evidence, the committee ruled in her favor. Iselin offered to resail the race but Dunraven peevishly refused.

Dunraven, who never ceased to claim that it was *Defender* that fouled *Valkyrie*, then wrote a letter to the club threatening not to sail the next race if the course were as jammed with steamers. An old problem, this crowding had been addressed by "Keep Away" signs held up by the competing crews and, in 1895, by a fleet of yacht club patrol boats. There had been little improvement. The club tried to talk Dunraven round, but *Valkyrie* dropped out of the third race after starting.

That was the match, with only one completed race. But when the Earl returned to England he continued to criticize the yacht club. More serious, he accused Iselin of cheating by adding ballast after the original measurement and taking it out before the remeasurement. *Defender*, he said, was at least one foot longer during the first race than her measurement indicated. He knew this to be true, he said, because he himself had seen *Defender*'s crew working all night stowing the ballast and, the next morning, noticed a drain hole and the bobstay fitting sitting lower than usual. To settle this charge and its broad-ranging implications about American honor, the club appointed a blue-ribbon panel of distinguished members with strong trans-Atlantic ties, among them the banker J. Pierpont Morgan and the naval strategist Alfred Thayer Mahan. Testimony from Herreshoff, consulting engineers, and Haff boxed Dunraven into a corner: the work he had observed involved restowing ballast already on board; the two fittings could be lowered or raised simply by moving the crew and the boom on deck; and it would take fully 13 tons of additional lead to increase *Defender*'s waterline length by a foot. Iselin was cleared.

What was behind all this? Why would Dunraven stake his own reputation on the relative position of a drain pipe? We know that he had been angered by the way *Vigilant*'s speed had been artificially increased with extra crewmembers in 1893, and that some American friends had hinted that the tactic was typical of Iselin. With his freshly acquired knowledge of yacht design, Dunraven was overly proud of his ability to evaluate boats and, with that life-long, painful oversensitivity about his independence, he was not ready to defer to any authority. Most important, we think, is the fact that in *Valkyrie III* he had perhaps the best chance ever to take the cup back to Cowes, so he had to start finding or inventing excuses for losing even before he started winning. Lord Dunraven self-destructed on the eve of his greatest triumph. He was not the last America's Cup challenger to do so.

Edwin D. Morgan, one of the syndicate members, is in the center on the deck of Defender. *At the helm is skipper Hank Haff, a veteran of America's Cup races. This was to be his last Cup defense.*

Defender
Designer: N. Herreshoff
L.O.A.: 123'
L.W.L.: 89'

Valkyrie III
Designer: G.L. Watson
L.O.A.: 129'
L.W.L.: 89'

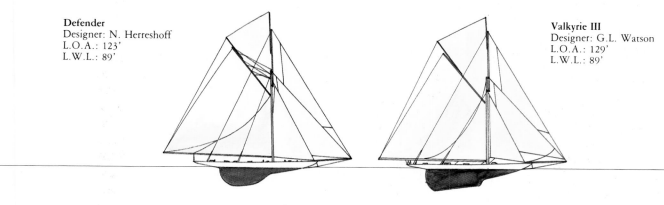

	date	course	allowance	elapsed time	corrected time	wins by
Defender	9/7	15 miles from mark, 3 miles N.E. of	00'29''	h. 05.00.24	h. 04.59.55	08'49''
Valkyrie III		Seabright, N.J. and return. 30 miles		h. 05.08.44	h. 05.08.44	
Valkyrie III	9/10	Equilateral triangle from Sandy Hook		h. 03.55.09	h. 03.55.09	00'47''
Defender		Lightship. 30 miles	00'29''	h. 03.56.25	h. 03.55.56	
Defender	9/12	15 miles to windward from Sandy Hook	00'29''	h. 04.44.12	h. 04.43.43	
Valkyrie III		Lightship and return. 30 miles		retired		

1899
Columbia-Shamrock

When the New York Yacht Club expelled the Earl of Dunraven as an honorary member on February 27, 1896, the chances of there being another English challenge seemed beyond hope. Already the Royal Victoria Yacht Club had sent and withdrawn a challenge on behalf of a certain Charles D. Rose — English criticism that they were collaborating with the enemy and denying Dunraven's rightful claims made the challenge a liability for both. The club tried to recruit a challenger (by one account, its members may have even offered to finance one), but with no apparent success until April 1897, when rumors of a challenge from Northern Ireland's Royal Ulster Yacht Club began to appear in the New York newspapers. The name most prominently mentioned in connection with the possible challenge was that of the Marquis of Dufferin, the club's commodore. Nobody seemed aware of the web of connections that made Dufferin the ideal midwife for a renewal of amicable relations. Then in his early seventies, he had behind him a distinguished diplomatic career, having served as governor-general of Canada, viceroy of India, and ambassador to France, Italy, Turkey, and Russia. He was also an active yachtsman, a member of the Royal Yacht Squadron and, since 1859, an honorary member of the New York Yacht Club. And he was the only man whose name was carried on the transom of a cup competitor since the 1876 challenger, *Countess of Dufferin*, had been named in honor of his wife during their tenure in Canada.

For more than a year, somebody kept the rumor active without any published denials until, on August 2, 1898, the carefully orchestrated overture ended with the dramatic announcement that there would indeed be a challenge from Ulster — not from Dufferin but from a much less aristocratic but equally diplomatic member named Sir Thomas Lipton. Dufferin, having found a sponsor for a challenge, was never heard of again in cup circles.

Who was this Lipton? Born to Irish parents in Glasgow, Scotland, in 1850, he was reared in poverty and emigrated to the United States as an adolescent. After wandering around for a while, he took a job in a New York grocery store. He returned to Scotland when he was nineteen and opened his own grocery store, which became a chain of shops, which became an inter-

Thomas Lipton in a period print. Of humble origins — he was a grocer's son — he did a great deal to calm the waters stirred by Lord Dunraven's accusations.

Shamrock *as seen from the deck of* Columbia *during a race. At the helm of the defender is Charlie Barr, the most famous helmsman at the time.*

national merchandising phenomenon with tea plantations in Ceylon and stockyards in the great plains and, behind it all, Lipton's simple faith in the customer's willingness to buy decent products at a low price if only he could be lured into the store. While advertising had existed long before Lipton opened his first store, he invented that strategy of ubiquitous publicity called the advertising campaign.

Lipton hoped this to be an all-Irish challenge (in fact, he had proposed such a project back in 1887), but all that was Irish about *Shamrock* were her name, club, and owner's blood. George Watson had sworn off Cup activity after the 1895 fiasco, so a Scot named William Fife designed the boat, which was built near London. In New York, Commodore J. Pierpont Morgan, his distant relative Edwin D. Morgan, and C. Oliver Iselin built a new Herreshoff boat called *Columbia*. A former commodore, Edwin Morgan was described by W.P. Stephens as a man who "thought no more of buying a yacht than

the average man does of picking up a paper as he passes a newsstand". J. Pierpont Morgan had recently become the most powerful banker — perhaps the most powerful man — in the world, and had just surprised his clubmates by handing over title to $200,000 worth of land on West 44th Street on which an opulent new clubhouse would be constructed. This syndicate of big spenders laid out an estimated quarter of a million dollars on *Columbia*, but *Shamrock* was believed to have cost Lipton as much as twice that amount by the end of the summer. Two men could not have been more unlike than the genial showman Lipton and the scowling introvert J.P. Morgan, but they played their parts well. In their luxury steamers *Erin* and *Corsair* they headed the triumphal parade in New York Harbor welcoming Admiral George Dewey back from his victories in the Spanish-American War. Since neither knew much about sailing, they watched the match from the same glamorous platforms, which also patrolled the course along with a

Five men of Shamrock's *crew on the bowsprit prepare to hoist a jib shortly before the race.*

dozen U.S. Navy warships. This innovation, which kept the course clear of spectator vessels, was the result of a special act of the United States Congress, but its roots obviously lay in the Dunraven affair, which also fertilized Iselin's suggestion that each side send a representative to the other to observe measuring. Joseph Chamberlain, the British colonial secretary, had begged Lipton to avoid straining international relations, but the last person needing that advice was the ever amicable Sir Thomas. The only strain he showed was boredom while thirteen days passed before a race could be completed.

When a race was finally finished, on October 16, *Columbia* was the winner by a large margin in less than 10 knots of wind. The next day, her skipper, Charlie Barr, steered right through *Shamrock*'s blanket after the start and was climbing out to a big lead when the challenger's topmast snapped and she dropped out. As required, *Columbia* sailed around the course. The crews endured another abandoned race after *Shamrock* took on several tons of lead to increase her waterline length by 1.3 feet, and then had an exciting race in fresh wind. *Shamrock* started on a run about a minute before *Columbia*, but, despite problems with her spinnaker, the defending boat slowly ground down the challenger, sailed through her lee, and led by only seventeen seconds at the mark. Beating back into 20 knots of wind, *Columbia* carried only her "lowers" — jib, forestaysail, and mainsail — while *Shamrock* lugged a topsail. In the chill green-black of an approaching late October storm, the defender shot across the line more than six minutes ahead. Not without some satisfaction, for he had become the toast of New York, Lipton sailed home with plans to rechallenge in the first year of the new century.

Columbia
Designer: N. Herreshoff
L.O.A.: 131'
L.W.L.: 90'

Shamrock
Designer: W. Fife
L.O.A.: 128'
L.W.L.: 90'

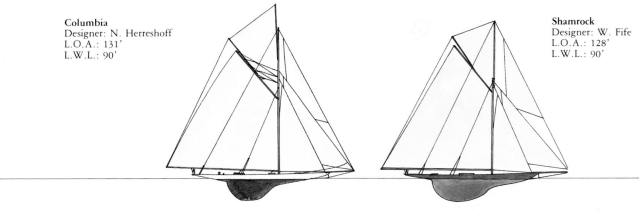

	date	course	allowance	elapsed time	corrected time	wins by
Columbia	10/16	15 miles to windward from Sandy Hook		h. 04.53.53	h. 04.53.53	10'08''
Shamrock		Lightship and return. 30 miles	00'06''	h. 05.04.07	h. 05.04.01	
Columbia	10/17	Equilateral triangle from Sandy Hook		h. 03.37.00	h. 03.37.00	
Shamrock		Lightship. 30 miles	00'06''	retired		
Columbia	10/20	15 miles to windward from Sandy Hook	00'16''	h. 03.38.25	h. 03.38.09	06'34''
Shamrock		Lightship and return. 30 miles		h. 03.44.43	h. 03.44.43	

In the past, as today, racing yachts were equipped with masts that had the unpleasant tendency to crash on deck. Columbia (above) and Shamrock II (below) after such accidents.

1901
Columbia-Shamrock II

Above: a room of the New York Yacht Club, moved to its present site on 44th Street in 1901 thanks to a generous offer by Pierpont Morgan. On the opposite page: Columbia *and* Shamrock *running on different tacks.*

When Sir Thomas Lipton returned, it was with a new boat designed by George Watson who, like everybody else, was unable to say no to the open-handed grocer and came back from retirement. *Shamrock II*'s departure for America was delayed by the collapse of her mast almost on the head of Lipton's friend King Edward VII, news of which only heightened interest in his challenge, but this year he had to compete for attention with a self-promoter from Boston and a modest Scottish-American professional sailor.

Thomas W. Lawson was a quixotic Bostonian who, though he knew even less about sailing than Lipton, decided that he wanted to defend the America's Cup. As was also true with Lipton, his motives were less than pure, however. Not a member of the New York Yacht Club and determined never to join it, Lawson claimed to be an average sort of man not in need of such connections. A self-made multimillionaire who had the gambler's instincts of the club's founders, he made his

first million at age twenty, lost it almost immediately, and went on to gather and be separated from several more fortunes with the kind of stock-market speculation that caused the Securities and Exchange Commission to be formed many years later. His enemies in these escapades frequently included J. Pierpont Morgan and his friends and colleagues, who were attempting to squash this kind of independent and frequently disruptive behavior. Not by coincidence, Morgan was a prominent member of the New York Yacht Club, so when Lawson claimed his right to enter the cup trials without being a member of the club, he was merely playing maverick in a new arena but with the same opponents.

He did not bother to inform the club's America's Cup Committee of his plans when he commissioned his suitably named *Independence*. When the chairman, a Wall Street lawyer, Commodore Lewis Cass Ledyard, wrote to inform him that if he wanted her to sail in the trials he would have to sell or charter her to a club

Measurers at work in a dinghy to check Lipton's
Shamrock II, *which had a handicap
of forty-three seconds.*

while and claimed that she handled as awkwardly as an ice wagon. She was broken up before the 1901 cup match even started.

The other product of the *Independence* campaign was *Lawson's History of the America's Cup*, a beautiful and generally authoritative account of *America*'s career and the nineteenth century matches. Winfield M. Thompson wrote the historical chapters and Lawson (who gave away three thousand copies of the book) was responsible for the colorful and highly prejudiced section about his own boat. Much of the strange correspondence with Ledyard is reprinted in an appendix — at least the letters that make Lawson come over well.

More enduring than Lawson's burst upon the yachting scene was the performance of the professional skipper Charles Barr. Born in Scotland in 1864, he came to America with his half-brother John Barr. His touch at the helm and authority with the roughhewn sailors who manned racing boats gradually earned him ever more responsible commands until he was hired to sail *Vigilant* in the 1895 trials against the new *Defender*. There, white-bearded Hank Haff initiated him to the big time with rough, sometimes illegal tactics. Haff won the trials and Barr learned a lesson. He was chosen by Iselin, who did not favor passive skippers, to sail *Columbia* in 1899, and now J.P. Morgan and Edwin D. Morgan (who had bought out Iselin's share) asked him to sail her again against the new boats, *Independence* and the Herreshoff-designed *Constitution*.

When an amateur steered a big boat around a course, it was headline news in the sports pages. L. Francis Herreshoff, Nat's son, once described one of these huge skimming dishes as having "one head or brain (the captain), several mouthpieces (the mates), and twenty or fifty bunches of sinew, muscle, and leather, which acted instantly at each order". No amateur, no matter how wealthy, would have the authority to command such a team and the 130-foot, 100-ton vessel that it operated. A good captain would earn $3,500 in a cup season — the price of a new mainsail — commanding deckhands who made $45 a month plus $5 a race. Sailors with dangerous jobs, like the topmastmen working 80 feet above deck, got bonuses. The work was long and hard. A jib change taking five minutes was considered exceptionally fast, and simply drying the acres of cotton sails required much more time than the four-hour races (of which there were only fifteen or twenty a summer anyway).

Going into the 1901 season, Charlie Barr had one big advantage: a good crew. His most dangerous competitor and the favorite to defend the cup, Uriah Rhodes of *Constitution*, had made the mistake of trying to choose his Deer Island, Maine, crew himself without going through local middle-men, with the result that he was unable to recruit anybody from that breeding ground of yachting deckhands and was left with poor sail-handling that plagued him all summer. But that was not his only

member, Lawson misrepresented the message. In the painfully polite exchange that followed, letter after letter from Ledyard made clear to any reader except Lawson that the only requirement was that *Independence* fly the club's burgee; Lawson and his people could remain on board and sail her just so long as a club member had titular charge of her. And letter after letter from Lawson stated his interpretation of Ledyard's requirement: "No American other than a member of the New York Yacht Club has a right to take part in the defence of an international cup, rightly named America's and belonging to all Americans".

Back and forth this correspondence flowed with no minds being changed, until Lawson finally volunteered to charter *Independence* to the cup committee itself. The exasperated Ledyard finally blew the whistle: "Your last letter", he wrote, "indicates a settled purpose on your part to misunderstand the position of the committee, which has been again and again stated to you in terms too plain to any but willful misconstruction". Ledyard declined further communication.

Of course, Lawson kept the press fully informed of his self-imposed plight, and he struck a sympathetic chord. Peter Finley Dunne's uneducated but shrewd social commentator "Mr. Dooley" interpreted his problem this way: "Yachtin' is a gintleman's spoort, an' in dalin' with gintlemen ye can't be too careful".

Two tangible objects came out of Lawson's sly quest. One was a failure. The $200,000 *Independence* had a radical scow-type shape, an extremely leaky hull, and few redeeming features. She did race in some contests organized by a Newport, Rhode Island, sailing association and though she showed bursts of speed, did poorly. Charles Francis Adams, a young amateur whose name will appear in greater glory later on, steered her for a

Above: Shamrock *crossing the Atlantic under jury rig so as not to strain the racing sails.*
Below: Thomas Lipton on board his Erin, *which he used as support to his Shamrocks.*

Charlie Barr at the wheel of Columbia. *The famous Scottish-born helmsman was to steer three defenders to victory.*

handicap. *Constitution* steered awkwardly, her rigging broke down all too often, her sails set poorly, and, without a commanding manager like Iselin in charge, Rhodes seemed distracted by advice from all quarters. His biggest problem, though, was Charlie Barr, who, knowing that his boat was theoretically slower than *Constitution*, hounded Rhodes all over the race course. "Handling *Columbia* as a man would a bicycle", wrote W.P. Stephens, who was there, "turning her as on a pivot, he took chances that would have been dangerous in the extreme for an average good skipper". His favorite position at the start, learned at the hands of Hank Haff six years earlier, was on his competitor's windward quarter driving her down and away from the line. It was not quite legal, but it was effective — especially when Rhodes did not know if *Constitution* would go where he aimed her and whether his crew would do what he ordered. According to one observer, Thomas Fleming Day, "Barr simply made a monkey of the other man. He forced him to do whatever he wished and shoved and jostled *Constitution*, the latter's skipper giving way in the most complaisant manner". The two boats split the races up to the trials, where *Columbia* won all three races but was protested for sailing all over *Constitution* at the start of the last one. On September 5, she and Charlie Barr enjoyed the special distinction of being both disqualified from a race and selected to defend the America's Cup.

For the Americans, the committee was right to choose the aggressive skipper. *Shamrock II*, the first cup boat designed with the help of model-towing in a test tank, was fast and with Edward Sycamore at the helm she was well sailed. Held in the shadow of the assassination of President William McKinley, on September 6, this was the closest match in cup history, with an average winning margin of only one minute fifty-two seconds. *Shamrock* was first to the first mark in each of the three races and actually finished first in the last one. All three races followed the same pattern. The starts were hard-fought, with Barr struggling to get his favorite windward-quarter berth; he gained it in the first start, but that race was abandoned in a calm and Sycamore never let him have it so securely again. On the beats to windward, Sycamore sailed for speed, Barr for the tactical advantage. Sometimes *Columbia* tacked twice as often as *Shamrock* to squeeze an extra few yards out of a windshift or to find a covering position on the challenger's windward bow. When given the opportunity to cover *Columbia*, which he often had since *Shamrock* usually led on the beats, Sycamore never took it for reasons summarized in his post-match statement, "I'll follow no amateurs' judgement again" — like Rhodes, he had too many advisers forced upon him.

The best race was the last one, a "Homeric contest", according to one newspaper, held on October 4. It was a running start and each boat tried to force the other to go first so as to be in the aggressive blanketing position. After delaying for more than two minutes, *Columbia* finally got off ahead and in the 9-knot wind. *Shamrock*, with some 800 square feet more in sail area, gradually passed her to lead by a minute at the mark. After a couple of tacks and a fifty-minute long board on the port tack, they traded tacks up the right-hand side of the beat, *Columbia* — which was allowed 43 seconds on handicap — never letting *Shamrock* get away, *Shamrock* — her afterguard perhaps fearing Barr's well-trained crew — unwilling to tack on her opponent's wind and thus start a tacking duel. The defender tacked eighteen times in the shifting wind, staying to the favored West; her opponent, pinned to the East, came about thirteen times. Finally they slipped toward the line on a final starboard board and luffed across it, *Shamrock* two seconds ahead but *Columbia* the clear winner on corrected time. As the huge spectator fleet let loose with a barrage of whistles, Charlie Barr casually pulled an apple out of his pocket and bit into it.

C. Oliver Iselin, in the center, and Nat Herreshoff, on his left, aboard Columbia
after her second defense.

Columbia
Designer: N. Herreshoff
L.O.A.: 131'
L.W.L.: 90'

Shamrock II
Designer: G.L. Watson
L.O.A.: 137'
L.W.L.: 89'

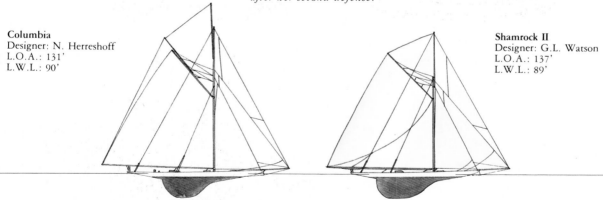

	date	course	allowance	elapsed time	corrected time	wins by
Columbia **Shamrock II**	9/28	15 miles to windward from Sandy Hook Lightship and return. 30 miles	00'43''	h. 04.31.07 h. 04.31.44	h. 04.30.24 h. 04.31.44	01'20''
Columbia **Shamrock II**	10/3	Equilateral triangle from Sandy Hook Lightship. 30 miles	00'43''	h. 03.13.18 h. 03.16.10	h. 03.12.35 h. 03.16.10	03'35''
Columbia **Shamrock II**	10/4	15 miles to leeward from Sandy Hook Lightship and return. 30 miles	00'43''	h. 04.33.40 h. 04.33.38	h. 04.32.57 h. 04.33.38	00'41''

1903
Reliance - Shamrock III

Greatly encouraged by the extraordinary closeness of the 1901 match, Sir Thomas Lipton tried to challenge with *Shamrock II* for 1902, but the club turned him down citing the deed of gift's prohibition against returning with a loser within two years. Since that provision had been introduced twenty years earlier to forestall another slaughter of Alexander Cuthbert's *Atalanta*, this was greeted with a certain amount of derision. It was probably true that the yacht club was both exhausted and frightened by its narrow win and needed time to regroup; since they were expensive and time-consuming, matches in consecutive years were ancient history. Despite rumors of an imminent Canadian challenge from Sydney, Nova Scotia, a new Lipton boat was expected to show up in 1903, and show up she did.

George Watson was tired and aging, but he helped William Fife with the design of *Shamrock III*, which, though drawn after considerable tank-testing, was as much a work of art as a work of science. Lipton's only white challenger — the other four were a bright Irish green — she was a beautifully proportioned melding of graceful sheer and rounded sections. By contemporary standards, she looked fast, and even after an early-season dismasting in which a deck hand was killed, the British were so optimistic that they tuned her up not

against *Shamrock II* but against Fife's earlier creation, the first *Shamrock*.

After racing in Scotland, both boats were towed across the Atlantic to New York and the tuning-up continued until the match started in late August. This was the first time that a challenger had the benefit of a trial horse in America, something the defender had automatically since she raced all summer in regattas sponsored by the New York and other yacht clubs. In any other year but 1903, this strategy might have made a major difference in the final results.

Meanwhile a millionaire's syndicate, including a Vanderbilt and a Rockefeller, commissioned a new boat from Nathanael Herreshoff. Coming out of retirement, C. Oliver Iselin volunteered to manage the boat. He had been impressed by *Independence*'s flashes of speed, and he urged Herreshoff to build a boat along her radical lines with flat, scow-like sections and a small fin keel. Herreshoff silently reflected and then, in only two evenings, carved out a model that seemed to him to represent the best improvement on *Columbia* and *Constitution*. He took offsets from the model, lofted her lines full-scale, and, under the usual tight secrecy, started to build. The result was *Reliance*, the largest single-masted racing boat ever built and the last of her kind.

Her huge crew lines her rail as the great Reliance *sails close-hauled. This many men were needed partly to set sails, partly to be ballast.*

For most people, the main fascination of the history of the America's Cup is the astonishingly varied cast of characters who have played upon its stage, the Stevenses and Dunravens and Liptons and Vanderbilts and Turners. Their heroics and their tragedies, strengths and foibles make this event one of the most fascinating of all human endeavors. But there are times when the men, no matter how interesting, must give way to the boats themselves, those metal and wood and cloth creations that, in moments of accidental or intentional genius, may turn out to be especially startling and dramatic. There have been three "super boats" in America's Cup history, three sloops that have so dominated the competition that, as Queen Victoria was purported to have said about *America*'s race around the Isle of Wight, there was no second. These yachts were *Reliance, Ranger,* and *Intrepid,* the defenders in 1903, 1937, and 1967.

Built to a simple length and sail area rule, *Reliance* and her immediate forebears were very different from Edward Burgess' compromise sloops. They were true "out-and-outers" whose only cruising amenity, as George Watson put it, was a coat of paint. Their long overhangs and towering rigs were not seaworthy; in the interest of reaching New York in one piece, challengers were always sailed across the Atlantic under special small rigs or, with the yacht club's permission (and sometimes without it) towed behind tugs or big yachts like *Lipton's Erin.* If their thin metal plating did not dent under the hammering of waves, it quickly corroded. Most defenders and challengers were broken up within a few years of their summer in the limelight even though their wooden and iron predecessors continued to give their owners pleasure. In fact, *America* was now back under the New York Yacht Club burgee and Lipton had been taken out for a sail in her.

Yachtsmen and writers grumbled with increasing irritation about the direction that yacht design was taking, not because these boats were expensive — if the Morgans wanted to lay out a fortune for these fragile yachts, it was their own business — but because they were becoming unsafe. This echo of the outcry against extreme centerboarders of twenty-five years earlier led to a new measurement system called the Universal Rule, which was devised by Herreshoff. Unlike the Seawanhaka Rule, which had governed racing until then, it penalized extremes in sail area, overhangs, and displacement to produce a more seaworthy boat. The yacht club promptly adopted the rule for all its races — except those for the America's Cup, which, it was thought, should be held in the largest, least regulated yachts possible.

Reliance was so extreme that some thought Herreshoff was trying to demonstrate the folly of this exemption. The only dimension that she had in common with *Columbia* was her waterline length of 90 feet. Otherwise, she had 3,000 square feet more sail area,

Shamrock III, designed by William Fife, met with no better luck than her predecessors and failed to win even one of the three races held, despite Lipton's being decidedly optimistic at the outset.

almost 2 feet more beam, at least 38 tons more displacement, and 13 feet more overall length. Her 16,159 square feet of measured sail area was about the same as those of *Puritan* and *Mayflower* combined, and the 202 feet stretching from the tip of her bowsprit to the end of her boom would have included both their hulls with 8 feet to spare. If we compare *Reliance* with a modern 12-Meter cup boat, which seems like a big vessel today, her extravagance is even more astonishing. Her topsail alone was larger than a 12-Meter's 1,800 square foot measured sail area; her waterline length was 25 feet greater than a Twelve's overall length; her displacement was more than four times that of a 60,000 pound 1980 vintage defender.

Her 54 foot overhang — an incredible 40 percent of her overall length — was rarely dry. In only 7 knots of wind, that huge wall of sail pulled *Reliance* over until her effective waterline was all of 130 feet long, giving her a theoretical hull speed of 15 knots. To keep her

69

aimed in the right direction, Herreshoff gave her two steering wheels and a hollow rudder that could be filled full of water or pumped dry in order to adjust the feel of the helm. To control all that sail power, he built a battery of sophisticated winches with ball bearings, automatically shifting gears, and other features that were considered revolutionary when they reappeared sixty years later. To lower at least some of the sixty-four sailors out of Charlie Barr's line of sight, he placed many of these winches below decks. Aloft, *Reliance* carried lightweight steel spars; the towering topmast could be retracted into the mainmast in order to save weight up high when the topsail was not set. It is a testimonial to the skill of both Barr and Iselin, as well as to Herreshoff's engineering brilliance, that the only damage that this monster yacht suffered all season was a minor breakdown of her topmast housing system.

The first impression one had of *Reliance* was her great size — 144 feet of white, rather ugly boat dominated by an immense rig stretching 175 feet into the air. She looked like a tightrope walker, her great cloud of canvas teetering over her hull. Knowing that her lead keel dropped almost 20 feet below the waterline, the observer became slightly more confident about her stability, but she would put her leeward rail under in only 12 knots of wind.

Up close and down below, the impression of sheer bulk faded into one of ingenious detailing. Each of her fittings was custom-crafted at Herreshoff's yard, where prototypes of rigging were thoroughly tested to destruction on special machines. Her structure was an intricate web of steel frames that tied her keel, bronze hull, and aluminum deck into a sleek ramrod of electrolysis. An immense mast step stretched almost one-fourth her length so as to spread the elephantine load of her spar.

In cross-section, her shape reminds a modern sailor more of a racing dinghy or scow than of a big keel boat. Inspired by the flat-bottomed lake and river scows that

Above: Reliance, Columbia *and* Constitution *in a race during the summer of the challenge.*
Below: the future crew of Shamrock III *at work on* Shamrock I *during a trial race in English waters.*

were becoming popular for smooth-water sailing, she and her breed were called "skimming dishes". However in rough water they did not so much skim as plow, squishing their endless flat bows into every wave as they wallowed along. That was *Reliance*'s only weakness, and in the first race of the cup match *Shamrock III* held her about even until Charley Barr tacked over into smooth water. From then on, there was no holding *Reliance* back until, two months after the last race, she was broken up and sold for scrap.

About the only innovation aboard *Shamrock III* was a steering wheel, the British finally deciding that a 12-foot tiller did not provide sufficient control for a large yacht. She had no winches for reasons parodied several years later by an English writer: "Winches, we say, are unseamanlike. New fangled gadgets, we bluster. Dammit, sir, they destroy the old tradition of the sea. Manpower is the right power".

Reliance sailed away in a match that took fifteen days to complete because of calms, fog, and gales. For the first time in cup history, a race was cancelled due to strong winds — everybody was nervous about the flimsy hull and rigs, and, besides the fatality during *Shamrock*'s dismasting, a man had been washed off *Columbia* and drowned during a tune-up race. *Reliance* won two races and then *Shamrock* got lost in the fog and did not even finish the third one. When people tried to console Lipton with assurances that at least *Shamrock* was lovelier than her opponent, he responded with uncharacteristic testiness, "I don't want a beautiful boat. What I want is a boat to win the cup — a *Reliance*. Give me the homeliest boat that was ever designed, if she is like *Reliance*".

Captain Nathanael Herreshoff, the "wizard of Bristol" who, during his career, designed six defenders between 1893 and 1920.

Reliance
Designer: N. Herreshoff
L.O.A.: 144'
L.W.L.: 90'

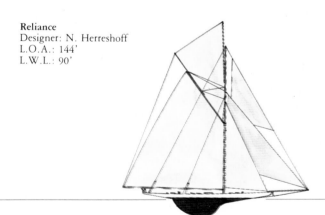

Shamrock III
Designer: W. Fife
L.O.A.: 134'
L.W.L.: 90'

	date	course	allowance	elapsed time	corrected time	wins by
Reliance	8/22	15 miles to windward from Sandy Hook		h. 03.32.17	h. 03.32.17	07'03''
Shamrock III		Lightship and return. 30 miles	01'57''	h. 03.41.17	h. 03.39.20	
Reliance	8/25	Equilateral triangle from Sandy Hook		h. 03.14.54	h. 03.14.54	01'19''
Shamrock III		Lightship. 30 miles	01'57''	h. 03.18.10	h. 03.16.13	
Reliance	9/3	15 miles to windward from Sandy Hook		h. 04.28.00	h. 04.28.06	
Shamrock III		Lightship and return. 30 miles	01'57''	retired		

1920
Resolute - Shamrock IV

Thomas Lipton, in the center, during a reception organized in his honor as a tribute to his sportsmanship.

Sir Thomas Lipton had asked for a homely, fast boat, and that is what he got from his designer for his next challenge in 1914. With her snub bow, squared-off stern, green slab topsides, and straight sheer she looked, Alfred F. Loomis wrote, "something like a cross between a tortoise and an armored cruiser". From our modern perspective, *Shamrock IV* looks merely efficient, but yachting aesthetics have changed drastically; even her designer, Charles E. Nicholson, called her "the ugly duckling".

Her appearance was closely related to the long interval between Lipton's third and fourth challenges. He and his yachting advisers were as appalled by the extremes of big-boat design as was Herreshoff, and, in 1907, he challenged, specifying that his new boat would be built to the J-Class rating under the Universal Rule, not to the 90 foot waterline length under the old rule. Herreshoff's Universal Rule assigned several classes, each with a rating and identified by a letter. The J-Class rating was

68 feet and it was thought that a boat in this class would be about 110 feet long. The club rejected his challenge at a special meeting during which former Commodore Lewis Cass Ledyard argued that yachts of such "insignificant power and size" would lower the America's Cup to second-rate status, and J. Pierpont Morgan (who had just ended a Wall Street panic singlehandedly) seconded his motion that the cup should be competed for by "the fastest and most powerful vessels that can be produced".

Lipton held off for another six years while rumors were scattered about Swedish and Canadian challenges, and then challenged. This time, he said he would bring a boat 75 feet long on the waterline, about the size of a J-Class boat. In another of those long exchanges of carefully-worded letters, the club kept insisting that its defender would be 90 feet long, since that, according to its interpretation, was the largest boat allowed under the deed of gift. When Lipton saw that he was not getting

Resolute, on the right, and Shamrock IV *vying for the best position before a start.*
For the first time both boats were steered by amateurs.

anywhere, he made his challenge unconditional. Now that it had once again successfully asserted its control over the cup, the yacht club dropped its own conditions and, citing the "mutual consent clause" in the deed, said it would produce a 75-footer built to the Universal Rule, after all. Except for some critics of the yacht club's negotiating tactics, everybody was happy: Lipton got the boats he wanted and the New York Yacht Club had not lost any authority.

The match was scheduled for September 1914. While three new American boats raced on the New York Yacht Club Cruise, *Shamrock IV* headed West under a short ketch rig. On August 5, she intercepted a German radio transmission announcing the start of what would be known as the Great War. Pausing at Bermuda, she went to New York, where she remained in a cradle until the thirteenth match was finally held in July 1920.

The yacht club wanted the series to be sailed off Newport, where there was less steamer traffic and the winds and currents were more fair than off Sandy Hook, but Lipton, who was no less eager for publicity at seventy than he had been at forty-nine, demurred, and the first cup match in seventeen years was held in the same packed arena.

This was the first cup match sailed by amateurs. In command of *Shamrock* — now even uglier since her cradle had broken and her bow and stern had drooped — was William Burton, thought to be Britain's best non-professional racing skipper. His boat was built with an ingenuity worthy of Herreshoff, with a spinnaker pole so light that two men could carry it, several weight-saving devices aloft, a special light-air jib, and the first speedometer ever used on a cup boat.

Unfortunately for Lipton, while Charles Nicholson knew how to design a fast boat, he was not as familiar with the Universal Rule as its inventor and *Shamrock* had to allow the Herreshoff-designed defender seven minutes on handicap.

73

Resolute's skipper was Charles Francis Adams, a descendant of presidents who was called "The Deacon" because of his calm formality and who was widely respected as America's best sailor, amateur or professional, since Charlie Barr's early death in 1911. He had been in charge of the boat since her launching and had the big advantage of having sailed her in competition for three summers — 1914, 1915, and 1919 — while *Shamrock* was untested. Therefore he probably was the most surprised person in New York to see the challenger win the first two races.

Shamrock lost the first start and, in shifty wind and a rain squall, kept dropping back until she was more than five minutes behind (twelve minutes on corrected time). That was when *Resolute*'s throat halyard broke and her gaff came down and jumped off the mast. Burton and his afterguard argued the protocol of the situation and finally decided to finish. In the second race, which turned into a 30 mile reach around a triangle, *Shamrock* showed that she had speed on at least one point of sail and, by sailing into an increasing wind first, demonstrated that a challenger could have defender's luck.

Now with only one win needed to take the cup home, *Shamrock* battled *Resolute* up a tightly-fought beat, tacking nineteen times but never able to shake Adams' close cover. *Resolute* rounded the mark almost two minutes in the lead, but then the challenger's extra 1,750 square feet of sail area pulled her down and over the defender on the 15 mile run to the finish to cross the line nineteen seconds ahead. In those days, when races were sailed on handicap, a boat was counted as starting when she crossed the starting line (so long as it was within two minutes after the gun). Since *Shamrock* had started nineteen seconds after *Resolute*, this race was counted as a dead heat, though of course the defender won handily on corrected time. *Resolute* next tied the

Above: of all the Shamrocks, *the fourth was the only one which gave Sir Thomas Lipton the satisfaction of winning any races.*
Below: Resolute *with Charles Francis Adams at the helm.*

match at two races each by beating *Shamrock* to the windward mark, holding her off on the reaches, and keeping her lead through a confusing series of wind shifts after a thunder squall. *Shamrock's* crew, guided by an equally confused afterguard (or so it was whispered), tried sail after sail but could not catch the other boat. The rubber race was cancelled the next day because the wind was piping up to 25 knots. Plenty of people who had no idea about how foolish and dangerous it can be to race around the buoys in a small gale in any vessel (much less a 110 footer) made sure that everybody else knew their dark opinions of these boats. The actual finale was a letdown: in more light air, *Resolute* took the lead part-way up the first leg and stretched it out to finish at dusk some thirteen minutes ahead on elapsed time and twenty on corrected. Besides reminding the New York Yacht Club that even a slow challenger could find a way to win a race (in this case and for the first time, two races), the 1920 match is important for the many ''lasts'' that it marked: last match held in gaff-rigged yachts; last match held on handicap, so great here that it left everybody confused; and last match held off New York, that cauldron of fluky weather and, in this July match, of thunder-squalls. It was not, however, the last match for Sir Thomas Lipton, whose aging hands still itched to carry the America's Cup back to its native land.

A great number of ladies were invited aboard Lipton's motor yacht, Erin, *despite his reputation for being a confirmed bachelor.*

Resolute
Designer: N. Herreshoff
L.O.A.: 106'
L.W.L.: 75'

Shamrock IV
Designer: C.E. Nicholson
L.O.A.: 110'
L.W.L.: 75'

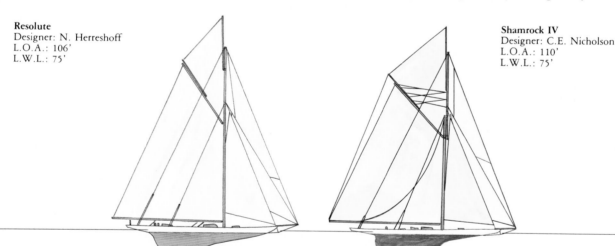

	date	course	allowance	elapsed time	corrected time	wins by
Shamrock IV **Resolute**	7/15	15 miles to windward from Ambrose Channel Lightship and return. 30 miles	06'42''	h. 04.24.58 retired	h. 04.24.58	
Shamrock IV **Resolute**	7/20	Equilateral triangle from Ambrose Channel Lightship. 30 miles	07'01''	h. 05.22.18 h. 05.31.45	h. 05.22.18 h. 05.24.44	02'26''
Resolute **Shamrock IV**	7/21	15 miles to windward from Ambrose Channel Lightship and return. 30 miles	07'01''	h. 04.03.06 h. 04.03.06	h. 03.56.05 h. 04.03.06	07'01''
Resolute **Shamrock IV**	7/23	Equilateral triangle from Ambrose Channel Lightship. 30 miles	06'40''	h. 03.37.52 h. 03.41.10	h. 03.31.12 h. 03.41.10	09'58''
Resolute **Shamrock IV**	7/25	15 miles to windward from Ambrose Channel Lightship and return. 30 miles	06'40''	h. 05.35.15 h. 05.48.20	h. 05.28.35 h. 05.48.20	19'45''

1930
Enterprise-Shamrock V

Harold Vanderbilt, Enterprise's *financer-skipper, invaluable above all for his considerable organizing ability.*

Weary, frail, but still game, eighty-year-old Sir Thomas Lipton built his last *Shamrock* and returned for his last America's Cup match in 1930. The world, just beginning to feel the cold fingers of economic depression, hoped more than ever before that the Scottish-Irish grocer would finally win, but his and their dream, as always, was not realized. While Newport and the boats, with their tall Bermudan rigs, seemed worlds apart from the old cup days, and although the aging Nat Herreshoff had retired after designing five winners, there was a remarkable sameness about Lipton's fifth and the cup's fourteenth match. Once again, the challenger was prepared thoughtfully and sailed skillfully. But, once again, she was massacred by a boat of overwhelming technological superiority. Murmuring, "I can't win, I can't win", Lipton distractedly accepted a huge loving cup paid for by public donation and went home to die.

Lipton's sympathy for his fellow humans extended even to an appreciation of the plight of the winning

skipper, Harold Vanderbilt, who knew as well as Lipton did that few if any Americans were cheering for him. Not the least of Vanderbilt's extraordinary achievements was his public admission of grief. "Our hour of triumph, our hour of victory, is all but at hand", he wrote at the finish of the last race and later recorded in his book about the match, "but it is so tempered with sadness that it is almost hollow. To win the America's Cup is glory enough for any yachtsman, but why should we be verging on the disconsolate?" Vanderbilt was a fifteen-year-old schoolboy when the first *Shamrock* came over in 1899, a member of the second generation of cup sailors that grew up near Lipton's fabulous aura and that now took the torch and carried it through the great challenges of the 1930's. Vanderbilt's father and uncle had financed cup defenders around the turn of the century. His own defenders, *Enterprise, Rainbow* and *Ranger*, were designed by Edward Burgess' son and sailed against boats designed by sons of Charles Paine

The loft of Ratsey and Lapthorn at Cowes. The men are completing work on a
J Class mainsail.

and Nathanael Herreshoff. To quote the cliché, the more things change, the more they remain the same.

In Harold Vanderbilt were combined the managerial skills of a Paine and an Iselin, the ruthless competitiveness and skillful helmsmanship of a Barr, and the wealth of... well, of a Vanderbilt. His great-grandfather, Cornelius van Der Bilt (called ''Commodore'' due to his commanding presence), had exploited the steamship and railroad inventions of the Stevens family to create America's greatest fortune. Within two generations, however, the Vanderbilt family became a quarrelling pack of social climbers more famous for their mansions and divorces than for any achievements. Harold's father, William Kissam, had forced his daughter Consuelo to marry the Duke of Marlborough in order to bring a title into the family. That was about the limit of his aspirations, as even he admitted. Money, William Kissam Vanderbilt sadly confessed, only left him ''with nothing to hope for, with nothing definite to

seek or strive for. Inherited wealth is a real handicap to happiness. It is as certain as death to ambition as cocaine is to morality''. By some miracle, the father's misery was not passed on to the son. Born in 1884, Harold Stirling ''Mike'' Vanderbilt went through Harvard in only three years, earned a law degree, and, at the age of twenty-nine, succeeded the late J. Pierpont Morgan as a director of the Vanderbilt-controlled New York Central Railroad.

Vanderbilt is best known for his contributions to games, which he approached as seriously as the old Commodore had planned a new steamship line. While in college, he became an expert at playing cards and between 1910 and 1920 was a member of the strongest pair of bridge players in the country. In 1925, at the beginning of a steamship cruise from Los Angeles to Cuba, he told his companions, ''Gentlemen, let me show you a new game. It may interest you''. The new game was contract bridge, which Vanderbilt melded from bridge,

whist, and the French game of Plafond, and which, to be played well, required "the memory of an elephant, the boldness of a lion, endurance of a bulldog, and killer instinct of a wolf", as a commentator once wrote. Harold Vanderbilt was a very good contract bridge player indeed, winning many championships.

He applied the same energy and character traits to yacht racing. In 1910, when he was twenty-six, Vanderbilt won a race to Bermuda in his Herreshoff schooner *Vagrant*, and he went on to build a series of large boats that culminated in *Enterprise*. Designed by the ingenious William Starling Burgess, Edward's son, she was an engineering marvel, a floating showplace of technology. Starting aloft, she carried a complicated duralumin mast held together by more than eighty thousand rivets and weighing one-third less than her competitors' steel and wooden spars. Her "Park Avenue" boom — so called because two men could walk on it abreast — was covered with tracks and slides that allowed the crew to optimize the shape of the mainsail. She carried twenty-six professional sailors (the new rigs were much smaller than the old gaff rigs), eight of whom were never seen on deck during races because they ground away at winches below — like a steamer's coal stokers, they were known as "the black gang".

Enterprise's crew was organized with equal efficiency. Each position was numbered; each sailor wore a jersey with a number corresponding to his position. When sails were set or doused, numbers, not names, were called out. Aft, Vanderbilt assigned tasks to his four amateur assistants: he would steer at starts and upwind; somebody else would steer off the wind; one man — Sherman Hoyt, a wonderfully talented sailor — was in charge of sail trim; and there were three-man committees to decide on tactics, strategy, and sail-selection. In short, her afterguard was a small model of the modern American corporation, and like the modern American corporation at its best, this company of mariners was successful. Once her tricky mast was tuned and all the numbered deck (and sub-deck) hands had sorted out the complicated rigging, *Enterprise* swept by her four American rivals and then beat *Shamrock V* in four straight races (one of which *Shamrock* withdrew from due to a broken main halyard). All this in spite of being the smallest of the J-Class yachts at Newport with a waterline length of 80 feet, 4 feet shorter than that of *Yankee* (designed by Frank Paine) and 6 feet less than that of *Whirlwind* (designed by L. Francis Herreshoff). In the prevailing light winds, a long waterline length did not give a great advantage. But the main reason why *Enterprise* won in 1930 was that Harold Vanderbilt was a fanatic about efficiency and details, the small things that, added up, make a boat a winner. It is historical justice that the man who engineered her phenomenally effective mast was Charles Paine Burgess, the brother of her designer and the namesake and son of the two men whose managerial and creative geniuses had won three cup matches half a century earlier. With the 1930 match as a warm-up, the Vanderbilt-Burgess team would reach even higher peaks of glory in 1934 and 1937.

The crew of Shamrock V *preparing to hoist a jib in stops. When the sheets are trimmed it unfolds in the wind.*

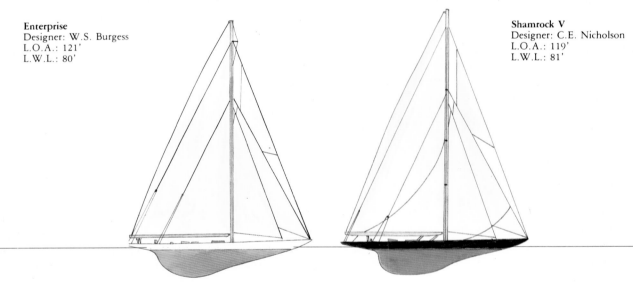

Enterprise
Designer: W.S. Burgess
L.O.A.: 121'
L.W.L.: 80'

Shamrock V
Designer: C.E. Nicholson
L.O.A.: 119'
L.W.L.: 81'

	date	course	allowance	elapsed time	corrected time	wins by
Enterprise Shamrock V	9/13	15 miles to leeward and return at a mark 9 miles S.E. from Brenton Reef Lightship		h. 04.03.48 h. 04.06.40		02'52''
Enterprise Shamrock V	9/15	Equilateral triangle. 30 miles		h. 04.00.44 h. 04.10.18		09'34''
Enterprise Shamrock V	9/17	15 miles to windward and return 30 miles		h. 03.54.16 retired		
Enterprise Shamrock V	9/18	Equilateral triangle. 30 miles		h. 03.10.13 h. 03.15.57		05'44''

1934
Rainbow-Endeavour

One of the few people who could afford a $400,000 yacht in the middle of the Great Depression, Thomas Sopwith had made a fortune building airplanes — the famous Sopwith Camel was the most successful fighter plane in World War I with 1,294 kills. He developed into an excellent big-boat skipper in England, where J-Class and other huge yachts raced all summer in a kind of traveling circus that went from harbor to harbor, performing on short courses before thousands of paying spectators. The financial proceeds went to the professional crews (a successful boat might win $5,000 in a season), the glory to the millionaire owners, not all of whom knew more about sailing than Sir Thomas Lipton did. Applying his keen engineering intelligence as he sailed around many race courses, Sopwith made many innovations entirely independent of America, where the J-boats remained in their cradles. In 1934, representing the Royal Yacht Squadron, he challenged.

The only new American boat was Harold Vanderbilt's *Rainbow*, supported by a huge syndicate of eighteen. Designed by Starling Burgess and sailed by most of the afterguard that had helped Vanderbilt in 1930, she lost race after race to *Yankee*, commanded by sixty-eight-year-old Charles Francis Adams. But Burgess and Vanderbilt accepted neither steady defeat nor their

boat's apparent inferiority. Adding tons of ballast to improve her stability, setting larger sails, and rigging a bendy boom that shaped the mainsail even more efficiently than the Park Avenue boom, they steadily improved her. They were lucky, too: the New York Yacht Club's selection committee was about to choose *Yankee* to defend when she dropped out of a race after a piece of rigging broke. Three days later, *Rainbow* won by only a second, but it was her fourth triumph over *Yankee* in five starts and she was selected. Adams, the imperturbable old Deacon, wept.

Meanwhile, Sopwith's Nicholson-designed *Endeavour* was proving to be very fast in trials. The aggressive Sopwith made it clear how serious he was by protesting *Rainbow*'s skimpy accommodations. The ostensible issue was whether she should be required to carry a bathtub, as *Endeavour* did. The *real* issue, obviously, was whether the challenger would allow himself to be taken advantage of (many Englishmen thought) as all too many predecessors had been. The symbolic bathtub issue was resolved by removing *Endeavour*'s tub, and Sopwith's confidence only increased.

After one race was abandoned due to calm, *Endeavour* sailed a close windward leg, rounded the mark only eighteen seconds behind, and proceeded to

Endeavour's crew posing for a keepsake photo together with Sir Thomas Sopwith, the owner, and his wife in the center. On the opposite page, Endeavour *under sail. Overleaf,* Rainbow.

sail right away from *Rainbow* on the run to the finish to win by two minutes. Sopwith won the next race, too, sailing faster in 15 knots of wind and covering Vanderbilt tack for tack to arrive fifty-one seconds ahead.

Down by two races to a faster boat, even Harold Vanderbilt was feeling a bit hopeless. By the time *Rainbow* reached the turning mark of the windward-leeward third race, he was almost in despair. More than six minutes ahead on a 15 mile close reach to the finish, *Endeavour* could fetch the committee boat without tacking. All Sopwith had to do was to stay on the starboard tack for a couple of hours and he would have a three-race lead. It was an impossible situation that would force most leaders to abandon their organization charts and systems, to stay at the helm and play the role of the noble martyr — but Vanderbilt did neither. According to his system, Sherman Hoyt always steered in light wind when the genoa jib was set because he had the best feel for the boat. Vanderbilt turned the helm over to Hoyt and went below to mourn. Hoyt sailed a little high of the course in search of wind. Sopwith, seeing this and unsure of his position, panicked and tacked to sail up to *Rainbow* to cover — and in the light wind, *Endeavour* was now headed away from the finishing line at very low speed. When she tacked back, Hoyt headed off to increase *Rainbow*'s speed and sailed right through *Endeavour*'s blanket. Never tacking, *Rainbow* won the race by more than three minutes, gaining more than ten minutes on the leg. Vanderbilt later described this as "in many ways the most startling race I have ever sailed — a constantly changing panorama of breaks and mistakes". But what it all came down to was that Sopwith and not Vanderbilt had self-destructed.

Before the fourth race, *Rainbow* took on two more tons of ballast as well as a new crewmember — Frank

Endeavour (above) under sail. Note the particularly wide boom useful in giving the sail an aerodynamic shape.
Below: Charles Nicholson, builder and designer of Endeavour, astern while checking his boat's sails.

Paine, *Yankee*'s disappointed designer, who accepted Vanderbilt's invitation to help improve her downwind performance. Nobody on *Rainbow* felt comfortable trimming the new parachute spinnakers, but Paine had mastered these monster sails and even brought along *Yankee*'s best spinnaker. Spinnakers were not the issue in this race, however. The issue was protests.

After some close manoeuvering before the gun, *Rainbow* led up the 10 mile windward leg but was overhauled at the mark. She began to pass the challenger to windward. Sopwith luffed to keep Vanderbilt from sailing by, but Vanderbilt did not head up. Rather than collide with *Rainbow*, Sopwith headed off, and the unimpeded defender easily sailed over *Endeavour* to win the race. As she crossed the finish line, a red protest flag was hung in *Endeavour*'s rigging. The racing rules then required the windward boat to alter course if the leeward boat's bow would strike her forward of the mast. But the issue of whether Sopwith's or Vanderbilt's judgement was correct was never dealt with, since the race committee disallowed the protest because the flag was not displayed immediately, as the rules required. To many people, this citation of an apparently minor technicality was an obviously unfair protection of the cup. "Britannia rules the waves and America waives the rules", was one popular commentary. The decision stuck, and later Vanderbilt wrote a new set of racing rules that eliminated judgement calls and form the basis for the modern rules.

Whether because Sopwith was unnerved or because *Rainbow* was now the faster boat, *Endeavour* lost the fifth race by a wide margin. On the last day, *Rainbow* trailed after the end of the first leg, a 10 mile reach, gained the lead on a beat of the same length, and almost lost it all on the run to the finish.

For once, Vanderbilt went against his organization chart and gave the helm to Sherman Hoyt, who, knowing that Sopwith would try to cover *Rainbow* no matter what the course was, headed a mile to leeward of the finish in order to lure *Endeavour* into sailing a slow course by the lee to try to blanket *Rainbow* from astern. If Sopwith had simply steered for the finish, he would have passed *Rainbow* and won the race. The defender won by only fifty-five seconds, and both refused to press protests apparently connected with some fierce manoeuvering before the start. With some understatement, Vanderbilt observed of the 1934 cup summer, "it would seem that errors played the major part in deciding the issue". Of course, he was the one who made the fewest mistakes in the closest cup match ever.

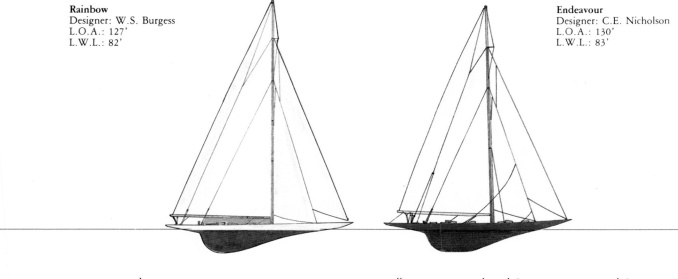

Rainbow
Designer: W.S. Burgess
L.O.A.: 127'
L.W.L.: 82'

Endeavour
Designer: C.E. Nicholson
L.O.A.: 130'
L.W.L.: 83'

	date	course	allowance	elapsed time	corrected time	wins by
Endeavour	9/17	15 miles to windward and return		h. 03.43.44		02'09''
Rainbow		30 miles		h. 03.45.53		
Endeavour	9/18	Equilateral triangle. 30 miles		h. 03.09.01		00'51''
Rainbow				h. 03.09.52		
Rainbow	9/20	15 miles to leeward and return		h. 04.35.34		03'26''
Endeavour		30 miles		h. 04.39.00		
Rainbow	9/22	Equilateral triangle. 30 miles		h. 03.15.38		01'15''
Endeavour				h. 03.16.53		
Rainbow	9/24	15 miles to leeward and return.		h. 03.54.05		04'01''
Endeavour		30 miles		h. 03.58.06		
Rainbow	9/25	Equilateral triangle. 30 miles		h. 03.40.05		00'55''
Endeavour				h. 03.41.00		

1937
Ranger-Endeavour II

The controversies of the match soon disappeared. A major factor in this happy development was an expedition organized by the commodore of the Eastern Yacht Club, Gerard B. Lambert, who eased the strain by taking his J *Yankee* to race in England in 1935. Toward the end of the summer, Thomas Sopwith, perhaps mollified by Lambert's warm-hearted gesture, announced that he would challenge again in 1937. This time Sopwith built his boat early, and in 1936 both *Endeavours* went at it with, it seemed, the same energy and competitiveness that honed the defender's skills during the American trials. The new *Endeavour* proved to be even faster than her predecessor.

Back in the United States, it was clear that a new defense candidate would have to be built, but with the economy in the state it was in nobody knew who would pay for her. Harold Vanderbilt approached both Starling Burgess and Olin Stephens and asked them to design a boat jointly while he tried to raise the necessary money. Thus was conceived the greatest cup boat ever.

The two designers made an interesting pair. Burgess was now a grizzled fifty-one years old with the equivalent of three careers behind him. He had dropped out of Harvard during the Spanish-American War to serve as a gunner's mate, and before returning to college had invented and patented a new type of machine gun. He wrote three books of poetry while at Harvard, opened a shipyard in Marblehead in 1905, and then, like many dreamer-technicians, was swept up in the new wave of aviation. In 1910, he built the first plane to fly in New England (it covered all of 2 miles); one year later, under contract from the Wright brothers, he opened the first licensed aircraft company in America at just about the time that Sopwith was getting started. He built the first seaplane to take off and land on water, and then sold out to Glenn Curtiss and went into partnership with Frank Paine as a yacht designer. In 1928 he designed a remarkably fast schooner named *Nina* that still won races thirty years later. His fascination with new building materials and his individualism drew him to the challenge of the huge J-boats as well as to working with R. Buckminster Fuller on a futuristic three-wheeled automobile called the Dymaxion, which looked like an egg on wheels. This combination of the impractical-looking and the practical-behaving intrigued Burgess.

On the mast of Ranger, *on the left, Rod Stephens, who had the habit of climbing all over the place for technical check-ups.*

Burgess was especially fascinated by the possibilities of model testing in towing tanks, and it was at the tank at the Stevens Institute of Technology (founded by *America*'s co-owner Edwin Stevens) where he and twenty-eight-year-old Olin Stephens II worked in 1936 testing models of their own designs against those of *Rainbow* and the first *Endeavour* (surprisingly, Charles Nicholson had traded the lines of his fast 1934 challenger for *Rainbow*'s plans). Though young, Olin Stephens was one of the most successful designers in the

Herreshoff's. The only hitch in her career was her dismasting as she was being towed to Newport. Once she started racing, there was almost no question in anybody's mind that she was all but unbeatable. When Nicholson took his first look at her out of the water, he said she was the most revolutionary boat in half a century, and the co-designers (later, Stephens gave Burgess the credit) claimed that only the test-tank results had kept them from discarding her design, so radical did it seem. *Ranger* was huge, powerful, and not very attrac-

Ranger, the last "J", with Harold Vanderbilt at the helm. Olin and
Rod Stephens were also part of the crew and were to make use of this experience
for their postwar 12-Meters.

world. After a year studying naval architecture at the Massachusetts Institute of Technology, he had dropped out; his interest was in yachts, not commercial ships. After designing some successful racing daysailers, he drew a yawl, *Dorade*, with which he and his younger brother Rod won the 1931 trans-Atlantic race by two days. They were greeted on their return by a ticker-tape parade up Broadway. He had sailed in an unsuccessful defense candidate in 1934, so was familiar with the type of boat, and his modest, focused demeanor seemed a healthy contrast to Burgess' diffused energies. They worked well together.

By the time that the designers and Vanderbilt chose a model, very little money had been raised, but Vanderbilt decided to go ahead on his own — a commitment, it turned out, of more than half a million dollars. The Bath Iron Works, in Maine, offered to build her for about its cost, so *Ranger* — as she was christened — was the first defender since *Volunteer*, in 1887, not built at

tive. With the immense new jibs now available (she had the first synthetic sail ever made) and a spinnaker made of 18,000 square feet of light cloth (an area even greater than *Reliance*'s measured area), this blunt-bowed, flat-sterned shark of a boat was pushed and pulled consistently fast, with no apparent weaknesses. To trim all this canvas, there was Vanderbilt's usual paid crew but also a new afterguard, three of whom — the Stephens brothers and Arthur Knapp Jr. — were hard-driving, small-boat racing sailors in their twenties with few outside commitments. According to Knapp, he and Rod Stephens spent one three-week period on board *Ranger* without going ashore, leaving only to eat and sleep on board Vanderbilt's power yacht. She may have been the first big yacht to be sailed like a small one. *Ranger* sailed in thirty-four races in her one and only summer; she won thirty-two of them, by an average of 7'4" — or more than a mile.

In the first cup races, Vanderbilt sailed with atypical

conservatism. To do otherwise in a superior boat is to take too great a risk, and everybody was nervous about another international controversy. She was behind at the first two starts, and won those races by seventeen and more than eighteen minutes. Then Mike Vanderbilt's natural aggressiveness swamped his sense of protocol and *Ranger* controlled the third start and pushed *Endeavour II* over the line early at the fourth one. Having made his point, he pulled back on his champion's reins to keep the races close, at least on paper.

Two years later, Vanderbilt wrote in his book *On the Wind's Highway* that none of his three cup triumphs had given him much pleasure beyond the satisfaction of having won. *Enterprise* and *Ranger* won in walkaways, *Rainbow* surrounded by bickering. What bothered him, too, was the thought of having ended J-Class racing by doing it too well. Looking back on the post-match New York Yacht Club Cruise, where five of these 135 footers raced against each other in the class's last appearance, Vanderbilt wrote: ''Presently, their season's work over, they will pass by in review. As they have come out of the distance, so they shall go into the distance.'' The fair wind, their never weary white wings, carry them on — on the wind's highway, 'homeward bound for orders' — on, to destiny''.

By 1942, *Ranger* and most of her sister J's were piles of metal and lead on their way to different destinies in different shapes — as Spitfires and battleships and bullets.

Above: from left to right: Starling Burgess, Olin Stephens, Rod Stephens and Drake Sparkman discussing the Ranger *project. On the opposite page:* Endeavour II, *for the last Sopwith challenge failed to win even one race.*

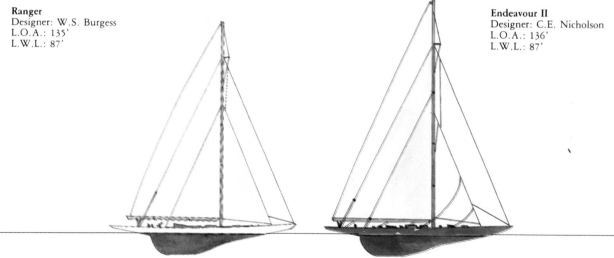

Ranger
Designer: W.S. Burgess
L.O.A.: 135'
L.W.L.: 87'

Endeavour II
Designer: C.E. Nicholson
L.O.A.: 136'
L.W.L.: 87'

	date	course	allowance	elapsed time	corrected time	wins by
Ranger	7/31	15 miles to windward and return		h. 04.41.15		17'05''
Endeavour II		30 miles		h. 04.58.20		
Ranger	8/2	Equilateral triangle. 30 miles		h. 03.41.33		18'32''
Endeavour II				h. 04.00.05		
Ranger	8/4	15 miles to windward and return		h. 03.54.30		04'27''
Endeavour II		30 miles		h. 03.58.57		
Ranger	8/5	Equilateral triangle. 30 miles		h. 03.07.49		03'37''
Endeavour II				h. 03.11.26		

THE 12-METER ERA

Even though the America's Cup yachts are now smaller,
the fight for the trophy has become more
and more unrelenting. The 12-Meters have become
floating technological showcases.
Challengers come from all over the world in an attempt
to unsaddle American supremacy.

1958
Columbia-Sceptre

Harold Vanderbilt was right: big-class racing was dead. The J-boats never sailed against each other again. Prescient as ever, Vanderbilt invested his competitiveness in a much smaller type of boat where he knew he could find some action. This boat was the 12-Meter designed to the International Rule, which for more than thirty years had been Europe's system for classifying racing yachts.

Under the International Rule, boats were grouped by their rating in meters. The classes stretching from 6 Meters (about 35 feet long) to 23 Meters (approximately 130 feet in length). One of the most popular was the 12-Meter, about 60 feet overall and 45 on the water. The International Rule encouraged the design of boats with shorter overhangs, a narrower beam, a more V-shaped hull, and a smaller sail area than Universal-Rule yachts. It also banned the use of centerboards, which in the J-Class boats were used to make minor adjustments in sailing balance rather than to increase stability. Although both rules required their boats to be built to the demanding scantlings of Lloyds Registry of Shipping, which assured the strength of the hulls, only wooden construction could be used under the International Rule, possibly because it was less expensive and complicated than metal construction.

So Vanderbilt commissioned Olin Stephens to design a new Twelve called *Vim*, and in the summer of 1939 she was shipped to England where, skilfully sailed by her owner, Rod Stephens, a young 6-Meter champion and sports car driver named Briggs Cunningham, and a crew of carefully drilled professionals and amateurs, she won nineteen of the twenty-seven races that she sailed in. Returning to the United States, she continued her winning ways against a small fleet of well-sailed Twelves and, after the 1940 season, was laid up at City Island and forgotten for a decade.

So, too, was the America's Cup until 1948 when the commodore of the New York Yacht Club, DeCoursey Fales, and the commodore of England's Royal Ocean Racing Club, John Illingworth, unofficially agreed that the matches should be resumed in ocean-racing yachts,

Sceptre, *the first British challenger after Sopwith, designed by David Boyd. At the time large spinnakers were considered very useful, but later were proved to be inefficient.*

Briggs Cunningham, skipper of Columbia, *was an innovator and is famous for having invented the Cunningham hole, an important sail control.*

Graham Mann, a Royal Navy officer and skipper of Sceptre, *was at a disadvantage because his boat could not point as high as* Columbia.

which would have a life after the cup races were over. That was all well and good, but no Britisher or American volunteered to build a boat with a waterline length of 65 feet, the minimum specified by the deed of gift. The largest boats then racing were only 72 feet long overall and about 51 feet on the waterline. By the early 1950's, post-war prosperity and the revival of international yachting in small boats gradually led to renewed interest in the cup. Now a century old, it remained yachting's deepest well into which the dreams of every sailor inevitably flowed. Advised by the Royal Yacht Squadron that it would consider challenging in 12-Meters, Commodore Henry Sears produced a fourth deed of gift that was approved by the Supreme Court of the State of New York late in 1956. It had two new conditions: the boats could be as small as 44 feet on the waterline and they could be shipped, rather than sailed, from the challenging country. A few months later, the squadron challenged for 1958.

At seventy-four, Vanderbilt was too old to compete, but from the vantage point of a seat on the club's America's Cup Committee, he observed some of the best trials racing in the cup's history between boats with which he had close personal ties. *Easterner*, potentially fast but a loser all summer, was owned by Chandler Hovey, whose *Yankee* had been *Rainbow*'s nemesis in 1934. *Weatherly*, which won in streaks, was commanded by *Ranger*'s sail-trimmer, Arthur Knapp Jr. His old boat *Vim* was sailed beyond her supposed potential by an aggressive young crew headed by Emil "Bus" Mosbacher and funded by her new owner, John Matthews. And the eventual winner, *Columbia*, was designed by Olin Stephens, rigged by Rod Stephens, skippered by Briggs Cunningham (with the Stephens brothers' help), and owned by a syndicate that included Gerard B. Lambert. *Columbia*'s crew had other ties to the cup's long history. Pulling halyards and sheets in what had become a mostly amateur endeavor were Colin

Columbia, *the first Twelve designed by S&S, won the privilege of defending over* Vim, Weatherly *and* Easterner *in some of the best match races ever sailed.*

Americans got their first look at *Sceptre*, the challenger, they shook their heads in disbelief. Bulbous forward where the American boats were sharp, fine aft where they were full, she seemed a modern-day product of the "cod's head and mackerel tail" theory that *America* had so convincingly disproved in 1851. Her sail cloth was stretchy, her rigging not aerodynamically refined. Without the luxury of a summer's close competition (*Columbia* had sailed forty trial races), her crew had no way to find out where they were weak. For example, they relied on circus tent spinnakers long after the Americans had discovered how much faster smaller downwind sails actually were. She was badly beaten.

As always when a cup challenger is dramatically unsuccessful, her performance was interpreted as a symptom of the Anglo-American technology gap, but one or two observers believed that if Thomas Sopwith could almost lift the cup twenty-four years earlier, some Britisher could at least bring over a reasonable 12-Meter.

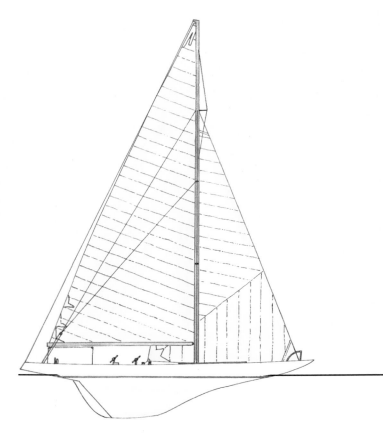

Ratsey, whose ancestors had made *America*'s jib boom and cut sails for most challengers and defenders, and Halsey Herreshoff, grandson of old Nathanael.

Vim and *Columbia* were the pick of the lot. All summer their bows were even; most of the summer it was the older boat's bow that usually stuck a few inches ahead thanks to aggressive tactics by Mosbacher (he tacked thirty-six times in one 8-mile windward leg against *Columbia*) and excellent sails made of the then brand-new Dacron sail cloth by her sail trimmer, Ted Hood. If the winds had stayed light, she would have won, but it was a summer of fresh air off Newport and the slightly more stable new boat finally began to grind her down after a trying summer of experimentation with different helmsmen and sails. The average winning margin in the *Vim-Columbia* final series, the best set of match races ever sailed, was only thirty-two seconds.

Most people — perhaps even Cunningham — hoped the match itself would be as exciting, but when the

	date	wind (mph)	start	finish
Columbia	9/20	8	h. 12.30.10	h. 17.43.56
Sceptre			h. 12.30.11	h. 17.51.40
Columbia	9/22	7	h. 12.21.32	Time limit
Sceptre			h. 12.21.34	expired
Columbia	9/24	8/10	h. 12.20.03	h. 15.37.43
Sceptre			h. 12.20.05	h. 15.49.25
Sceptre	9/25	15/20	h. 12.10.04	h. 15.27.27
Columbia			h. 12.10.05	h. 15.19.07
Columbia	9/26	12/17	h. 12.10.10	h. 15.14.22
Sceptre			h. 12.10.23	h. 15.21.27

1962
Weatherly-Gretel

After the embarrassing 1958 match, the rumor machine began to churn once again. Englishmen outside the Royal Yacht Squadron began a challenge that, they anticipated, would be better organized and manned than *Sceptre*'s. Working under the auspices of the Royal Thames Yacht Club (which, as the Cumberland Sailing Society, was founded in 1775 — forty years before the squadron), they methodically planned a challenge for 1962. Then out of the Southern Hemisphere there appeared a challenge for the same year from the Royal Sydney Yacht Squadron, which the New York Yacht Club promptly accepted to howls of rage from London. At one stage, the Duke of Edinburgh tried to rebuild cordial relations with a proposal for a Commonwealth effort, but the Australian challenger, Sir Frank Packer, stuck to his guns, arguing that although he might not improve on the English record, "every now and again you have to give the young fellow in the family his head."

Packer was an antipodean version of John Cox Stevens, a blunt, ambitious, powerful gambler who had made his fortune in the twentieth-century battleground of entrepreneurs, communications, which was as successful for him as transportation had been for Stevens, Charles Paine, Harold Vanderbilt and Thomas Sopwith. He chartered *Vim* for use as a trial horse, both full-scale off Sydney Heads and part-scale in the towing tank at the Stevens Institute of Technology, where his designer, Alan Payne, conducted extensive model tests with the blessing of the yacht club. The only yacht designer working in Australia, Payne was as tactful and attentive to basic issues as his backer was gruff and freewheeling; not only did he persuade the club to let him use the New Jersey test tank, but he also talked them into allowing his boat to use sails made of American sail cloth, which was far superior to Australian and British cloth. (In fact, in the match *Gretel* ended up setting American-made sails trimmed to many U.S. winches.) Payne did not stop there. Realizing that in match racing the crew that could trim its sails quickest would win a tacking duel almost independent of its boat's inherent speed, he designed two "coffee grinder" jib-sheet winches that could be linked together by a clutch to allow four men instead of two to grind the drum. When *Gretel* was finally launched and allowed

Weatherly to the leeward of Gretel, *the first Australian boat ever to sail at Newport in an America's Cup race.*

Gretel at the finishing line. The Australians managed to win one race, but the crew was adverserly affected by the energetic management of Frank Packer, the Australian press tycoon.

by Packer to sail against *Vim*, the Australians realized what Payne knew all along — that the first Aussie Twelve ever built was faster than the second-fastest boat of 1958.

So little did the Americans fear the Sydney challenge that only one new boat was built, *Nefertiti*, from Boston. Designed and canvassed by the multi-talented Ted Hood, she was also co-skippered by him and Don MacNamara — an odd pair, Hood taciturn and technically minded and MacNamara emotionally extravagant and perpetually charging up San Juan Hill. Big and broad, *Nefertiti* was at her best in fresh wind and under spinnaker. At first she did well against fellow New Englander *Easterner*, *Columbia* (in new hands), and *Weatherly*, now with Bus Mosbacher in command and greatly modified by A.E. Luders Jr. from her Philip Rhodes design. Things started to go wrong on the new boat in mid-summer and MacNamara was fired. *Weatherly*, which might have been the slowest of the

four under equally competent management, gradually improved. One ingredient was her sails, cut and altered by Mosbacher's main competitor, Hood. Another — and more important — ingredient was Mosbacher.

Known best for his aggressive starting tactics, Bus Mosbacher was able to control his boat, his crew, his opponent, and (not least important) himself from one end of the race course to the other. Like Charlie Barr in 1901 and Harold Vanderbilt in 1934, he had a slower boat that would win only if he could force the other boat to make more mistakes than he did. He also had a deep understanding of what the cup meant to the New York Yacht Club, and of the importance of the America's Cup Committee. Defenders are chosen by the committee; they do not automatically earn their way by winning a series of races. He knew that if *Weatherly* was to be selected, she should show competence in extreme conditions. Already faster than *Nefertiti* in light air, she was honed and refined all summer until she finally beat the

Weatherly, *the American Twelve, which was not selected four years before, made it to the finals with Bus Mosbacher at the helm.*

Boston boat to a windward mark in a fresh wind.

Once in the cup match against a boat that turned out to be faster on almost every leg, Mosbacher found himself improvising. In one way he was lucky. Frank Packer, an autocrat who was uncomfortable when out of the limelight, seemed unwilling to lose control of *Gretel* when she left her dock. He did not name the skipper, Jock Sturrock, until the eve of the match and he changed navigators on the morning of the first race, when *Gretel* went out with a crew of twelve men who had never sailed as a team before. Only the brilliant Alan Payne was given some responsibility, and just two weeks before the match he boldly moved *Gretel*'s mast step 19 inches in order to improve her balance.

The first race, sailed in front of 2,500 spectator boats, showed how good Payne's work was. Despite being pushed early over the line and restarting, despite carrying a light-weather mainsail in a wind that built to 18 knots, despite crew confusion and a broken backstay,

Gretel lost the first formal race she ever sailed by less than 4 minutes — bad, but not a *Sceptre* - like disaster.

In fresh air, *Weatherly* narrowly won the second start by being under *Gretel*'s leeward bow, and then a tense duel stretched out over a dozen back-breaking, spray-flying, hair-raising tacks as *Gretel* searched for clear wind and Mosbacher refused to let her have it. Her yoked winches spinning more powerfully than *Weatherly*'s single coffee grinders, the challenger slowly gained until Mosbacher realized what was happening and broke the duel off to cover loosely. This was one time when he could not afford to play to the committee, who would expect him to cover tack for tack. *Gretel* was clearly too fast, so by minimizing the number of tacks, he cut his losses. "We knew when we made the decision we would have to live with it," Mosbacher later acknowledged. "Our strategy worked out perfectly. Can you imagine the howl that would have gone up if it hadn't?"

Weatherly led by only twelve seconds at the end of the

8-mile beat, held on down the first 8-mile reach, then jibed for the reach home. Slow in setting their spinnaker, his crew was shaken by the roar of a war cry. Looking up, they saw *Gretel* surfing madly down a great wave, a crewmember named Norm Wright standing at the mast shrieking his lungs out. *Gretel* thundered by, taking *Weatherly*'s wind, and when the Americans headed up to attack their afterguy broke, the spinnaker pole folded around the headstay and they were beaten. "Waltzing Matilda" rocked Newport all night long.

If they had sailed the next day the conditions would have been the same but a layday forced them into light air, when *Weatherly* won easily after *Gretel* took the start. In more wind in the fourth race, Mosbacher again refused to bite into Sturrock's offer of a tacking duel and held the challenger off on the reaches much the way *Rainbow* had beaten *Endeavour* in the last race in 1934. Seeing *Gretel* gain rapidly as they sailed under spinnaker toward the finish, Mosbacher decided to lure Stur-

rock away from his fastest point of sail. *Weatherly*'s spinnaker came down and she squeezed up to windward under genoa. If he had known how much faster his boat was, and if he had been aware that a race can be won without sailing in close quarters, Sturrock would have simply let *Weatherly* go and sailed serenely (and rapidly) to the finish. But he doused his own chute and went up after *Weatherly* — his advantage lost.

When he finally realized how he was being mislead, Sturrock bore off for the finish and set his spinnaker. Too late: Mosbacher, to windward, sailed down and over him and won by only twenty-six seconds. *Weatherly* won the last race with relative ease, and to Mosbacher's great relief the match was over. Soon after, the director of the Stevens test tank confirmed what he already knew was true, that *Gretel* was faster than *Weatherly*. Like Vanderbilt, Mosbacher would not sail for the cup again unless he had the fastest boat under him.

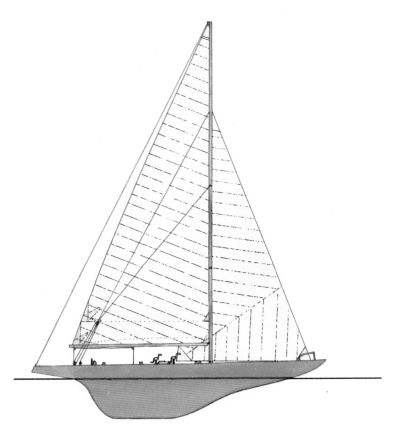

Bus Mosbacher was chosen as Weatherly's *helmsman after having proved himself an accomplished skipper on board* Vim *in 1958.*

	date	wind (mph)	start	finish
Weatherly	9/15	12	h. 13.10.12	h. 16.23.57
Gretel			h. 13.10.26	h. 16.27.43
Gretel	9/18	22/28	h. 12.20.11	h. 15.06.58
Weatherly			h. 12.20.17	h. 15.07.45
Weatherly	9/20	10/11	h. 12.51.24	h. 17.11.16
Gretel			h. 12.50.21	h. 17.19.56
Weatherly	9/22	9/11	h. 13.05.19	h. 16.27.28
Gretel			h. 13.05.23	h. 16.27.54
Weatherly	9/25	9/11	h. 13.10.13	h. 16.26.17
Gretel			h. 13.10.09	h. 16.29.57

1964
Constellation-Sovereign

Sovereign, *with Peter Scott at the helm, outdistanced on the lee of* Constellation, *skippered by Bob Bavier.*

Alan Payne's design genius, coupled with his exploitation of American sailing technology, had almost taken the cup on Australia's first try. Not quite accustomed to the truth that its sailmakers and winch manufacturers were not just slightly better than the foreign competition but actually stood head and shoulders above it, the New York Yacht Club suddenly realized that the trophy might be lost to a challenger that was Australian or British in name only. On December 7, 1962, the club's board of trustees voted on a new interpretation of the deed of gift's requirement that the boats be "constructed" in their home nations. Henceforth, all equipment, sails (including sail cloth), and design research would have to originate in the competitors' homelands. The club believed that this interpretation was consistent with the *America* syndicate's goal of establishing "a perpetual Challenge Cup for friendly competition between foreign countries." Of course, others saw it as only the latest outgrowth of the ninety-year-old conspiracy to keep the cup in New York. Put in the paradoxical position of having to interpret the rules governing an event in which it also competed, the club was (and is) always vulnerable to the charge of engaging in conflict of interest. The reality was (and is) that it usually interpreted the deed of gift about as equitably as possible. But when conflict of interest is an issue, appearances are more important than reality and the club's brusque, businesslike way of handling cup matters sometimes may seem prejudiced from the point of view of an enthusiastic potential challenger based thousands of miles from Manhattan.

Sometimes, too, challengers hopefully and willfully misconstrue the yacht club's statements. In 1960, the disappointed Royal Thames Yacht Club was told that its challenge might be accepted for 1963, a year after the Australian match. The Englishmen interpreted "might" as "will" and got to work, squeezing in some tank-testing at Stevens Institute before the new limitations took effect. However, the Americans were so exhausted (emotionally and financially) by the 1962 match that they told the new challenger, a young tycoon named Anthony Boyden, to wait until 1964. Boyden tried to arouse public sympathy but failed.

Designed by David Boyd, who had been responsible for *Sceptre*, Boyden's *Sovereign* was not much of an im-

provement over the 1958 challenger even after extensive trials against a new sistership, *Kurrewa*, and a year of sailing before she reached Newport. Her skipper, Peter Scott (son of the great Antarctic explorer Robert), apparently was chosen more for his ability to get along with the temperamental Boyden than for his match-racing skills. Believing that brawn was more important than sailing experience, Boyden chose the crew from a group of rugby players. *Sovereign* seemed reasonably competitive when the water was smooth, but the water is almost always rough off Newport and she was very badly beaten — the twenty-minute margin in the second race was the largest in the cup's history. The English were embarrassed once again; the Americans were downright angry that they had spent a great deal of money and time on two new boats when one of the 1958 Twelves could have beaten *Sovereign* handily.

But the racing that went on between those new boats! *American Eagle* was designed by A.E. Luders Jr., who

The crew of Constellation at the ready.
Harold Vanderbilt was one of the syndicate members.

had so improved *Weatherly* in 1962, and sailed by a brilliant technically-minded skipper named Bill Cox, and *Constellation*, the new Olin Stephens boat, was commanded by Eric Ridder, a somewhat successful 6-Meter sailor. Each boat was supported by immense syndicates of as many as eighteen members; Pierre S. du Pont, of the chemicals family, headed *American Eagle's* long list of backers and Walter Gubelmann, heir to an office machine fortune, and Ridder, a successful publisher, organized *Constellation's* funders. Neither boat lacked money. Until August, however, it looked as though *Constellation* was short of sailing talent. Her record was only six wins against sixteen defeats, and she was consistently beaten by Cox, who at one stage ran up a fourteen-race winning streak. Ridder guessed that the source of her failure lay not with *Constellation's* design or sails but with himself. He asked his relief helmsman, Robert N. Bavier Jr., to take over at first for a start, then for a weather leg, finally for most of a race — and she improved radically. The syndicate then named Bavier helmsman and asked that Ridder stay on as titular skipper. Bavier, who liked to control his boat, warily agreed once Ridder granted him that control. It was a brave thing for both men to do, and it worked. Ridder had never beaten *American Eagle*; now Bavier was beating her almost all the time.

Bavier and Cox had sailed against and with each other for decades, Cox the master of minute technological refinements and Bavier the aggressive tactician. Now in boats where technology and tactics were equally important, they fought through a series of superb races with the fierceness that surfaces when gentlemen play games. Shaken out of their early cockiness by *Constellation's* late, hard charge, *American Eagle's* crew started to make small mistakes that Bavier and his navigator, Rod Stephens, pounced on. Bavier won the first race in the final trials after her opponent's jib fell apart. Still needing a decisive win to provide the confidence necessary to sweep on to selection, Bavier won the start of the second race but lost the lead to round the mark just two lengths behind. He hung off *American Eagle's* stern as though being towed, and then on the last 4½-mile beat began a tacking duel. Stephens noticed that *Constellation* gained very slightly with each tack as Cox nervously jammed his boat's helm over while Bavier swung more gracefully through the wind's eye. Cox continued his close cover in order to keep *Constellation* in his wind shadow, which only played into Bavier's hands. Tack, tack, tack, tack — forty times *Constellation* came about and forty-two times *American Eagle* mimicked her as their exhausted crews swung their arms mechanically around the radii of the winch handles. With only a mile to go, *Constellation* broke through to win. Bavier predicted that this loss had broken the hearts of *American Eagle's* previously high-flying crew. He was right. She won only one more race, and that due to a major wind shift on the course. *Con-*

stellation was selected to slaughter poor *Sovereign*.

Three new developments in 1964 foresaw new trends in cup sailing. One was Eric Ridder's replacement as *Constellation's* helmsman by Bavier. Later syndicates would fire helmsmen if they were not producing up to expectation — and with many more hurt feelings all around. Another was the appearance of the first boat not from the East Coast. This was the old 1958 defender *Columbia*, now owned by Southern Californian Pat Dougan and sailed by Briggs Cunningham (who lived in that area) and a crew that included a young San Diego sailmaker named Lowell North. West Coast sailors would soon be manning and owning other Twelves. The third innovation was the use of a six-leg Olympic course instead of the old triangle and windward-leeward courses. The length was still 24 miles, but with shorter legs and more buoys to round, tactics and sail-handling became increasingly important. A fast boat would have to be sailed at least as competently as a slow one.

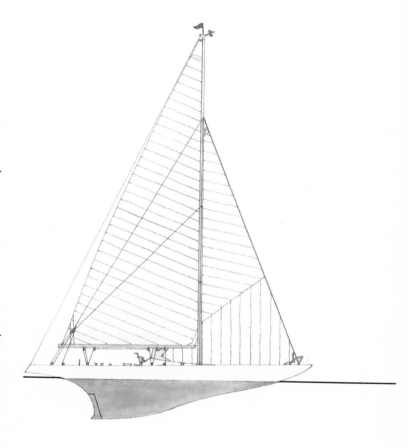

	date	wind (mph)	start	finish
Constellation	9/15	7/9	h. 12.35.08	h. 16.05.41
Sovereign			h. 12.35.10	h. 16.11.15
Constellation	9/17	17/20	h. 12.10.21	h. 15.56.48
Sovereign			h. 12.10.23	h. 16.17.12
Constellation	9/19	15/17	h. 12.10.03	h. 15.48.07
Sovereign			h. 12.10.43	h. 15.54.40
Constellation	9/21	21	h. 12.10.11	h. 16.22.27
Sovereign			h. 12.10.02	h. 16.38.07

Above, Constellation, *on the right, engaged in a jibing duel with* Nefertiti *during one of the selection trial races. Below,* American Eagle *after she was reconverted to an offshore racing yacht.*

103

1967
Intrepid-Dame Pattie

This was the year of *Intrepid*, which — with *Reliance* in 1903 and *Ranger* in 1937 — is one of the three "superboats" in America's Cup history. She won twenty-three of the twenty-four trial and cup races that she finished, and her only shortcomings were the navigator's error that caused her sole loss and two broken masts resulting from an overeagerness to save weight aloft. Unlike the two great boats that preceded her, *Intrepid* did not kill off her breed. Rather, she created a whole new generation of 12-Meters, and her radical hull, layout, and sail plan set a standard in yacht design that still applied sixteen years later.

Despite her revolutionary design, *Intrepid* was conceived and gestated as most successful cup defenders are: in the company of a small number of wealthy men, a creative yacht designer, and a dedicated skipper. We know this because several months after she destroyed the Australian challenger, *Dame Pattie*, her principals described her genesis in unusually frank interviews that Robert W. Carrick and Stanley Rosenfeld later collected in a fascinating book, *Defending the America's Cup*. More than any other source, these interviews provide a clear window into the privileged board-room of American cup syndicates. Since an important factor in the continued dominance of American defenders is their financial and manpower organization, a glance at the structure of *Intrepid*'s 1967 syndicate can suggest some of the important ingredients of a successful cup campaign.

The spark plug of the *Intrepid* effort was a wealthy yachtsman named William Strawbridge, who had caught the highly contagious America's Cup fever while aiding the *American Eagle* syndicate in 1964 (his original aim had been to help his son find a position in her campaign). Not impressed with the way that she and *Constellation* had been managed or with the cumbersomeness of the immense syndicates, he outlined a plan for a new campaign involving Olin Stephens and, at Stephens' suggestion, Bus Mosbacher. But he was unable to quickly raise the seed money that would win Stephens' commitment because Mosbacher was unable to say definitely if he could sail. Finally, in June 1965, pushed by Stephens, Mosbacher agreed. Strawbridge then, as he put it, had "something to sell" and while visiting with friends in a Florida resort and on a

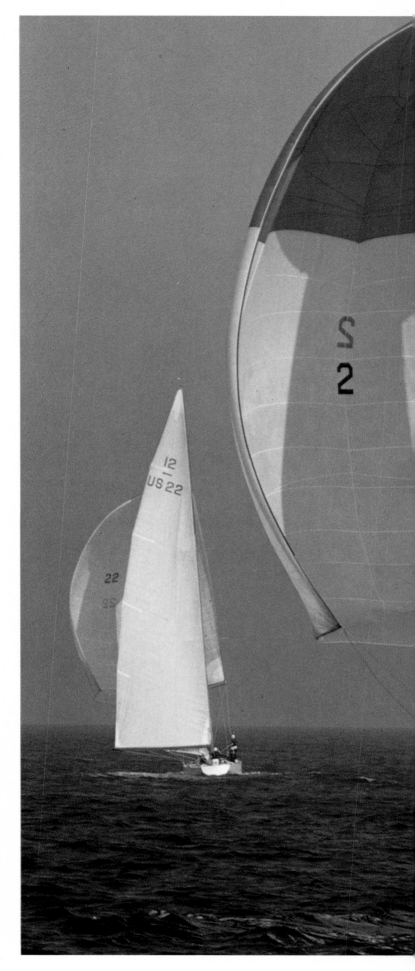

Maryland hunt was able to put together a $700,000 syndicate. It was small, with only four principal members at $150,000 each, because the huge 1964 syndicates had given little pleasure to their members; and it was selective because they wanted nobody who would challenge either Strawbridge's managership on shore or Mosbacher's leadership on the water. One of the four principals was none other than Harold S. Vanderbilt, with whom Bill Strawbridge had once sailed on *Ranger* and who more than anybody else knew the right formula for a successful campaign. Another was Patrick E. Haggerty, who had helped make Texas Instruments one of the most successful electronics companies in the world and who came in because of Olin Stephens, whom he called ''not only something of a genius but as fine a human being as I've ever met.''

Haggerty was also attracted by the special nature of the cup, which he called an anachronism. ''In this day and age, it seems ridiculous to try so hard with a mechanism of movement which is so relatively slow,'' he said after the match. ''The efficiency of a sailboat in terms of distance covered is not very high. But maybe this is one of the exciting things about it... There is an exquisiteness about the preparation, certainly in contemporary contests.'' At one time or another, these sentiments — voiced by a man who was revolutionizing the way people did calculations — might have been expressed by John Cox Stevens, Charles J. Paine, Sir Thomas Lipton, Thomas Sopwith, Harold Vanderbilt, and Briggs Cunningham, other cup principals who were at the forefront of development in transportation, marketing, and race-car manufacturing.

''The whole thing is just fascinating,'' is how another syndicate principal, Burr Bartram, explained his sizeable commitment — which was not tax-deductible until the 1970's. ''I don't think it's a waste of money. Certainly it is not a business venture by any means — I guess maybe some people go into it with the idea of getting publicity or renown, or whatever the word is. I don't think anyone in our syndicate had that idea. They just wanted to keep the cup here''.

Eventually, more than $700,000 was needed and a few smaller donations of $50,000 were accepted for a total that may have reached $1 million. Vanderbilt was so impressed by *Intrepid*'s performance that he offered whatever funds the syndicate needed; sadly, at age eighty-three, he was unable to complete the circle by going out for a sail in her. Strawbridge was not a principal but did pay some costs, and he signed an official document giving him complete control. As manager, his jobs were to supervise the boat, solve problems, and keep costs down. His loyalty, he said, was primarily to the syndicate. ''My sense of responsibility to the New York

Dame Pattie, with Jock Sturrock at the helm, too far away to be able to blanket Intrepid *which has a safe advantage and proved very fast.*

Yacht Club was not all that great — I figured they should be darn glad we were there. That isn't the way they like to look at it," he admitted, "but it was the syndicate that was putting on the show."

Indeed, what a show they put on. With more than a year available for tank-testing (which ended up costing more than $30,000), Olin Stephens was able to pursue some new directions. One of these was to make the keel smaller in order to reduce wetted surface, for good light-air speed, and put the rudder far aft of the keel. This was not a new idea: Nathanael Herreshoff had tried it on small boats in the 1890's, it had been the basis for a failed defense candidate in 1893, and it had been used on small racing boats for years. But it had been counter-productive in boats larger than about 40 feet because the small keel reduced the lateral area so much that big boats slid sideways. To make the short keel as effective as a long one, a Boston-based designer named Dick Carter had begun attaching flaps to the trailing edge. By turning the flap to leeward, the crew could improve the water flow over the keel and increase its hydrodynamic lift. Having decided to use this radical concept, Stephens experimented with various hull shapes in the Stevens Institute towing tank to find the correct combination of low wetted surface and high stability he knew from experience to be key to a successful racing yacht.

Meanwhile, Mosbacher and his right-hand man, Vic Romagna, were rethinking the common wisdom about equipment layout. The traditional arrangement had men standing on deck and in the cockpit aft. This, they thought, not only obstructed the helmsman's view but also spread more than a ton of crew weight far above and aft of the hull's center of gravity. So using a full-scale mock-up, they designed a lay-out with almost all the winches ground below deck.

Of course, Reliance and Enterprise had had winches below, but not so many important ones; here, even the jib-sheet coffee grinders would be there, the pedestals dropping down from the deck. In all, only the helmsman, the tactician, and the two men tailing the jib and spinnaker sheets would have their heads in daylight. The other seven men would be below much of the race — some the entire race. Olin and Rod Stephens and their colleagues at Sparkman & Stephens were at first dubious about this startling innovation, but Mosbacher and Romagna met their objections. Eventually, only one winch was replaced all summer — a remarkable statistic since most new Twelves undergo major gear alterations as a matter of course.

The third major innovation was to lower the boom until it was at the level of Mosbacher's shoulder. Advice from aerodynamicists and research by Halsey Herreshoff, who taught at the Massachusetts Institute of Technology, suggested that a low boom would create something called an "end plate effect", which would greatly improve the mainsail's power upwind.

When Intrepid was launched at the Minneford yard,

on City Island, New York, in the spring of 1967, she looked as startling as America appeared to the Marquis of Anglesey back on the Isle of Wight in 1851. Her keel was absurdly small, her steering wheel was covered with clutches and handles for manipulating the flap, and her deck was ridiculously clear of sail-handling equipment. Afloat, she sailed without any visible means of crew support, her boom threatened to decapitate her skipper, and, when Mosbacher put her helm down, she spun like a racing dinghy.

Those who liked their cup defenders long and graceful were disappointed by her snubbed bow. Like Reliance and Ranger, she was an ugly duckling. Also like them, she was very, very fast.

On the water, Mosbacher was in charge. Following standard procedure, her designers wanted to assign a project engineer to the boat for repairs and equipment problems, but Mosbacher demurred because "we were not going to have somebody who was not going to sail telling us what to do." He chose Ted Hood as exclusive sailmaker and the inventory, though small, was superb. Contrary to his practice in 1958 and 1967, he sailed very conservatively in winds above 6 knots. "Anything less and we had to work a little," he remembered fondly. Intrepid's crew consisted of friends with whom Mosbacher and Romagna had sailed in other boats, and from the beginning he delegated responsibility that other skippers might have reserved for themselves. On her first sail, they approached a buoy on Long Island Sound. The crew wanted to make their first spinnaker set a tricky "tack-jibe" manoeuver — about the most difficult sail-handling exercise of all. Mosbacher had doubts but went along because, as he put it, "If you're going to delegate responsibility, you've got to learn to live with it." He tacked around the buoy, threw Intrepid into a quick jibe and, pop!, the spinnaker was up and full. "You know, there's something special about that crew," Mosbacher said thirteen years later, using the present tense to hint that his team continued to perform perfect tack-jibe spinnaker sets on the inner 12-Meter of his memory.

However, to Olin Stephens, Mosbacher was the one who was special. "Bus was responsible in an inspirational way for getting the group together, and he's the kind of guy you really want to be associated with," he told Carrick and Rosenfeld. Then a forty-five-year-old real estate investor and oil and gas producer, Mosbacher had attended Choate School and Dartmouth College and had served in the Navy during World War II. As a boy, he had learned to sail and race under the tutelage of a professional seaman hired by his father, a man who demanded excellence in his son's activities. After winning junior championships on Long Island Sound,

A birdseye view of Dame Pattie *close-hauled. She was the second Twelve designed by Alan Payne and was owned by a syndicate of Australian corporations.*

Intrepid, *above, and, below, her crew. At the helm is Bus Mosbacher, who like Charlie Barr and Harold Vanderbilt successfully defended in both a slow boat and a fast one.*

Mosbacher sailed extremely successfully in keel daysailers and frostbite dinghies, racing almost every weekend all year, before moving on to Twelves and ocean racers. There his extraordinary powers of concentration, intimate feel for a boat's capabilities, aggressive tactics, and leadership strengths combined to make him a master-skipper.

Despite his easy selection in the trials against *Constellation* and *Columbia*, Mosbacher approached the match against *Dame Pattie* with some nervousness. The challenger, designed by Alan Payne's chief assistant, Warwick Hood, had easily beaten *Gretel* in the first-ever set of challenger's trials in Australia. Owned by a syndicate of Australian corporations headed by Emil Christensen, she was well-funded. Mosbacher had the most to lose not only because he was the defending skipper but because he was partially responsible for his boat's radical design. The Australians annoyed him by quibbling about *Intrepid*'s measurement certificate and the resulting bitterness left him pacing his bedroom floor at night, muttering, "It's only a game, it's only a sport." A man who was known to lose as much as seven pounds during a race due to nervous energy alone, Mosbacher now was strained simply by the preliminary build-up. His worries were wasted: *Intrepid* easily won four straight.

The only events to make the series interesting were the threat of a hurricane and the intrusion of a bumbling small sailboat that was promptly capsized in front of *Intrepid* by the wind blast from an equally bumbling U.S. Coast Guard helicopter. The hurricane dodged Newport and Mosbacher dodged the swamped boat, and it was all over. Like Charlie Barr and Harold Vanderbilt, he had won the cup first in a slow boat and now in a fast one.

Unlike them, Bus Mosbacher retired from serious racing. He had climbed his personal Everest twice and now he could move on to other mountains.

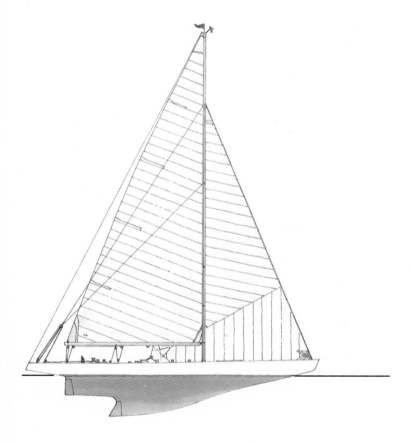

Rod Stephens aloft on Intrepid *handling a stay. Maintenance work on Twelves is of vital importance and the crew works at it all the time when ashore.*

	date	wind (mph)	start	finish
Intrepid	9/12	17/21	h. 12.30.16	h. 15.55.03
Dame Pattie			h. 12.30.06	h. 16.01.01
Intrepid	9/13	8/16	h. 12.35.15	h. 16.04.21
Dame Pattie			h. 12.35.14	h. 16.07.57
Intrepid	9/14	14/18	h. 12.20.07	h. 15.40.14
Dame Pattie			h. 12.20.06	h. 15.44.55
Intrepid	9/18	9/14	h. 14.00.04	h. 17.27.39
Dame Pattie			h. 14.00.01	h. 17.31.14

1970
Intrepid-Gretel II

Above, Intrepid, *after having crossed the finish line with Bill Ficker at the helm. On the opposite page,* Gretel II *which was skippered by Jim Hardy. This Twelve was equipped with two wheels and during the racing was at the center of fresh controversy.*

In some ways, this was the most successful of all the 12-Meter matches; in others, it was the most discouraging. It never ceased to be the most dramatic.

Surprisingly, considering the drubbings handed the invaders in the previous two matches, four countries challenged: Greece, Britain, France, and Australia. The first two dropped out and an international committee was organized to run trials off Newport between Sir Frank Packer's *Gretel II* and Baron Marcel Bich's *France*. Bich, who had made an immense fortune by selling cheap Bic pens to the world, had bought the failed British challenge candidate *Kurrewa V* as a daysailer for his nine children back in 1964. Entranced by the power and feel of even this bad Twelve, he then purchased *Constellation* and *Sovereign*, and, planning a challenge for 1970, commissioned a boat from the American designer Britton Chance Jr. *France* was a French design inspired by Chance's boat. Bich brought most of his fleet of 12-Meters to Newport along with support vessels, sixty sailors, two chefs, and an immense quantity of French wine. Each of *France's* spinnakers carried the crest of a different province in her home country. Unfortunately, this colorful Gallic feeling also permeated the more technical aspects of Bich's campaign. He switched skippers and crews around all summer and, in the trials, tried two different helmsmen before he himself took over in the fourth race. In a formal yachting outfit that included white gloves, he succeeded in getting lost in the fog and finally accepted a tow. His $4 million campaign ended ignominiously with Bich angrily attacking the race committee for allowing the contest to continue in the poor visibility. However, he allowed *France* to be used as a tune-up boat by *Gretel II*, which was vital to the Packer group because Alan Payne continued to make major alterations right up until the eve of the match.

Her competitor would be *Intrepid*, but a very different *Intrepid*. Test-tank work since 1967 had convinced American designers that they could pare away at keels even more than Stephens had done while simultaneously making the boats longer and heavier to increase their maximum speed. Under the International Rule, this meant that sail area had to be reduced, but it was thought that the trade-off would work favorably. With Stephens committed to a new boat, the *Intrepid* syndicate had Britton Chance Jr., the young man responsible for Bich's trial horse, alter their boat, and she came to the starting line almost 2 feet longer on the waterline and heavier. Her main opponent, the new Stephens boat, *Valiant*, was even larger. *Valiant* also carried the "black gang" below-deck gear idea to its furthest extreme, having only one winch out in the sun. The other new boat was a flashback to Alexander Cuthbert's second Canadian challenger ninety years earlier — a yacht owned, designed, built, sailed, and canvassed by one and the same man, in this case a St. Petersburg, Florida, sailmaker and boatbuilder named Charley Morgan. *Heritage*, as she was called, carried the hopes of not only the South but also of many people who admired Morgan's quixotic spirit. Unfortunately, she was no more successful than Cuthbert's *Atalanta* had been.

The trials, then, came down to *Valiant* (sailed by Rear-Commodore Robert McCullough) and *Intrepid*

The crew at work to trim a sheet after a tack. Before 1977 the winches could be set below decks. This rule was then altered for safety reasons.

(with Californian William Ficker, *Columbia*'s 1967 co-skipper, in charge). Some observers were disturbed to see that little old *Weatherly*, appearing ostensibly so that two trial races could be held each day between four boats, was often competitive with these big high-tech Twelves eight years after she had won the 1962 match. By all rights, assuming that the test tank had been correct, they should have been slaughtering her. Once *Weatherly* and *Heritage* were eliminated, *Intrepid* and *Valiant* went at it. The older boat won out and became the only twice-defender other than the Herreshoff-designed *Columbia* and, later, *Courageous*.

There was another controversy about measurement. This time, though, it was substantial. Chance had fitted plastic sheets around the rudder that effectively lengthened *Intrepid*'s waterline. The American measurer had declared them legal, to the Australians' apparent surprise, and after some negotiation they were altered. Packer also made it known that he considered

the fact that *Intrepid*'s toilet was not enclosed to ensure privacy a violation of the spirit as well as the letter of the International Rule. Once required to have extensive cruising accommodations, Twelves were now pared down to minimum facilities that the American crews worked hard to make as unobtrusive as possible. That *Intrepid*'s people had tried to cut this corner is an indication of the ways in which cup racing was tending toward ruthless efficiency. Like the plastic sheets, her head was altered, and the two boats got down to serious business on the water.

Race one was an unmitigated disaster for the challengers, who tangled their spinnaker and then lost a man overboard. They lost two minutes recovering him, were beaten by almost six minutes, and seemed all but eliminated as a threat. But an event before the start indicated that *Gretel II*'s crew had the aggressiveness needed to win the cup. As she on starboard tack approached *Intrepid* on port, her skipper, Jim Hardy,

The first challenge of Baron Bich at the helm of France, *who got lost in thick fog during the last of the trail races. Eric Tabarly can be seen on the right.*

altered course to prevent Bill Ficker from passing clearly to one side. At almost the last moment, Hardy tacked and both boats sent up protest flags. Since there was no collision, and undoubtedly because they were wary of creating a dispute, the race committee disallowed both protests with the comment that they were bending over backwards to be fair. However, they could easily have disqualified *Gretel II*, which had broken a cardinal rule by not allowing the boat that did not have right of way sufficient room to stay clear. Whether the Australians actually knew that rule — subsequent events indicated that they were more than casual about other regulations — was an open question.

This became even more clear in the second race. At the start, Ficker tried to squeeze between *Gretel* and the committee boat. Martin Visser, now the challenger's starting helmsman, headed up (as he thought he had the right to do) and just after the starting gun was fired, *Gretel*'s bow smashed against *Intrepid*'s port side — in

fact, a false bow broke off onto *Intrepid*'s deck. Ficker shot ahead in the light air but *Gretel*, now helmed by Hardy, immediately began to gain. Clearly faster than *Intrepid*, she gradually closed the gap and passed her on the run. (Ficker had another disadvantage: his tactician, Steve Van Dyck, had been taken off before the start after being stung by a bee and was replaced by a man who was unfamiliar with *Intrepid*. Ficker, a skipper who delegated authority as systematically as Vanderbilt had, may have been distracted.) *Gretel* won the race, and the next morning the principals met to argue the protest. In the end, *Gretel* was disqualified.

Although there was a slight ambiguity in the rules, most experienced sailors agreed with the committee's decision that *Gretel* was at fault. She had sailed above a close-hauled course after the starting gun and that, clear and simple, was illegal. If she had held to her proper course, there would have been no collision. The New York Yacht Club's race committee chairman, B.

113

Devereux Barker, was astonished at how poorly the Australians knew the racing rules, which are an integral part of all sailboat races. But the public reaction, led by Packer, was entirely different. "*Gretel* Robbed" was one of the more tame headlines in Australian newspapers. The American ambassador to Australia, hundreds of newspaper editorialists and columnists, and any number of public officials sent up a great howl of anguish. The overriding theme was the by now familiar one of conflict of interest. Packer chose an imaginative simile: "An American skipper protesting to the New York Yacht Club committee is like a man complaining to his mother-in-law about his wife." Visser said, "We feel we can't beat the New York Yacht Club, but we feel we can beat *Intrepid*." At one point, the club's America's Cup Committee actually considered resailing the race and asked Bob Bavier, the president of the North American Yacht Racing Union, for his opinion. He demurred; as he put it elsewhere: "The Australians deserved to win on the race course. They simply don't know the rules."

Why was Bill Ficker, no gambler, willing to try for the hole? If his timing had been off by just five seconds, the Australians would have had every right to squeeze *Intrepid* out. He took the chance because he knew how fast *Gretel II* was and he was alert to every opportunity to grab an advantage. Smaller, lighter, and with the same if not more sail area, the challenger was a superior boat in the prevailing light conditions. As Mosbacher had done in 1962, Ficker throughout the rest of the match ignored traditional covering tactics, sailed pretty much his own boat races and even set different sails than the Australians did on downwind legs. He squeezed out a win in the third race, lost the fourth one on the last part of the last leg, and caught Hardy part-way up the first leg of the last race and held on to take the cup. Apparently, the Australians had repeated their 1962 mistake of never fully realizing how much faster their boat was than the Americans'. If they had trusted in their boat speed instead of their fierce starting-line tactics, Hardy and his crew might well have won the match four races to one. Make that a clean sweep if they had taken the time to learn the racing rules.

A forty-two-year-old architect from Southern California, Bill Ficker had won a Star Class world championship. His skillful co-skippership of *Columbia* in 1967 had earned him control of the rebuilt *Intrepid*, and he put together a young crew that became superbly proficient at tactics and sail-handling through the long summer of defense trials. The only man on board over thirty, he concentrated on steering; this was absolutely vital in the new Twelves since they tracked about as poorly as a runaway skateboard and felt dead in the helm. If there was ever a series where patient, confident reliance on a crew was important, it was the 1970 America's Cup match. Once again a slow defender beat a fast challenger; once again the American system prevailed.

Gretel II close hauled. *This Twelve, the second to be sponsored by Sir Frank Packer, was designed by Alan Payne.*

	date	wind (mph)	start	finish
Intrepid	9/15	14/18	h. 12.10.06	h. 15.36.03
Gretel II			h. 12.10.08	h. 15.41.55
Intrepid	9/18	11	h. 12.30.11	Abandoned
Gretel II			h. 12.30.08	due to fog
Intrepid	9/20	7/11	h. 14.00.00	h. 18.38.10
Gretel II			h. 14.00.00	h. 18.37.03
Intrepid	9/22	12/21	h. 12.10.09	h. 15.34.43
Gretel II			h. 12.10.14	h. 15.36.01
Gretel II	9/24	5/12	h. 12.10.21	h. 15.33.59
Intrepid			h. 12.10.13	h. 15.35.01
Intrepid	9/28	6/11	h. 12.10.11	h. 16.39.03
Gretel II			h. 12.10.10	h. 16.40.47

Intrepid *on a reach with the hull hidden by a wave. The boat,*
designed by S&S, was modified for this challenge by Britton Chance.

1974
Courageous-Southern Cross

Seven challenges flowed into the New York Yacht Club in the fall of 1970, but only Baron Marcel Bich, from France, and Alan Bond, from Australia, built boats. Bond was a thirty-two-year-old entrepreneur who had emigrated from England at the age of thirteen and, in twenty years, had moved from a small sign business to a $200 million corporation developing the hills of Western Australia. He made no bones about using his challenge to promote his housing projects. Pugnacious and ambitious, he exploited the bad feeling that still hung in the Australian air about the 1970 foul and pressed every possible claim of unfairness onto the yacht club's back. His champion was the yellow Bob Miller-designed *Southern Cross*.

The match was postponed from 1973 to 1974 partly because designers wanted more time to study the use of aluminum hulls, which had become legal under the International Rule, and due to major international financial worries. So serious was the recession that William Strawbridge had trouble finding money for his syndicate's boat and he urged the yacht club to announce another postponement. It refused, construction stopped on the new boat, an Olin Stephens design, and Bill Ficker, who had planned to sail her, made business commitments. By the time Vice-Commodore Robert Mc-Cullough had reorganized the syndicate, Ficker was no longer available so Bob Bavier, the 1964 defending helmsman, was signed on as skipper. The other new American boat was managed by former Commodore George Hinman, *Weatherly*'s skipper in 1970. To attract donors, he developed a scheme whereby the boat was owned by a tax-exempt foundation so that donations could be deducted from personal income taxes, a system originally intended to encourage gifts to hospitals, schools, and charities. Britton Chance Jr. would design and Ted Turner would sail her.

Few people were more unlike than the two opposing skippers, Bavier and Turner. At fifty-five, Bob Bavier was the quintessential American yachtsman, a leader of the yachting establishment and publisher of the sport's most important and successful magazine, *Yachting*. It is

France II should have been Baron Bich's 1974 challenger but was delayed due to disagreements with Paul Elvström, the project manager designate. In 1977 she was, however, slower than France I.

*Southern Cross was the first Twelve to be designed by Bob Miller and the first to be
sponsored by Alan Bond, a real-estate developer from Perth.*

interesting irony that despite his apparent compatibility
with tradition, he was the first of a new breed of
amateur sailors who had earned their reputations almost
solely within the boating community. For his
predecessors, sailing had been a part-time relaxation
that was sometimes stretched into a summer's campaign. Bavier, however, lived, breathed, and earned his
salary around boats. Thirty-four years old, Ted Turner
had burst upon the yachting scene ten years earlier by
winning a Southern Ocean Racing Conference and then
going on to spend much of the money he made from his
Atlanta, Georgia, advertising, television, and sports empire on fast yachts. One was *American Eagle*, which
Bavier had beaten in 1964 and which Turner sailed to a
world ocean racing championship. Rambunctious, often
crude, Turner seemed the exact opposite of the
withdrawn, stiff Bavier; but the New England elder
statesman had taken the Southern rebel under his wing,
had helped him get into the New York Yacht Club, and

would one day make him a corporate director of
Yachting. What they had in common was boyish enthusiasm about racing sailboats.

Their 12-Meters were very different. Bavier's
Courageous was classic Stephens. Lighter and smaller
than the lumbering *Valiant*, she also had a lot of *Gretel
II* in her lines. Chance was not patient with minor
refinements. In *Mariner*, he produced the most radical
boat that had ever appeared in cup competition — a
stubby hull mounted on a tiny keel, with lines that
swept back to a huge squared-off slab that looked like a
massive submerged transom. Chance had learned in the
test tank that his sliced-off stern would "fool the water"
into behaving as though the hull was longer that it really
was. So persuasive was his evidence that Hinman
ordered her stablemate *Valiant* rebuilt to the same
shape so that she would be fast enough to provide some
competition in tune-up trials. The only thing that was
fooled, it turned out, was the syndicate. *Valiant* and

Overleaf, a ceremony repeated every America's Cup year: the spectator fleet follows the contenders at a respectful distance.

Mariner were even, all right, but they were badly beaten by *Courageous* and the other contender, *Intrepid*. Chance blamed Turner's helmsmanship. Turner pleaded for hull alterations ("Damn, Brit," he said with exasperation, "even a turd is tapered at both ends!"). Finally, *Mariner* was withdrawn from the trials and her entire after underbody was cut off and replaced by one more conventional. An improvement, but not enough.

Meanwhile, Bob Bavier was unexpectedly losing races to the seven-year-old *Intrepid*, which her skipper, San Diego boatbuilder Gerald Driscoll, had returned to her 1967 lines with some modifications. Many observers thought her North sails superior to the new boat's Hood sails, so Bavier ordered some Norths and saw some improvement. The situation became complex, however, when Ted Hood himself came on as his tactician. That was not the only crew change made by syndicate manager Bob McCullough. Dennis Conner, *Mariner*'s thirty-one-year-old tactician, had replaced Turner and

dominated the starts against Bavier and Driscoll. In late August, after *Mariner* was excused from the trials, McCullough appointed Conner as *Courageous*'s starting helmsman.

On face value, this move confused an already complicated command structure. Under McCullough's orders, Conner started, Hood steered upwind, and Bavier steered downwind. Nobody — least of all Bavier — was very clear who was in overall charge. It was a Harold Vanderbilt type of organization except that the man taking Vanderbilt's role, McCullough, was not aboard. Bavier lost confidence and the crew apparently lost confidence in him. On the morning of the second-to-last trial race, McCullough fired Bavier and named Hood as skipper and Conner as tactician and starting helmsman. The America's Cup was getting to be serious business indeed. With the final trials scorecard reading four races won by each boat, it all came down to the last race, sailed in fresh winds, and *Courageous* won.

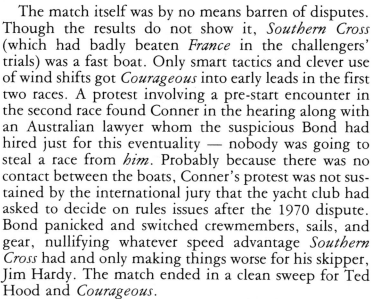

Gretel II *and* Southern Cross, *on the right, ready to be both shipped back to Australia.*
On the right, Dennis Conner at the helm of Courageous.

The match itself was by no means barren of disputes. Though the results do not show it, *Southern Cross* (which had badly beaten *France* in the challengers' trials) was a fast boat. Only smart tactics and clever use of wind shifts got *Courageous* into early leads in the first two races. A protest involving a pre-start encounter in the second race found Conner in the hearing along with an Australian lawyer whom the suspicious Bond had hired just for this eventuality — nobody was going to steal a race from *him*. Probably because there was no contact between the boats, Conner's protest was not sustained by the international jury that the yacht club had asked to decide on rules issues after the 1970 dispute. Bond panicked and switched crewmembers, sails, and gear, nullifying whatever speed advantage *Southern Cross* had and only making things worse for his skipper, Jim Hardy. The match ended in a clean sweep for Ted Hood and *Courageous*.

The only major controversy to survive the 1974 match was between two American sailmakers. Before the first race, Ted Hood refused McCullough's orders to lower his own company's mainsail and replace it with a North sail that McCullough and others believed was superior. Conner, who relayed McCullough's instructions and Hood's responses over a radiotelephone, reports that Hood's last words on the subject were, "You tell Bob I'm the skipper and that we're going with what we have up." *Courageous* won the race and the Hood sail stayed up, and after the match a North sailmaker, John Marshall (who had been in *Intrepid*'s crew), publicly criticized Hood for placing business considerations above sporting ones.

Dennis Conner, however, saw it as an expression of the skipper's right both to run his own boat and to use equipment in which he had confidence. This, it seemed, was an issue that had haunted the American defenders all summer long in one guise or another and would crop up again.

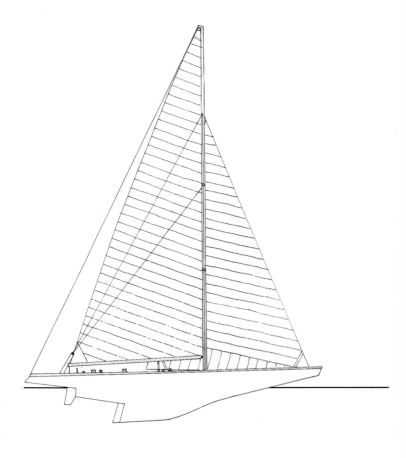

	date	wind (mph)	start	finish
Courageous	9/10	7/11	h. 14.10.06	h. 18.22.03
Southern Cross			h. 14.10.08	h. 18.26.57
Courageous	9/12	11/16	h. 12.10.09	h. 15.42.37
Southern Cross			h. 12.10.08	h. 15.43.48
Courageous	9/16	11/12	h. 12.11.01	h. 15.43.02
Southern Cross			h. 12.11.17	h. 15.48.29
Courageous	9/17	12	h. 12.10.07	h. 15.42.25
Southern Cross			h. 12.10.27	h. 15.49.44

Courageous, *on the left to windward, and* Intrepid, *which was skippered by Gerald Driscoll, during a selection trial race. Old* Intrepid *was nearly selected for the third time.*

1977
Courageous-Australia

The twenty-third challenge introduced a fourth generation of sailors to the strains and satisfactions of cup sailing. The first generation consisted of the late nineteenth-century railroad tycoons and professional skippers, the second was the small group of wealthy amateurs led by Harold Vanderbilt, and the third was the wave of businessmen who took leaves from their jobs to man the Twelves. Now a bevy of young sailmakers, boatbuilders, and others in the middle or on the fringe of the burgeoning boating industry were chosen to sail the defense candidates — men who had won their spurs in Olympic and ocean racing competition and had found a living making equipment for an expanding market of sailors. Companies like Lowell North's and Ted Hood's sail lofts had expanded across the country and around the world and, like missionaries, had brought whole new groups of people into major league sailing. One consequence of this trend was the growing internationalization of sailboat technology. Linked by computers, sail lofts in the North and Hood organizations could exchange information about sail cloths and designs, and there had to be understandings about which privileged information belonged to which client so that security could not be breached. Employees of the same company now found themselves on competing boats, and old friends who had shared long watches on ocean races now realized that one might be sailing on the cup challenger and the other on the defender.

In the American camp, you could sense how much times had changed by listening to the voices of the 12-Meter crews. On the J-Class boats and their predecessors, most orders were given and acknowledged in Scandinavian accents. The crews of the early Twelves talked and shouted in nasal New Englandish or the mid-Atlantic tones of upper-class boarding schools. But now each crew was a melange of accents, some flat Californian, others slow Southern, and a few (still) broad Eastern. At least in this way, the America's Cup had finally become American.

The one link to the earlier generations was Olin Stephens. This time he was in partnership with Lowell North — an ideal team, most people thought, since the sailmaker had won dozens of championships with just the kind of attention to technological detail that the old master thrived on. Ted Hood, too, would be at

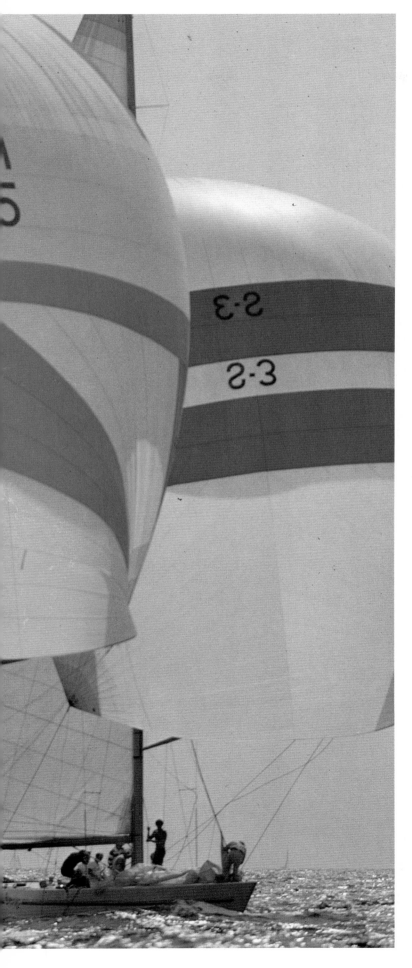

Newport, this time in a boat of his own design — his first 12-Meter since the 1962-vintage *Nefertiti*. Both syndicates were well-financed through tax-exempt foundations, and both planned long compaigns that would start well before the first trials race. Previous candidates were not launched until the late spring of the cup year, partly because the crews were not available, but mainly due to their designers' passionate attempt to find just the right shape by squeezing every possible moment of useful time out of the Stevens Institute test tank. The discrediting of the tank as the last word (remember *Valiant* and *Mariner*?) and the simultaneous arrival of radically improved sail cloths and men who knew how to shape them into fast sails turned the emphasis from the boat's underbody to her rig. Now the two giants of the sail business, North and Hood, had control of boats to use as full-scale laboratories for their ideas.

Both boats were built of aluminum at the Minneford Yard in New York. Hood's *Independence* was launched in July 1976, almost a year before her first official race. Then the shop was cleaned up and work started on North's *Enterprise*. *Independence* tuned up all summer and fall and into the winter, sailing against *Courageous* and testing sails, rigs and rudders. When the harbor at Marblehead, Massachusetts, off Hood's home, finally froze up in January, she was hauled for alterations. *Enterprise* was completed at about that time and trucked West to North's home, San Diego, California. There she sailed several hours a day, testing sails against computer read-outs since *Intrepid* was not available as trial horse. When *Intrepid* finally appeared — the syndicate was forced to buy her — *Enterprise* was able to beat her quite handily before being sent back East.

The two-time defender's 1974 skipper, Gerald Driscoll, hoped to take *Intrepid* East but the new boat's syndicates dried up most of the necessary donations. She needed extensive alterations required by the International Rule, which now said that all winches had to be located on deck and, to forestall a sinking, limited the number and size of deck openings. Beyond that, she would be expensive to maintain. A cup campaign cost well over $1 million. *Enterprise*'s $1.5 million budget included the following large items: $375,000 for research and design; $300,000 for hull construction; $225,000 for winches, spars, and rigging; $220,000 for the boat's shipyard expenses and the crew's housing and transportation; $100,000 for sails; $50,000 for trailering back and forth across the United States; and $25,000 for a house in Newport. Considering inflation, this was less than the estimated $600,000 that Harold Vanderbilt spent on *Ranger* in 1937 and probably on a par with the $100,000 that went into *Vigilant* in 1893. While those boats were destined for the wrecking ball once their

On the left, Australia, *with Noel Robins at the helm, during a jibing duel against* Sverige, *skippered by Pelle Petterson, the most innovative boat at Newport.*

brief summers of glory were over, *Enterprise*'s backers could count on selling her for about $200,000 to another syndicate or, given the ease of working with aluminum, making alterations and campaigning her again in 1980.

Facing most of the same expenses plus that of *Courageous*, Hood's backers searched for a skipper who would campaign the old boat well and cover her costs. Dennis Conner was considered, but he was not a wealthy man; in addition, he might sail her *too* well. So Ted Turner became her skipper in the spring. His reputation discredited by his miserable showing in 1974, he had nothing to lose; anyway, he enjoyed being the underdog. Turner gathered a crew, many of whom had suffered through the humiliating *Mariner* summer with him, and signed on a young U.S. Naval Academy sailing coach named Gary Jobson as his tactician. If he suffered a disadvantage it was that Lowell North would not sell him copies of the sails being developed for *Enterprise*. North personally was willing, but his backers had come to the conclusion that *Courageous* had won in 1974 in part because she eventually took advantage of North Sails's research and development program for *Intrepid*, which some of the same men also supported. Not wanting to be burned again, they made North agree to an exclusive arrangement. Turner could have worked with North lofts other than the two that were making *Enterprise*'s sails, but he chose to do something that, in the long run, was much more helpful to his chances than a new mainsail or jib: exploiting his apparent role as the poor underdog, he began a long outspoken campaign against North and the unfairness of it all. This was a game that the charismatic, verbose Southerner was much better prepared to play than the introspective California engineer and, caught in the middle between his syndicate and his competitor, North showed some strain. His program having taken on the

Above, Enterprise, *skippered by Lowell North.*
Below, Independence, *designed and built by sailmaker Ted Hood.*
On the opposite page, Ted Turner, skipper of Courageous *shortly after the victory. Below, a view of* Courageous *below decks.*
On the following page, twice-defender Courageous.

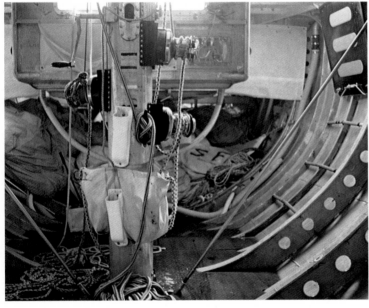

and frequently showed blinding speed. But she tacked more slowly than her competition because, to improve her straight-ahead speed, North had given her a smaller foretriangle through which the jib swung, and she continued to suffer tactical lapses. *Independence* never really got going well, despite the fact that almost all her syndicate's attention was lavished on her, not *Courageous*. Turner slipped slightly in the July trials, but dug into his own pockets to buy new sails (which crewmember Robbie Doyle, Hood's right-hand man at the loft, recut almost every night), recovered his boat speed, and cleaned up in the final trials, winning by small margins but winning all the same. North was fired as *Enterprise*'s skipper and the afterguard on *Independence* was shuffled — but too late.

Some thought that Turner would never be selected because of his uninhibited behaviour ashore, but wiser heads knew that what counted most was his demonstrated reliability behind *Courageous*'s wheel. The New York Yacht Club's America's Cup Committee now included five former defenders or contenders — Bob Bavier, Briggs Cunningham, George Hinman, Bob McCullough, and Bus Mosbacher — who certainly knew what the bottom line was in cup racing. Dubious about radically new technologies, impatient with any result other than winning, they continued with the final trials until, as one of them said, "Turner selected himself."

While Turner was beating the sailmakers, the four challengers held their own trials. Baron Bich was back with a new boat so slow that he replaced her with the original *France*; once again, she did not win a single race. For the first time, there were two boats from the same country, the almost successful 1970 challenger *Gretel II* and Alan Bond's new *Australia*. The old boat beat the new one in the only race they sailed, but *Gretel* was nipped in the semi-finals by the new girl on the block, the Swedish Twelve *Sverige*, which was the most innovative boat in Newport. Her winches were ground by leg-power using bicycle linkages, and her skipper-designer, Pelle Petterson, steered using a huge tiller rather than a wheel. An industrial designer, Petterson had organized a large syndicate of sixty Swedish businesses, and from her name to her colors, *Sverige* was a frank advertisement for her homeland's commercial prowess. Petterson was a former world champion of the highly competitive Star Class, like North, Driscoll, Conner, and Bill Ficker (*Intrepid*'s skipper in 1970), so he had sailing as well as design and managerial skills. In the semi-finals, he beat *Gretel II* and Gordon Ingate in a tight series that went the full seven races, but *Sverige* lost all her races against *Australia* in the finals.

The thinking behind *Australia* reflected a new strategy on the part of the challengers. Co-designed by Bob Miller (who, for unclear reasons, had changed his name to Ben Lexcen) and a Dutch alumnus of the Sparkman & Stephens office named Johan Valentijn, Bond's new challenger was conceived as a fast boat in

guise of a moral crusade, Turner surprised everybody (even, perhaps, himself) by beating both North and Hood in the March Congressional Cup match-racing championship held in California. Three months later, setting some perfectly good Hood sails, Turner and *Courageous* almost swept the June trials. That was only the first skirmish in the summer-long war, but Turner — who often pictured himself as a Civil War commander — knew the value of drawing first blood. At least he was winning races, which was a major improvement over his performance in 1974.

North and Hood, meanwhile, seemed preoccupied more with their technology than with winning. It looked almost as though they were slowing down and losing races intentionally — North threw away several big leads by not covering — in order to mislead each other about their boats' speeds. In the July trials, *Enterprise* set a variety of strange-looking sails, including a green jib that was the first sail made of Mylar material,

Courageous, which for the second time proved a successful defender, was skippered by Ted Turner who three years earlier had tried to qualify on board Mariner.

light winds. Close followers of cup history had developed a theory that a challenger's best hope was to turn up with a boat that was speedy in an extreme condition. If that condition prevailed, she would dominate the defender, which had to be a good all-round boat in order to survive her summer-long series of trials. Since winds off Newport in September, when the matches were held, tended to be light to moderate, the challenger should be especially good when it blew less than about 10 knots, according to this theory. She would lose if it blew harder, but if history was any indication she would probably lose then, anyway. The introduction of long challengers' trials complicated things to some extent, but since one boat usually dominated the trials she probably could be a good light air design and hang on to win in stronger winds with good tactics and boat-handling.

Of course, this is exactly what had happened in 1970, when *Gretel II* would have won over *Intrepid* in light air

if the human element had not interfered. This year, Bond's *Australia* was another relatively small boat with a large sail area. Miller/Lexcen and Valentijn had even cut several inches off her topsides to make her hull lighter; the International Rule penalized this ingenious innovation by requiring a shorter waterline, but the trade-off seemed worth it. With Bond more sedate and patient than he had been in 1974, the boat had a good, experienced crew led by skipper Noel Robins, who was courageously coming back from a near-fatal accident that still affected his walking ability.

Unfortunately for the Australians, while the wind was light, *Courageous* was both fast and near-perfectly handled and won four straight races rather easily. The American defender was faster than the challenger, which seemed not be well-balanced and carried her sails oddly trimmed. More important, Turner and his tactician, Gary Jobson, picked every shift and puff exactly right, possibly because they had almost lived on the

Australia, like Courageous, *had two wheels to allow the skipper to check the sails more easily. In designing the boat Ben Lexcen was helped by Johan Valentijn.*

America's Cup course all summer and knew its quirks intimately, but also because they had strong backgrounds in dinghy racing, where anticipating shifts is quickly rewarded. They were especially good at forcing their competitor into the fluky wind and sloppy seas that hugged the huge spectator fleet; since the defense trials usually drew a larger pack of observers than the challengers' eliminations, this was a problem that they knew better than the Australians did.

Having risen from ignominy to glory in six short months, Turner arrived at the dock brandishing a bottle of rum with inebriated good cheer and later collapsed in a drunken stupor at the post-match press conference — that is to say, he behaved as most men would after a great accomplishment, and his wild celebration endeared him to the world of non-sailors who had been forever put off by the cool detachment of stiff-upper-lip New England yachtsmen. America's Cup sailing now seemed human.

	date	*wind (mph)*	*start*	*finish*
Courageous	9/13	12/17	h. 12.10.24	Courageous
Australia			h. 12.10.12	by 01'48''
Courageous	9/15	10/3	h. 12.10.07	Time limit
Australia			h. 12.10.06	expired
Courageous	9/16	11/15	h. 12.10.02	h. 15.54.07
Australia			h. 12.10.03	h. 15.55.10
Courageous	9/17	8	h. 12.10.15	h. 16.33.23
Australia			h. 12.10.21	h. 16.35.55
Courageous	9/18	14/9	h. 12.10.09	h. 15.42.31
Australia			h. 12.10.09	h. 15.44.56

131

1980
Freedom-Australia

The long campaigns of *Enterprise* and *Independence* had a much greater influence on cup racing than Ted Turner's short, but more successful, tenure at the helm of *Courageous*. Now that the design gap had been narrowed so that most Twelves were modified versions of *Courageous*, every syndicate focused its energy, time, and money on full-scale sailing rather than testing.

Seven boats raced at Newport in the 1980 defenders' and challengers' trials; of them, only one was built that year. Of the invaders, the British *Lionheart* and *France III* were the newest, having been launched and raced in 1979. Pelle Petterson and Alan Bond were back with their three-year-old Twelves, *Sverige* and *Australia*, each considerably modified. Four American boats were available, although only three would be sailed. Ted Turner had bought *Courageous* and, although he was busy with his new satellite- transmitted television news network, planned an even longer campaign than the one he had put in during 1977. The backers of *Enterprise*, working under the aegis of the Maritime College at Ft. Schuyler Foundation, Inc., chose Dennis Conner to sail her and commissioned Olin Stephens to design a new boat as a trial horse. After a minimum of tank-testing, Stephens produced the lines for *Freedom*, which was launched in the spring of 1979 and spent the summer tuning against the older boat before both were trailered to San Diego. The only boat launched after the new year was *Clipper* and, technically speaking, she was only half-new since her keel, rig, steering gear, and sails were cannibalized from *Independence*, whose hull was broken up. This ingenious strategy allowed *Clipper* to be built faster and less expensively than other Twelves. Her designer was David Pedrick, who had worked on *Courageous* and *Enterprise* while employed by Olin Stephens; her skipper was Russell Long, the young heir of a shipping fortune created by his father Sumner A. Long, owner of several big ocean racers named *Ondine*, and the aluminum empire built by the Reynolds family, on his mother's side.

Of the Americans, Conner was favored no matter which boat he chose to sail. At thirty-seven he was the

Freedom, designed by S&S and skippered by Dennis Conner, Olympic medallist in the Tempest class and starting helmsman with Ted Hood in 1974.

most successful racing skipper in the world, a master of whichever type of boat he commanded. Twice world champion of the Star Class, he had also won an Olympic bronze medal in the Tempest, another keel one-design boat, in 1976. His ocean racing championships included several Southern Ocean Racing Conferences. But it was as a match racer that he had earned his first fame, starting out in the annual Congressional Cup series in California and then as the starting helmsman and tactician in *Courageous* in 1974. Aggressive yet tactful in command, he had a loyal crew that followed him from boat to boat — ''my guys'', he called them. Many were in the boating business, but Conner himself owned and managed a drapery manufacturing company he somehow continued to run when he was not sailing (which was not often). Unlike many cup sailors, Conner did not grow up with a sailing heritage. As a boy, he joined the junior program of the San Diego Yacht Club, which was just down the street from his house. Finding success and enjoying it, he was soon badgering older sailors into taking him aboard their boats as a crewmember and gradually became a regular hand on winning ocean-racers and one-designs. His idol was Lowell North, so it was natural that he would devise a mammoth campaign for the 1980 match that at times included North's aid and, much of the time, his sails. *Freedom* and *Enterprise* tested more than a hundred sails during some one hundred and fifty days of tuning and practicing before the trials even began. In the old days, a defense candidate might have a sail inventory of only two dozen sails and, if her builder stuck to his schedule, would warm up for just a few weeks.

The search for incremental speed advantages was expensive as well as time-consuming and sophisticated. A mainsail built of the space-age materials Kevlar and Mylar cost $7,000, a genoa jib or spinnaker $4,500. Two complete eleven-man crews were needed to man the two

From top to bottom on the opposite page: British challenger
Lionheart, Sverige, and France 3 with Bich at the helm. The ball-
point Baron gave up after this last fruitless effort. Above: a typical
after-race press conference. From right to left: Dennis Conner,
Bob Bavier, moderator, Alan Bond and Jim Hardy.
On the following page: Lionheart and Australia as sparring partners
for the 1983 syndicates.

Twelves and they were supported by a large technical staff that ran the tow boats, set marks, started races, fixed broken gear, and supervised sail selection. There was even a physical trainer, Arnie Schmeling, the grand-nephew of the great German boxer Max Schmeling, who ran forty-five minutes of calisthenics and stretching exercises each morning. Plenty of big, talented sailors were available to man the boats. Some were experienced older men like Herreshoff, a naval architect, and John Marshall, the president of the North Sails international operation who had sailed in *Intrepid* in 1974 and *Enterprise* in 1977, and for them winning the cup was a sign of professional expertise as well as a matter of pride. Others were men in their twenties with less authority both on board and ashore. Their sailing résumés already showing tens of thousands of miles spent in racing boats, these winch-grinders and line-pullers found a thrill in the challenge that belied the tedium of their jobs, which hardly varied during the eighteen-month campaign. Here was a small mountain against which to pit both body and brain — a cliff that, if surmounted, would allow them to prefix their names with the holy words "America's Cup winner".

Money came harder than manpower. Edward du Moulin, the Ft. Schuyler Foundation's hard-working and imaginative project manager, exploited its tax-exempt status as well as the cup's high visibility to the fullest. More than $300,000 worth of in-kind services were provided by businesses eager for publicity. For example, there were five hundred Izod T-shirts whose little green alligators were surmounted by the two boats'

numbers. Powerboats, food, bicycles, hot tubs, foul weather gear, rope, shoes, formal clothes, automobiles — all seemed to be necessary, all donated or loaned in exchange for the right to claim status as an exclusive supplier. *Clipper* went further; her name reflected support given by Pan American Airways, whose clippers were among the first long-distance planes, and when practicing she sometimes flew a spinnaker that carried the logo of a rum distiller. Even the New York Yacht Club got in on the commercialism, selling $15,000 "official sponsor" shares to help cover the over $250,000 cost of running the races. "The future of the America's Cup rests in the hands of corporate sponsors," Russell Long stated flatly. Perhaps thinking of the nine sailmakers, gear suppliers, and other boating professionals in Conner's crew, Long also predicted the end of the age of the sportsman-sailor like Ted Turner and himself. Halsey Herreshoff put it in a slightly different way: "The days when a New York stockbroker will leave his business for a month or two and race in the America's Cup are over."

No longer an underdog since his win in 1977, Turner tried to make himself one by criticizing these new trends, and especially Conner's exploitation of them. Conner simply responded, "If people don't want to pay the price at the top of the sport, they shouldn't compete," and in his *Freedom* proceeded to destroy *Courageous* and *Clipper*, losing only four of more than forty races. Young Russell Long's *Clipper* was next best, her speed and record improving after Tom Blackaller, who ran a North Sails loft near San Francisco and who was yet another Star Class world champion, came aboard as tactician. Turner compounded his failure on the race course by taking the Australian designer Ben Lexcen out for a sail — a clear violation of an agreement between the syndicates. The America's Cup Committee punished him by excusing *Courageous* from the last two races in the July trials; after that, her fate was absolutely

Clipper, the Twelve designed by Dave Pedrick for Russell Long, and Freedom *on the windward leg of a race.*

Courageous *after having rounded a windward mark ready to hoist the spinnaker. This time Turner did not each the finals.*

clear, and the committee stretched out the trials just long enough to give *Clipper* a chance to show some encouraging bursts of speed and then selected *Freedom* before she sustained any damage.

Over in the challenger's trials, there was a new closeness to the competition. *Sverige* was a disappointment, but the British boat, *Lionheart*, showed good speed in light air. Unlike the other Twelves, she had a mast that hooked aft several feet at its tip, almost like a half-gaff, to allow a mainsail about ten percent larger than the ones carried on conventional masts. Another 100 square feet of sail area made quite a difference when there was not much wind, but poor management, a switch of skippers, and undistinguished performance in winds stronger than about 12 knots eventually took their toll. The great — and to many people, most satisfying — surprise was Baron Marcel Bich's *France 3*. Not only did she break the baron's eighteen-race, three-cup losing streak that began in 1970, she actually made it to

the final trials against Alan Bond's old *Australia*. Designed by Johan Valentijn, *Australia*'s co-architect, *France 3* had been sailed off Newport all through the summer of 1979 against *Intrepid*. Starting out with a radical articulated keel flap, or trim tab, she had been gradually simplified. With Bruno Troublé, France's best small keel-boat skipper, in charge, she beat *Australia* in one race (due mainly to a major wind shift) but lost the series one race to four.

This was perhaps the most low-key of Alan Bond's three campaigns. At forty-two, he had begun to look more to long-run than to overnight improvements. When asked why he kept returning to Newport, Bond came up with a surprisingly statesmanlike reason. "You get out there," he said, "and you're as good as the next guy, who might be a Vanderbilt. You get out there and all you've got is a common element — the wind and the sea — and everybody's equal." No more screams about the New York Yacht Club's boat being more equal than

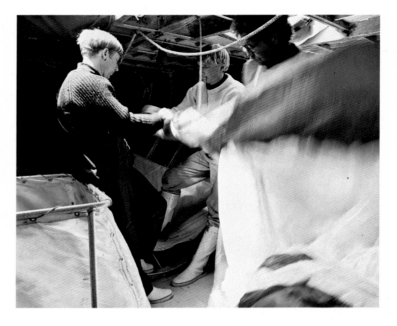

Above, Freedom *becalmed at sunset in the race won by* Australia.
Top right, stopping a spinnaker below decks on Freedom.

the others. Sir Thomas Lipton could not have been more diplomatic.

While the Aussies continued to play the humble underdog before the press, they were secretly hard at work on a mast that was a copy of *Lionheart*'s. Once again, the light-air strategy had sprung to life and seemed to have a good future, since *Australia* was already fast and *Freedom* was not at her best until the wind started to blow more than 10 knots. Once the hooked mast appeared on *Australia*, the challengers shifted their public relations campaign to a subtle attack on Conner. Bond worried out loud about whether the defending skipper might crack under the intense self-inflicted strain of taking on too much responsibility. His skipper, Jim Hardy (back for the third time), genially claimed that while he himself was quite relaxed, "the poor old defending helmsman, ouch, he's got heaps of fear of defeat."

What Conner really had heaps of fear of was light air, for he knew that the extra sail area made *Australia* faster

than *Freedom* unless there was good wind. His strategy showed it, as tactician Dennis Durgan directed him not onto *Australia*'s wind in the traditional tight cover but toward puffs and shifts. This strategy worked most of the time. *Freedom* had a ten boat-length lead after only eleven minutes of sailing in the light-air first race simply because Durgan played the shifts correctly, and *Freedom* held on to win even though her steering gear broke and she was steered with a block and tackle jury rig up the last windward leg. *Australia* sailed right away in the second race, which could not be finished within the time limit, and after the start of the rematch, Hardy could squeeze up under Conner's leeward bow and force him to tack. *Australia* led for four legs, was caught on the run, and then overhauled *Freedom* on the last leg to win with only seven minutes to go before the time limit expired. (They finished in the dark and Conner protested the challenger for not carrying navigation lights — a petty issue that showed, more than anything else, the pressure he was under; the protest was withdrawn the next day.) Conner gave the start away in the third race to allow him freedom to sail toward a shift, led narrowly (despite a spinnaker tangle), and won by less than a minute in a freshening wind.

Because they had built their radical mast in secrecy and delayed revealing it until they were sure that Conner would not follow suit, the Australians had not been able to conduct thorough testing of the larger sails they had made for it. Their sailmakers recut the mainsails each night, but they were always a day or so behind and lacked the necessary confidence in them. In the fourth race, they put up the wrong sail and lost. In the fifth and final contest, the wind blew hard enough to cancel out their sail area advantage and they lost again, but once again a fast challenger had scared the daylights out of the defender and the New York Yacht Club, and only unorthodox tactics kept the match from running its full seven-race length — or from being lost.

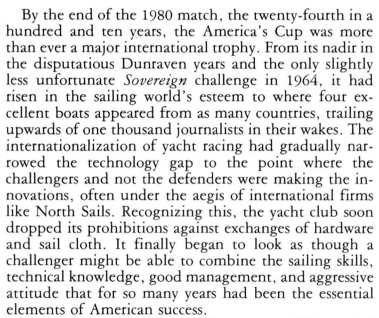

Above, the ceremonial dunking of all the crew plus skipper after the victory of Freedom. *On the right, Dennis Conner at the helm. On the opposite page:* Freedom *to leeward of* Australia.

By the end of the 1980 match, the twenty-fourth in a hundred and ten years, the America's Cup was more than ever a major international trophy. From its nadir in the disputatious Dunraven years and the only slightly less unfortunate *Sovereign* challenge in 1964, it had risen in the sailing world's esteem to where four excellent boats appeared from as many countries, trailing upwards of one thousand journalists in their wakes. The internationalization of yacht racing had gradually narrowed the technology gap to the point where the challengers and not the defenders were making the innovations, often under the aegis of international firms like North Sails. Recognizing this, the yacht club soon dropped its prohibitions against exchanges of hardware and sail cloth. It finally began to look as though a challenger might be able to combine the sailing skills, technical knowledge, good management, and aggressive attitude that for so many years had been the essential elements of American success.

The last connection with the cup's middle period ended with the retirement of Olin Stephens, who had been partially or wholly responsible for every defender but *Weatherly* from 1937 through 1980 — six boats and eight matches. In fact, Stephens was also the last living link with the cup's ancient history, since he had worked intimately with Starling Burgess and Harold Vanderbilt, whose heritages were rich with cup lore. Much had changed in those forty-three years. Once a clubby affair, its participants held accountable only to their commodores and their bankers, a match was now a commercial extravaganza with major nationalistic overtones. The boats were subsidized by businesses and, in the case of the American foundation-owned boats, by taxpayers. Soon Dennis Conner would be saying, "I have three hundred million Americans to represent. I have a lot to think about, and I don't want to let them down." Such sentiment would have seemed strange to a Charles Paine, a Harold Vanderbilt, or a Bus Mosbacher.

	date	wind (mph)	start	finish
Freedom	9/16	10	h. 12.10.29	h. 15.58.32
Australia			h. 12.10.24	h. 16.00.24
Freedom	9/18	6/2	h. 12.25.06	Time limit
Australia			h. 12.25.16	expired
Australia	9/19	6/8	h. 14.10.14	h. 19.16.42
Freedom			h. 14.10.09	h. 19.17.10
Freedom	9/21	12/16	h. 12.10.02	h. 15.45.07
Australia			h. 12.10.05	h. 15.46.00
Freedom	9/23	12	h. 12.10.08	h. 15.51.20
Australia			h. 12.10.21	h. 15.55.08
Freedom	9/25	17	h. 12.10.08	h. 15.38.00
Australia			h. 12.10.15	h. 14.41.38

THE LATEST CHALLENGE

The challenging fleet is expanding.
For the first time ever, in 1983 seven Twelves vied
for the privilege of a duel with the Americans.
The British, Canadians, Australians
and French were all old hands whereas the Italians
were newcomers.

The United States

The 1983 defense campaign — nearly three years long — played out slowly like a discordant fugue, with several key themes. First, four new 12-Meter sloops were built by the two defending syndicates, yet none of them broke new ground when compared to the 1980 defender, *Freedom*. Second, the complex technique of cutting apart a 12-Meter, remodeling it, and welding it back together again so that it still conformed to the 12-Meter Rule, was raised to a new and glorious art: the Twelves that sailed in the defense eliminations resembled their original selves in name, number and color only. Third, the public and verbal rivalry between the two star contenders — Dennis Conner and Tom Blackaller — was as intense as their competition on the water. Fourth, the New York Yacht Club finally conceded that corporate sponsorship and the collateral promotion for profit was not such a cardinal sin.

Above all, the awesome effort of the challengers placed an unprecedented burden on the Americans. With the likelihood of ten or more Twelves sailing a bristling competition for the right to take the Cup, the Americans had good reason to expect that one or more of them would match or exceed *Freedom*'s overall performance. (*Australia* might already have done so in 1980 had the Aussies not blundered by their last-minute switch to a bendy, *Lionheart*-type mast.) With tank testing, new computer techniques and awareness of *Freedom*'s faults, challenging designers were almost certain to produce a breakthrough in rig, underbody or keel configuration.

These facts, coupled with the New York Yacht Club's lifting of the formal restriction against use by the challengers of U.S. materials and off-the-shelf gear, further closed the narrowing gap that had kept the Cup in New York for so long. That, at least, was the perception.

Still, not all the threats were extraterritorial. There was potential weakness in the defense as well. *Freedom*'s clear superiority in 1980 — she won 47 of her 52 races — indicated that hull design might have reached its limits and that Conner's sails and tactics were unbeatable. If *Freedom* defended again in 1983, Conner might lack a fast sparring partner to tune against — *Courageous*, the only remaining competitive Twelve, after the others had been sold to challengers, would be ten years old in 1984. Conner and the *Freedom '83* syndicate began their

campaign in confidence, nonetheless. Through the Maritime College at Fort Schuyler Foundation, Inc., which owned *Freedom*, fund raising was started to cover the proposed $4 million budget. Most important, in order to incite a spirit of competition within the campaign, the *Freedom '83* hierarchy made the extraordinary decision to commission *two* new Twelves. One was to be drawn by Dutch-born Johan Valentijn (who had been recently naturalized an American and was thereby eligible to do so); the other by the prestigious firm of Sparkman & Stephens (designers of five Cup defenders).

Blackaller and Jobson, veterans of *Clipper*'s failed attempt to defend in 1980, slowly organized a campaign, eventually to be privately financed with considerable assistance from the People-to-People Sports Committee, a sports funding group founded during the Eisenhower years. The campaign accelerated mid-1981 when Dave Vietor (of Horizon Sails) and Leonard Greene bought *Courageous* from Ted Turner and agreed to join in forming a two-boat syndicate. With an infusion of some $400,000 from Nick and Jane Heyl, ardent Cup supporters, and eventual contributions of $100,000 or more from a dozen friends and lesser contributions from nearly 900 supporters, Conner's sole competitors came alive. They commissioned Dave Pedrick, *Clipper*'s designer, to draw their new boat. They restored *Courageous* to her original shape by replacing her old bow, and gave her an elliptical rudder. She was earmarked as the new Twelve's trial horse, but the syndicate soon decided to campaign both boats equally, a practice, however, that had yet to produce a Cup winner.

The design requirements of the competing syndicates contrasted sharply. Blackaller and his group asked Pedrick to be conservative: to simply refine *Clipper*, which had never been proved either fast or slow. Conner, however, asked his designers to take risks — to reach new limits through the dictates of their instincts, tank tests and computer analyses — not look to refine *Freedom*, but to break through her. Conner prescribed only that they draw identical deck layouts for efficient crew interchanges during the two-year campaign.

Spirit of America was designed by Bill Langan of S & S, but she has never impressed Dennis Conner who decided to shelve her in favor of other Twelves.

Otherwise, he informed neither designer of the other's intentions, to keep them competitively tense.

The S&S design, *Spirit of America* (US 34), conceived by Bill Langan, emphasized stability as the means to extend the upper speed range. Despite her fullness and high freeboard, which made her seem heavy, Langan characterized her as a "large, light Twelve."

Valentijn chose to culminate his long quest — begun with *Australia* and *France 3* — for a small, light-displacement Twelve. After extensive tank tests of computer-varied models in his native land, and fluid-flow studies of rigs and keels at Boeing's Seattle wind tunnels, he reached his goal with (black) *Magic* (US 38). She was several feet shorter than *Spirit*, and displaced a mere 45,000 pounds (about three-quarters of most recent Twelves). *Magic* and *Spirit* were commissioned at Fort Schuyler, N.Y., on April 17, 1982.

Pedrick, as requested, tried no extreme ideas for Blackaller. He drew his Twelve, *Defender* (US 33), after tank tests of several models, MIT propeller tunnel tests of keel shapes, and correlation of physical tests by theoretical computer analysis. *Defender*, the only "ordinary" Twelve among the three, was commissioned on June 26, by Newport Offshore, her builder.

Through the early summer off Newport, both syndicates tuned their Twelves, tried new and old sails, adjusted rigs and tested crews. Conner sparred with Jack Sutphen, who skippered the boat that Conner did not sail and was eventually replaced by Malin Burnham. Blackaller sailed *Defender*, against Dave Vietor on *Courageous*. And a strange thing happened — the older boats won races. Though Pedrick, Valentijn and S&S had tirelessly sought answers from tanks, tunnels and computers, all their new boats seemed to ask more questions. In particular, they seemed to ask if *Freedom* was indeed the ultimate Twelve: she dominated her bright new stablemates.

There was little jubilation in Newport. In fact, the probable high point of the summer came courtesy of Peter de Savary and the British *Victory* team. The *Victory* folk dogged Conner's Twelves all over Rhode Island Sound in an inflatable boat, taking photos and videotapes of his practice sessions. Conner became outraged, but could not shake the little "rubber duck." His entourage resorted to trailing lines that wrapped the duck's propeller and threatening more violent action. Though clearly legal and proper, such action is frustrating to the victim. Conner (like all Cup helmsmen) is particularly sensitive to being followed while sailing to windward; he fears an observer's peering into his boat's "slot." A sharp observer (spy) can learn a great deal about a Twelve's rig, tuning, sails and crew

Above: Magic, *designed by Johan Valentijn.*
Below: the launching of Liberty, *the new brainchild of Valentijn, after the poor show of* Magic, *which is one of the smallest and lightest 12-Meters. Both boats were commissioned for the* Freedom *syndicate.*

work by studying that sensitive and vulnerable space between main and genoa. Shaking off de Savary's "unsavories" became a matter of life or death.

It need not have been. By mid-summer it was public knowledge that *Magic* did not have it in a breeze, and *Spirit* would need major surgery to become agile. On September 8, Conner announced that *Magic* would be sold and that Valentijn would be drawing an unprecedented third Twelve for the *Freedom '83* syndicate, to be paid for by the proceeds of the sale (if a buyer was found). That simple but stunning announcement, however, masked a bitter controversy that had run its course during the preceding weeks.

The syndicate's earlier reaction to the new yachts' disappointing performance, short of panic, had been to ask S&S and Valentijn to pool their experience and collaborate on a third boat. But yacht designers operate in a framework of jealously guarded data and secret conceptions that would have to be violated for such a col-

laboration to take place. The violation, even if voluntary, is a certain invitation to conflict.

Following grudging debates and sensitive negotiations, nonetheless, Valentijn and Langan abandoned their radical ideas and agreed to jointly work toward a refined version of *Freedom*. The designers exchanged precious tank-test data and lines drawings — an act tantamount to exposing one's worst dreams, fears and frailties to a hostile world. But the collaboration was not to be; it collapsed in a sea of acrimony. Thus ended the design of a new Twelve that was already being publicly called "a committee boat."

Valentijn offered to resign, but remain as the syndicate's project manager to complete work on spars and the on-board computer. The syndicate fathers met in high council and refused Valentijn's resignation, asking him instead to design the new Twelve alone (with input from Conner's navigator, Halsey Herreshoff, a designer as well). They also allotted S&S $100,000 for the complete redesign of *Spirit*. Unfortunately, S&S, through its founder, Olin Stephens, took strong exception to the plan, and Stephens remained estranged from the *Freedom '83* camp for the duration of the Cup defense — his firm, however, continued to cooperate with the *Defender* people to effect improvements in *Courageous*.

Meanwhile, Blackaller's start-up was not without its difficulties. The flamboyant skipper and his group found finances somewhat unsure; they fell some $700,000 in the red before *Defender* was even launched. But, by early 1982, a new group of backers had joined the ranks — including some Texas oilmen.

During the summer of '82, *Defender* and *Courageous* tuned up off Newport. By summer's end the group had learned all it needed to know about the new boat. Pedrick had improved on *Clipper*'s stability, but not her speed, particularly in the moderate-to-heavy-air range, which was *Clipper*'s strength. But the summer was not otherwise wasted. Because the two Twelves carried equal rigs, they were able to test and interchange sails from the North loft, and experiment with new instrumentation designed to measure performance.

In October, Pedrick steepened the leading edge of *Defender*'s keel by shifting some lead from the top of the keel, to improve her stability on the wind. *Defender* and *Courageous* were then shipped to California for winter training in Balboa, not far from where *Freedom* and the rebuilt *Spirit* were also sparring for the winter, in San Diego. During the winter, Blackaller kept up the needling of Conner by frequently challenging him to a match-race series, knowing that Conner would refuse. Pedrick's changes worked — *Defender* became more powerful in a seaway and pointed higher.

Tom Blackallaer, Star Class world champion, was
Dennis Conner's archrival in the quest for the privilege
of defending the cup.
They spared no means when it came to sarcasm
even off the water.
On the right, two views of his Defender,
designed by Dave Pedrick, like Clipper in 1980.

Still, there were rumblings and internal pressures in Blackaller's camp, and the management at one point considered replacing him with Buddy Melges or Ted Turner. Blackaller remained, but he made other organizational changes. Vietor was replaced by John Kolius (who had no Twelve experience); *Courageous* was promoted from a trial horse to an equal partner and Kolius was encouraged to go all the way.

In late January, Valentijn's burgundy-red *Liberty* arrived at the *Freedom* camp. She was a spectacular sight — beautifully faired and finished by Newport Offshore. She was commissioned, rigged and entered into the *Freedom* sweepstakes. Early results were mixed — she was no breakthrough, but was sufficiently better than *Spirit* to retire the modified S&S boat.

Before the spring of 1983, when the chips were finally down, both Pedrick and Valentijn made major modifications to their boats. Pedrick continued to improve *Defender* by moving her keel and rig aft which,

according to the designer, "fooled the water into thinking she was a bigger boat." Valentijn, on the other hand, needed to steady *Liberty*'s seaway motion and bring her into *Freedom*'s league in the upper range of wind speeds. He cut three feet from her sharp stern and moved her keel and rig a bit forward.

Both alterations worked. With the boats back in the water in Newport, the competition tightened in both camps, and the summer of the Twelves heated up. Kolius, the low-key underdog in the entire complex, simply went forward without fanfare. Final alterations to *Courageous* included some keel modification by S&S. Her proud crew worked tirelessly to improve her and the local populace, with America's Cup fans all over the U.S., began rooting for *Courageous* to come from behind and take it all. Those who would never forget *Intrepid*'s glorious history saw a similarity between the two "old" Twelves.

However, the cost of operations in 1983 became a

149

larger factor than ever before. Rents for Newport housing had increased sharply since 1980. With food inflated and the cost of sewing and repairing the new Hood, North and Sobstad Kevlar/Mylar sails, and all the hull modifications, the *Defender/Courageous* group faced a monthly bill of $200,000. New masts cost between $50,000 and $70,000 each with a new mainsail about $15,000. (One of *Freedom*'s new mains was reported to have cost $70,000, including development). Conner's campaign, in fact, owned about 115 active sails and a total inventory of about 180 by North and Sobstad. But with four boats, why not?

Though the groups had enormous expenses in common, they operated in quite different styles. Conner disciplined his crew sharply. They exercised together daily, and were severely restricted in their Newport social life (which, in a Cup summer, is a deprivation not easily reckoned with by a young, healthy man). Kolius also kept his crew under control, but their come-from-behind spirit seemed to override any discomfort. Blackaller, by contrast, allowed his men to exercise voluntarily, live "off campus" (away from the syndicate's rooms at Salve Regina College) and some of them even got married during the campaign.

As the Preliminary Trials approached, both organizations seemed in good health, good spirits and in financial health as well. Corporate donations increased. The New York Yacht Club's new spirit of gentlemanly commercialism encouraged donors, who were allowed to associate themselves publicly with their donations and use the logos of the defending syndicates in advertising.

With *Defender* and *Courageous* well tuned and ready for the racing to begin on June 18, the only question that remained prior to the Preliminary Trials was: "Which boat will Conner choose?" To answer that question he called a press conference on June 9. Assembled before the press and television, Conner disappointed the multitudes by begging the issue and announcing only his crew. His two-year campaign to find a winning boat would not be rushed into such a decision. Instead, he waited until the night before the first race to tell the world that he was sailing *Liberty*.

After all the science and technology. After all the money spent and the bills yet to be paid. After all the cutting and re-cutting of lead, aluminum, Mylar and Kevlar. After all the open and behind-the-scenes personal skirmishes. After all that and more, the Preliminary Trials leading to the selection of the 1983 defender of the America's Cup began on a typically foggy New England Saturday, June 18. The selection process began. Who would be selected? The long, slow climb to the pinnacle of selection had entered its next tense stage.

Above, Liberty, *the Twelve chosen to sail.*
Below, "Old" Freedom, *winner over* Australia *in 1980.* 151

Great Britain

From the outset, even with the *Lionheart* fiasco of 1980 still fresh in the minds of critics, it was plain to see that the man behind the British challenge for the 1983 series was deadly serious.

Peter de Savary will have earned his place in the history books of yacht racing as the man most likely to have succeeded with any British 12-Meter challenge since 1958. In terms of hard cash, no one had put up so much; in terms of effort, no one had worked harder or longer and in terms of organisation, no battlefield commander could have bettered de Savary's enthusiasm for welding such an aggressive team of sailors.

Born in Dengie Manor in 1945 near Burnham-on-Crouch, de Savary's early recollections of life are of Venezuela where he went to live with his step-father and divorced mother until his tenth birthday. Upon returning to England for schooling, at sixteen he decided to go to Canada for four years; between studying he worked as a self-employed gardening contractor, car salesman, and truck driver.

On returning to England and having married a young Canadian girl, he joined his father's business, producing furniture, hi-fi cabinets and pre-cast concrete.

At the age of 27 and realising that manufacturing Elmstyle garden furniture was clearly not especially remunerative or adventurous, de Savary borrowed some money and set off for West Africa where he soon became involved in the import-export business, trading in foodstuffs and oil. From there he travelled to the Middle East. After the Yom Kippur war of 1973, real money began to flow through de Savary's Kuwait based Independent Oil Company and using the experiences of Africa he saw the possibilities of financial matchmaking.

His wealth has been amassed through deals made in commodities trading, in oil brokerage and in real estate, a field in which he has been considerably involved for the past seven years. In 1977, de Savary moved his whole operation to the Bahamas where he now lives. How this international adventurer became involved in a campaign to try and wrest the world's oldest and probably ugliest sporting trophy from its plinth in the New York Yacht Club is another story.

One of the major problems which plagued the British 1980 challenge was money – or, more to the point, the lack of it. The British Industry 1500 club which had been set up specially to gather much needed funds in the form of a 1,000 guinea membership fee from patriotic companies all over Britain was always pitifully below target. Sir John Methven, Chairman of British Industry 1500 and *Lionheart* campaign public relations adviser Kit Hobday approached Peter de Savary at what was described as a 'chance social outing' and asked him if emergency funds could be raised. De Savary not only agreed, but raised a total of £60,000 for the campaign as a sort of topping-up operation. Until then, de Savary's involvement in the 'sport' of sailing had been minimal.

Sport or pleasure, de Savary had now purchased a large stake of 'interest' in the America's Cup campaign. De Savary was so fascinated and excited by the quality of America's Cup match racing that the possibility of mounting a British challenge began to emerge.

He was hooked. His father was also partly responsible for helping to make the decision to challenge. Son would call father from time to time, long distance, trying to help relieve the inevitable outcome of a terminal illness. During one conversation in September de Savary's father said, "why not have a go next time?"

Throughout the finals of 1980, rumours had been buzzing around the press corps that the British would be back in '83 with a challenge.

The trouble was that no one had any idea of who the new benefactor was or what he looked like. Finally, at a press conference held in the hall of the Rhode Island State Armory on Thames Street on the afternoon of September 22, 1980, a deeply tanned and balding then 36-year-old de Savary announced the formation of the *Victory* Syndicate and his challenge for the Cup in 1983 to be made through the Royal Burnham Yacht Club. De Savary's father died the same day.

Several days later, the *Victory* Syndicate headquarters in London told the world that Peter de Savary meant business. He had purchased *Australia*.

Ed Dubois, a Lymington – based yacht designer of some note had already been called to Newport by de Savary to discuss a basis on which he would draw the lines for an IOR boat capable of leading a three boat

When Victory *was launched on March 26, 1982, owner Peter de Savary let it be known that he had every intention of commissioning another Twelve if the first did not prove fast enough.*

British team in the following year's Admiral's Cup series at Cowes. He was now commissioned to produce the lines for a new 12-Meter. In a way, this was a strange choice in view of Ian Howlett's already considerable experience with *Lionheart* and other 12 and 6-Meter projects, notably the 6-Meter *Kirlo*, winner of the 1981 world championships with Lawrie Smith at the helm. With the right crew and the right sails, it is possible that *Lionheart* would have done better and in fact it was later shown at the winter training camp in Nassau that *Lionheart* could trounce *Australia*.

Howlett, who must have felt somewhat irked that his services were not immediately called upon, did nevertheless indicate that he would be willing to co-operate with design and research matters pertaining to the new Dubois designed yacht. According to close associates of de Savary, Howlett's offer was not thrown out. He was added to the syndicate's retainer list in January 1981 and told to work on research for a possible second boat.

Howlett did go to work (especially at Southampton University's test tank), but it was to be eighteen months before he was called in to produce a report for a possible new boat. Ed Dubois in the meantime produced *Victory of Burnham* which was campaigned in the 1981 Admiral's Cup series and led the British team to first place.

While boats were being built and tuned, Peter de Savary spent every available hour with deputies, advisers, tacticians, designers and administrators paving the way for a monumental challenge. The original budget of £1.25 million had long since been revised to a more realistic figure of nearer £5 million. No one knows exactly how much, but what observers are sure of is the way in which the money is and has been spent. *Kalizma*, a 1905, 135 foot (40m) motor yacht once owned by the Burtons, Richard and Elizabeth, was bought to serve as headquarters in Newport. Launches, rubber inflatables, a 2,000 horse power Magnum 55, workshop equipment

"It will be the best of the Twelves" announced de Savary about Victory '83, *the latest Twelve fielded by the British, designed by Ian Howlett and built in record time in England. The keel project had in mind a winged version somewhat like* Australia II's. *Below: Rodney Pattison, one of the three skippers of the British Syndicate, at the helm.*

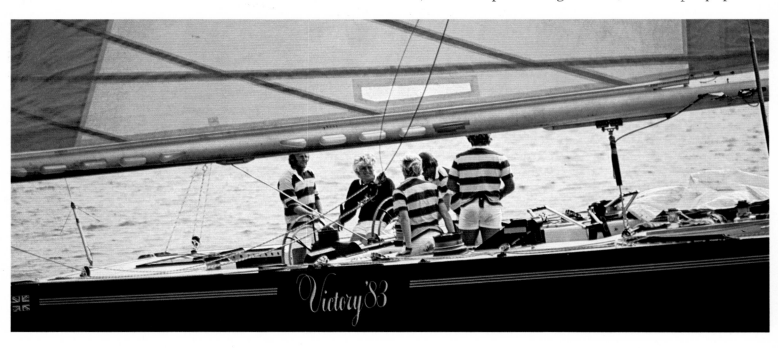

Phil Crebbin was one of the other two candidates to become helmsman.
Top right: de Savary established a small British
"Empire" in Newport plastering his bulldog, the symbol
of his challenge, everywhere. Below: Kalizma, once
owned by Richard Burton, is a luxurious motor yacht
completely remodelled to serve as tender to Victory '83
in the America's Cup operation.

and all the paraphernalia needed to keep four very expensive Twelves on the water and in fighting trim were ordered by the truckload. Eventually there would be seventy people in the *Victory* camp. De Savary and his deputies spent hours watching film and video of 12-Meters sailing, taking the America's Cup Rule book apart with the help of lawyers in New York and evaluating just about anything and everything that had ever been written about 12-Meter racing. After attending a de Savary party in Manhattan, Alan Bond told a London Times journalist: "The outcome will be decided in the jury room. My lawyers have already been briefed. De Savary is, rightly, approaching it like no-one ever before."

On 26th March 1982, Ed Dubois' 63 ft (18.9m) challenger *Victory* built for the syndicate by Souters was ceremoniously named in time-honoured fashion by HRH Princess Michael of Kent.

The new boat was not at all like *Lionheart*. Snubbed off at the nose and an almost straight sheer put her more

on a par with Conner's 1980 winner *Freedom* and Bond's *Australia*. There were no trials held on the water in England. The whole of de Savary's campaign had been geared to start and finish in Newport, with a winter training period in Nassau.

There followed an intensive sailing programme through the summer of '82 during which time, *Victory, Lionheart* and *Australia* sailed some 4,000 miles. In five months, much information was pumped into the syndicate's computer. It was clear from the outset of trials off Newport that syndicate leaders and helmsmen alike were not overawed by the new boat's performance.

Clearly, the British were not happy with their lot. Some decisions had to be made; whether to modify the existing boat or whether to build another one.

De Savary wanted a boat with a slightly different shape and one that was somewhat lighter than the Dubois boat. Modifications to *Victory* would only partly accomplish the need, so in October, while *Lionheart* and

Peter de Savary, 38, international financer and millionaire, had made an unlimited budget available for the British effort along with near perfect organization and management. Born in 1945, the British syndicate leader moved to Africa when still very young and later to the Middle East where he became a highly successful businessman.

Australia were being driven by truck to Florida to sail the short haul to Nassau, de Savary announced plans to build a new boat. Work had, in fact, already started on the building of *V '83* at Fairey Allday's yard at Hamble Point in England. The designer? Ian Howlett.

The boat was ready and waiting in Newport when the camp returned there in late April and allowed six weeks to fine-tune the boat before the trials began.

Victory I had not entirely disgraced herself. She had, after all, won the Xerox World 12-Meter Championships which ended that year's summer sailing off Newport. The Americans declined to take part in the event, de Savary says, because orders came down from the heirarchy of the NYYC to defending syndicates to stay away. Later, he was to elaborate on this theme, issuing a public warning to the American yachting establishment to end an alleged campaign of 'dirty tricks'.

Speaking from his Nassau base in early December '82, de Savary said that the 'dirty tricks' campaign had been aimed at him personally, his worldwide financial interests, the *Victory* Syndicate and the Royal Burnham Yacht Club. He said a few influential members of the American yachting establishment group, who had all been closely associated with the defense of the America's Cup, were responsible for the campaign. De Savary listed a number of items he said had caused unnecessary harrassment to the syndicate. Problems with United States Immigration over why a large contingent of Britons were working in Newport through the summer without Immigration Green Cards. Efforts which were made "to see that the U.S. Coast Guard gave us trouble". Lobbying conducted by the Americans to try and persuade the Royal Sydney Yacht Club to re-write the rules to disallow surveillance of a rival's boat. The Royal Sydney declined to give in to reported American pressure.

By now, progress on the new Howlett yacht was well under way. A naming ceremony took place inside one of Fairey's huge sheds at the Hamble in late March '83 and a few days later she was dropped into the water. Aside from general modifications to the hull, Howlett had produced a boat that was considerably lighter than her predecessor. When she hit the water, the discrepancy between designed and actual weight was a mere 50 lbs.

On arrival in America, riggers, boatswains and workshop craftsmen worked 18 to 20 hour days to finish fairing the new boat, paint her and have her in the water by May 1st. But before the new trials could begin, a conflict of opinion between de Savary and his first choice helmsman Harold Cudmore over priorities and strategies ended with Cudmore's departure. In his place came former Finn Gold Cup winner Chris Law. He had resigned his job at British Olivetti and travelled to the States not really knowing whether he would become a main sheet trimmer or a member of the afterguard.

In a little under six weeks from the time *Victory '83* had made her first outing into Newport waters, any weak spots in the boat had been ironed out, although some observers thought the new boat just as sluggish in manoeuvres as the earlier *Victory*. But with Cudmore's sudden departure and Law's late arrival so soon before the start of the elimination trials, there were more problems. Law found it difficult to integrate with the afterguard. Phil Crebbin, Lawrie Smith and Rodney Pattison, he said, had 'squeezed' him out. Two days after the first round had started, Law packed his bags, collected his family and flew home to England, the offer of a 'business' proposition by de Savary still under his belt.

De Savary had also reserved until the very last minute, the right to name the afterguard. As Law departed, the syndicate head confirmed that Crebbin, Smith and Pattison would sail the boat on a shift basis, two members being aboard the yacht every day, the third in rotation would study the form of their next competition rival. Steering duties would be shared and allocated as and when required and by the dictates of circumstance.

Above: Australia, *the 1980 challenger, bought as a sparring partner by de Savary. Below:* Victory '83 *close-hauled.*

Australia

Australia has mounted seven challenges for the America's Cup in the post World War Two era of racing in Twelve Meter Class yachts. Three of these challenges, *Gretel* (1962), *Gretel II* (1970) and *Australia* (1980), were strong enough to worry the impregnable US defense and take a race off the defender on each occasion.

At the final press conference after *Freedom* won the 1980 series Alan Bond announced that he would challenge again and that John Bertrand would be the skipper. That day, organisation for the 1983 challenge began.

Australia II's challenge was the fourth headed by dynamic West Australian businessman Alan Bond. The continuity of Bond's efforts to win the Cup and his spare-no-expense approach attracted the best and most experienced Twelve Meter manpower available in Australia. This was her main strength and from the very beginning of the campaign made her the favourite.

Ben Lexcen in 1981 spent months tank-testing third-scale models (about 6.7m long) at the Netherlands Ship Model Basin in Holland before finalising the designs for both *Australia II* and the Royal Yacht Club of Victoria's *Challenge 12*. The Bond syndicate made no secret of the fact that Lexcen concentrated his testing on keel shapes. But following his decision to put a radical keel on *Australia II*, details of that keel remained secret.

The yacht was launched with the keel shrouded; a special box-like container was built to conceal the keel when *Australia II* was being shipped — first from Perth to Melbourne and then to Newport — and armed security guards kept watch on the yacht continuously, in Australia and in Newport.

From what could be seen of *Australia II* when sailing and had been seen and talked about out of the water, the keel was best described as a fin/bulb, something like those used on model yachts and Star Class yachts but with the bulb hollowed underneath and, in the after part of the keel, splaying out into fins either side.

The main benefits of the keel and lack of bustle are manoeuvrability and stability with the concentration of weight low down. *Australia II* showed in racing against *Challenge 12*, which is a refinement of *Australia* with a reasonably conventional keel, that she could spin in her own length in pre-start manoeuvring, was quick to tack and accelerate from a tack, and was more stable and very fast upwind in fresh winds.

Lexcen has described *Australia II* as having a long sailing length and a fairly short measured waterline. If the displacement figure of 55,000 lbs. issued by the syndicate is correct, she was the lightest Twelve at Newport.

The hull was superbly crafted in aluminium by Steve Ward who also built *Challenge 12* and before that the original *Australia*.

Australia II was launched in June and immediately began sail evaluation, from Fremantle, the ocean port for Perth. She lacked the continuity of information that retaining *Australia* as a trial horse would have provided. However, she did have accurate computer performance records from *Australia* and tuned against them utilising the Ockam computer system developed for *Clipper* in her 1980 defense campaign.

From *Australia II*'s sail-evaluation program, with Tom Schnackenberg of New Zealand co-ordinating the efforts of sailmakers from several lofts, *Australia II* left for Newport with 50 sails. Most of the working sails were from North with spinnakers from Sobstad and Hood.

The syndicate's open cheque-book approach — "if it looks fast, buy it and try it" — led it to this multi-brand inventory. When *Challenge 12* looked faster downwind, with Hood spinnakers, *Australia II* immediately ordered spinnakers from Hood.

Reasoning that up to 60 races in Newport would create a heavy maintenance burden, *Australia II* went there with a total spares package. In Australia, the crew did considerable work testing and recording breaking points of equipment and rigging. The crew was a mixture of Twelve Meter veterans and enthusiasts, strong new blood. Seventy per cent had been to Newport before.

The skipper, John Bertrand, 36, won a bronze medal in the Finn class at the 1976 and won selection as the skipper in the Soling class for the 1980 Olympics. The Australian Yachting Federation, however, withdrew the team for Russia to meet the wishes of the Australian Government as a protest against the Russian invasion of Afghanistan.

He is one of Australia's best all-round sailors with a strong technical background as well as natural flair for

The new Australia II *was the best of the three Australian challengers. She was designed by Ben Lexcen who now has four Twelves under his belt.*

sailing. He graduated in mechanical engineering from Monash University with a thesis on the aerodynamics of Twelve Meter sails. A year after he graduated, he joined the crew of *Gretel II*. After sailing in the 1970 challenge, he stayed on in the US for a masters degree at the Massachusetts Institute of Technology in ocean engineering. He teamed with Lexcen on the design of the rig for *Southern Cross* and sailed on her as mainsheet hand in the 1974 challenge, He began working for North Sails in the USA, established the North loft in Melbourne, sailed in the 1977 Admiral's Cup team aboard *Superstar* and, in 1981, skippered Bond's *Apollo V*.

In the opposing field, the Royal Yacht club of Victoria's challenge finished strongly after a nebulous beginning and an almost complete breakdown of its financial structure just before *Challenge 12* was launched.

When the challenge was announced, in March 1981, the syndicate chairman, Sir Peter Derham, said its budget was $2.8 million and that it would seek the support of the Australian people through the "Advance Australia" campaign. At the initial announcement, Sir Peter said Alan Payne would be the designer but was vague about likely skipper and crew.

Although the syndicate had lodged the required fee of US$10,000 with the New York Yacht Club, the challenge did not seem to have any firm financial base; it was launched rather as a good idea that would hopefully attract financial support.

For the Royal Yacht Club of Victoria syndicate, without any initial strong financial backing, the situation rapidly became desperate. It had, instead of going to Alan Payne, bought, through the WA syndicate, Lexcen's conventional advance on the *Australia* (1980) design. The WA syndicate, which at that stage still hoped to build a second, conventional-design Twelve to use as a trial horse for its radical-keel design, readily agreed to sell the design and co-operate with the Victorians.

Advance, above, after a race and, below,
Challenge 12, *designed respectively by Alan Payne*
and by Ben Lexcen, who was once
known as Bob Miller. The two boats challenged on behalf
of the Royal Sydney Yacht Squadron
and the Royal Yacht Club of Victoria, which
bought the design for Challenge 12 *from Alan Bond.*

Advance, shown here with spinnaker, was the slowest of the three Australian challengers and was also handicapped by financial problems. Top right is Iain Murray, 25, four times world champion in the 18-footer "Sydney Harbour" class, and below is John Savage, 30, the helmsmen for Advance *and* Challenge 12. *Savage comes from a sailing family which is owner of the leading Australian shipyard.*

Challenge 12 was to have been launched in October 1982, an event as eagerly awaited by the Bond syndicate as by the Victorians who were now gathering momentum and enthusiasm with former world Etchells 22 Class champion John Savage appointed skipper.

However, the Victorian syndicate was unable to come up with the money to pay builder Steve Ward, Lexcen's design fee, and the bill for a mast by Zapspar — a sum total of about $400,000.

Finally, on November 22, the WA syndicate announced it had entered into a charter arrangement with the Victorian syndicate to help it overcome its financial difficulties and get the training program — vitally important to both boats — under way.

With *Challenge 12* launched and sailing against *Australia II* from Fremantle through December, and proving equally fast in straight-line sailing, strong support gathered for the boat among Victorian yachtsmen. After John Savage gave a short talk at the Royal Yacht Club of

Victoria about the *Challenge 12* campaign a yacht-owner jumped up and offered $1000 to the challenge. Others made the same offer and within a few minutes $10,000 had been raised.

Large-scale corporate support, however, was still not there. A crisis was reached on January 26 when Bond announced that his syndicate would take over the sailing program of *Challenge 12*.

Bond said that his syndicate had contributed $150,000 over the previous two months to keep *Challenge 12* sailing and that the total indebtedness of the Victorians was more than $450,000.

Within a few days, however, Melbourne businessman Dick Pratt, who had already given $100,000 towards new sails, intervened and paid out $300,000 of the amount to retain *Challenge 12* for the RYCV syndicate.

He is a great believer in motivation and quickly revived the *Challenge 12* effort, with new sails and a new mast from Sparcraft added to the two Zapspars the boat

161

Above: strict security measures were taken to hide Australia II*'s keel, always screened by canvas when out of the water.*
Below: Alan Bond, the businessman fourth-time challenger with Australia II, *chatting with John Bertrand, possibly the best Australian talent for America's Cup races and skipper of* Australia II.

already had. He organised a unique lottery, for $10 a ticket with the Twelve itself, or $200,000, as first prize.

By the time the three Australian Twelves were shipped to Newport in April, *Challenge 12* had almost completely caught up on its preparation program, disrupted by the financial crisis.

Challenge 12's skipper John Savage, 30, has accepted the challenge of competing in the America's Cup with the same cool determination that he has used in the family business. J.J. Savage and Sons is now the biggest builder of small aluminium pleasure boats in Australia.

Advance, the third America's Cup challenger de-

signed by Alan Payne of Sydney, suffered from the beginning to the end of its campaign from a shortfall of funding. This contributed to a design gamble, delays in building and outfitting the yacht, plus a drain-off of the experienced Twelve Meter and big offshore-yacht sailors available in its home port, Sydney, to the West Australian and Victorian challengers.

The challenge was inspired by Syd Fischer, Australia's most successful ocean-racing owner-skipper of recent years, who was looking for a new challenge in yachting.

In 1980, he went to watch the America's Cup, with the knowledge that he had the financial resources to at least initiate a challenge. Also influencing his decision to have a crack at the America's Cup was his longstanding and sometimes bitter rivalry with Alan Bond in ocean racing. When Fischer appeared in Newport, the feud flared again. Bond has Fischer ordered from Australia's dock area at Newport Offshore and also from the Newport Armory while Bond was giving a press con-

ference. If he had not already made up his mind, that would certainly have decided the determined Fischer to challenge for the America's Cup.

He organised a syndicate to issue a challenge through Royal Sydney Yacht Squadron which announced in June that it would build two identical new Twelves, to an Alan Payne design, to "provide the intense competition needed to prove equipment and build the fitness and skills of the crews."

Sir William Pettingell, who headed the syndicate's fund-raising efforts, said he was "rather optimistic" that money could be raised within a few weeks from major corporate bodies to finance the building of the second hull. The syndicate aimed to raise about Aus. $3 million in funds, services and equipment.

Sir William's optimism was not realised. As the recession bit harder into Australian business, the syndicate had to abandon plans to build the second Twelve.

The limited budget led Payne and his partners to

gamble on a radical shape. His fee for the design, some building supervision and design of the mast totalled Aus $151,000 — a sum that would not have covered the tank-testing of some other wealthier syndicates.

Advance is designed to be at her best in light to medium weather. Payne said: "We tried to think about moderate breezes first, last and all the time, leaving the other performance ranges to come out to be whatever they would.

Helmsman was Iain Murray, 25, one of Australia's outstanding dinghy sailors and technicians. He won six consecutive "world" 18-footer championships in boats he designed before retiring from the class in 1982.

Tactician, supplying badly-needed America's Cup experience, was Martin Visser. He was tactician for Jim Hardy aboard *Gretel II* in 1970 and starting helmsman in most of the races including the famous one where *Gretel II* hit *Intrepid* after the start and was disqualified after finishing the light-air race 1min 7sec ahead.

163

France

Late August 1980, Newport. "If I win I shall stop, if I lose I shall stop all the same." Baron Bich, the man through whom France 'discovered' the America's Cup, made it quite clear: at the age of 68 he no longer felt like carrying on. He was an instinctive and practical figure, far from that class of millionaires who race their boats out of megalomania and therefore, after having invested, over a span of a decade, almost ten million dollars in building three 12-Meters and taking part in four challenges, Marcel Bich stood down.

For his last challenge, despite the immense pleasure he gained from being personally at the helm, he entrusted Bruno Troublé with this role, pointing out, however, that "should there be nothing more to lose, I shall take the helm again". However, for the first time the Baron was not to be disappointed. Bruno Troublé and a top-level crew with *France 3* first eliminated the Swedes, then the English with *Lionheart* to reach the challengers' final, the best result ever obtained in the America's Cup.

This historical reminder is indispensable to understand how the 1983 French challenge came about. Until 1980, the America's Cup and 12-Meters were completely unknown to the French public at large. The French were to begin to take an interest in the cup in the wake of the victories in the elimination trials culminating in the only victory against the Australians in the final. Later, however, Australia was to earn the right to challenge the Americans and, as far as France was concerned, there prevailed the serious risk that the America's Cup would fall back into oblivion.

At this point Yves Rousset-Rouard, the film producer, came onto the scene. He had the successes of "Emanuelle" and Losey's "Don Giovanni" to his credit and was at the head of the leading French company in the field of video cassettes. It was in August 1980, in Paris, that he learnt of the retirement of Marcel Bich and had no hesitation in taking the first Concorde for New York and in less than twenty-four hours he was negotiating the purchase of *France 3* with the Baron. They soon agreed on an all-inclusive price of $300,000 which showed in no mean way that the Baron was more than pleased for another to carry on his good work.

Rousset-Rouard had also weighed up the situation well, or at least he thought so. With the dollar at 4.10 francs, the forthcoming support of the Giscard d'Estaing government and the promised backing of various Parisian industrialists, the French producer was optimistic. His programme had already been put into effect by the Swedish Syndicate in 1980: he had to win over the leading industrialists and build up widespread popular support and investment. At the Paris Boat Show in January 1981 promises were forthcoming but France was in the midst of one of those crises that have regularly upturned developments in the country. Following a heated electoral campaign, on May 10 1981, Giscard d'Estaing was defeated and the socialists under François Mitterand took over. This is not exactly what Yves Rousset-Rouard had hoped for, but fortunately for him and for French sailing, one of the most influential politicians, an old friend of Mitterand, was a keen sailor. Gaston Defferre, the Mayor of Marseilles, was an excellent racer in the IOR class as well as being owner of some splendid boats. Thanks to his backing, the Home Office set up the "Defi Français pour la Coupe de l'America" association. French citizens could deduct their donations to *France 3* from their taxes; however, results did not come up to expectations. France is a country with die-hard traditions not readily changed and Rousset-Rouard was to meet with bitter disappointment.

Only a dozen French cities answered his appeal with donations varying from 100,000 to 500,000 francs, while a number of ministries offered a total of over 500,000 francs: however, by the end of April 1983, the syndicate had already spent 11 million francs, seven of them coming from the Chairman's own pocket. Yves Rousset-Rouard kept on repeating: "Since the very first cheque arrived I've sworn to carry on till the bitter end."

While, on one hand, the search was on for men prepared to invest money in the undertaking, there were, on the other hand, already those prepared to dedicate their time free of charge. In effect, due to lack of funds, it had been decided against retaining the professional crew from Marcel Bich's time, since they did not care to carry on unpaid.

The demanding task of recruiting a group of young

France 3 was sold by Baron Bich to Yves Rousset-Rouard who was responsible for drumming up support for the French challenge in 1983.

FRANCE 3

talent and training them for a 12-Meter was given to Bruno Troublé, while the problem of getting them to work without pay for two years was in part solved by the Armed Forces. A military crew worked free of charge, to the delight of the syndicate and the young servicemen themselves, who no doubt preferred the life at Newport to that within the barracks.

After the glorious 1980 season, *France 3* returned to France for some alterations; the most important, the design of a new shape for the keel, was assigned to Jacques Fauroux, now very much in vogue due to his successes, as skipper and architect in the Quarter Ton Cup. The original project by Johan Valentijn was a keel with a dual trim tab, but the idea was abandoned by Baron Bich in 1980. It was logical to find a new shape since the single trim tab was to be used. Fauroux opted for a deeper and slimmer keel, to lessen the drift when coming out of turns, a defect which became evident during races in 1980. However, Fauroux went further and faced the question of a 12-Meter in a new way with considerable shrewdness, aiming at improving the performance of the boat while remaining within the limits laid down by the rules. In this way the new *France 3* has a kind of step on the aftersection so the mainsheet can be trimmed to deck-level and the mainsheet traveller is embedded, something which led to a few problems when the boat was measured in Rhode Island. Moreover, the whole deck level had been re-done: so as to give better weight distribution the helmsman's cockpit had been moved forward 1.4 meters, while the various positions of the crew were modified according to the dictates of modern times: the maximum rationalization, simplicity and communication between the members of the crew. *France 3*'s main problem in 1980 was that of the sails which, despite the efforts of Jean Paul Gattef, the sail-maker, were never in a position to match those of North or Hood. At that time the regulations allowed local branches of the two most important American sailmakers to rig out foreign 12-Meters, provided the sails were made in the same country as the syndicate. However, since 1980 the rules have become more flexible, the sails can be cut and stitched in America provided the sail-maker engaged is a citizen of the challenging nation. Following two years experience at North U.S.A. and one year at their Italian branch, Philippe Peché, without the slightest hesitation, asked Troublé and was allowed to take the sails of *France 3* in hand.

The case of the barely twenty-one-year-old Peché is somewhat symbolic, even characteristic of the 1983 challenge; the young men responsible for technical operations on board have also just started, their enthusiasm making up for lack of experience. However, the key man of the syndicate is without doubt Henri de Maublance, a thirty-four-year-old graduate of the Paris Polytechnic, who gave up an excellent job to become general secretary of the syndicate or rather the fund-raiser. He has undoubtedly had the most difficult role of all despite being young enough to grasp and solve the problems of the crew and being the right man to negotiate sponsoring. He is the first to admit that mistakes have been made and certain promotion proved disappointing. This was so with the advertising campaign launched in August 1981: a poster by Folon invited people to "take part in the history of France"; the cost of fifteen million francs was excessive when you consider the results obtained. In fact, despite a public opinion poll revealing that 51.7% of the population knew about the America's Cup and 65.3% were in favour of France taking part, the fund-raising campaign was another failure both as regards popular support and large scale sponsoring.

Perhaps a personality like Rousset-Rouard, a film producer who has become rich with films like "Emanuelle", was not the ideal person to ask for popular support, or it could simply have been a grave error of timing in a period of recession, when large scale industries are the first to cut advertising costs. Moreover, an America's Cup campaign also had to compete with the great ocean races in which the French had, for a number of years, obtained far better results. One only has to recall Marc Pajot and his *Elf Aquitaine*, not to mention Eric Tabarly in *Paul Ricard* or Alain Gabbay, second in the most recent Whitbread Round the World Race, who have for years been given wide coverage in the press, leaving little space for other sailing events and thus taking up a large proportion of the sponsors' budgets.

In the summer of 1982, *France 3* was on show in the center of Paris and later both boat and crew were transferred to Newport to take part in the Xerox Cup, a race which brought together most of the 12-Meters lined up for the 1983 Challenge, sparring partners included. The first disappointments at sea were come across when *France 3* was rammed by *Australia*, belonging to the *Victory* syndicate with de Savary himself at the helm.

Above: the boys from France 3, *all amateurs, worked hard even when ashore. Below: the French challenger's keel had been modified by Jacques Faroux, a designer very much in vogue at present in France.*

Yves Rousset-Rouard, the film producer, founded a "people's" committee to finance the challenge. On the right, France 3 *under sail.*

After the necessary period in dry-dock, *France 3* was transferred to Miami for the winter tuning period with the Canadian syndicate since the French could not afford a sparring partner of their own. The young crew set to work to learn all about the 12-Meters. They were not the cream of French sailors, but rather young men of talent and potential. However, Bruno Troublé, the skipper-helmsman, was not able to be present full-time. His work as marketing director for Bic Marine was to keep him away till early May in Newport, little more than a month before the beginning of the selection trials. *France 3*'s problem was typically French. "Put eleven Americans on board and you have a crew. Put eleven Frenchmen on board and you have eleven Frenchmen," Bruno Troublé was often heard to say.

However, in Miami the crew concentrated on the sails and rigging. Improvement was forthcoming but one had to await the help of Rhone Poulence along with the National Centre of Spatial Studies and Brochier Espace

before the question of the sails was resolved. Working together, a new fabric was prepared, Kevlar renamed Terphane, the quality of which was acknowledged by the Americans themselves. Unfortunately, sufficient quantity of the fabric arrived almost at the beginning of the Round Robin selection trials which *France 3* began with a set of old sails, incomplete furthermore; only the Chéret spinnaker was satisfactory. This, too, was typically French: able to do things well, even the impossible, but always too late, without the necessary means to match one's ambitions.

The same delay was evident with the rigging. The mast used in 1980 and designed by Alan Payne, had always been too heavy, partly because Baron Bich did not wish to run the minimum risk of dismasting. A second mast, dating from the previous challenge and which had been designed by Valentijn, which Bich considered too frail, was used for tuning after being modified. A third mast was therefore necessary and was made by Jean

*In the months of tuning in Florida the French boat, seen
here close-hauled, used* Canada 1 *as a sparring partner.
The French were also dogged by serious financial problems.*

Pierre Maréchal in the Poivreau shipyards from a project by Guy Ribadeau-Dumas.

However, as usual, it was a little too late: the new rigging arrived in Newport on April 15 and, though satisfactory, it was not able to be serviced properly. Moreover, it must be pointed out that the French syndicate was not sufficiently rich to be able to afford two complete riggings and, at every mast change the fixed rigging had to come from the old one. Then, early May, the final wave of the magic wand came late. Jacques Setton, who had bought up the Hood Yard, offered his contribution to the French syndicate. Together with his help, as the races gradually came nearer, a number of substantial offers were forthcoming, as if everyone wanted to give their offering so that it would not be said, at a later stage, that they had done nothing. Citröen manufactured a limited series of the famous "2 Chevaux" with the colours of *France 3*.

The crew are perhaps the only ones who have no-

thing for which to reproach themselves. To the contrary, they have done all they could with the means they have had at their disposal, as shown by the success in one of the very first races of the selection finals. *France 3* beat *Canada 1* and the Canadians were highly impressed above all by the frantic rhythm of their turns, so much so that they came to have a look at *France 3*'s winches that very evening, expecting to discover something new. They were, however, dumb-founded when the French showed them the date of manufacture: 1979, the era of the French ballpoint magnate, another epoch.

In conclusion, the glorious 1980 challenge led by one man did not, three years later, become a joint collective French effort. Unfortunately, nor was a suitable middle course found, despite the sound efforts and good will on the part of all those taking part in the challenge. Rather than seek out the guilty party, one must draw practical conclusions and hope for the best in the America's Cup next time out.

Canada

The Canadian coastline is, for the most part, *terra incognita*, and though one of the longest national coastlines in the world, it is largely inhospitable to man, let alone to yachting enterprise. As a result, sailing in Canada is centered around two major population centres, Vancouver in the West and Toronto in the East.

It must have been with some surprise, therefore, that the New York Yacht Club received a challenge for the Cup from an unknown Canadian group from the Western prairies, more than a thousand miles from the sea. Especially, let it be remembered, that the last Canadian bid for the Cup had been so incompetent in 1881 that the rules were changed banning all boats from entering that did not hail from the sea or an arm thereof.

Early in 1981, a group of Calgary businessmen who, for the most part knew next to nothing about sailing, used to meet at the exclusive 400 Club to discuss issues of the day. These were men of influence and forthright manner. Something, it was felt, needed to be done to give Canada a challenge to revive a spirit of unity and national confidence. Marvin McDill proposed challenging for the America's Cup. After it was explained what this was, a core group rallied, organized and applied to the New York Yacht Club for challenger status. NYYC were nonplussed. The syndicate was unknown, their club irregular, their credentials vague. To ancitipate the conditions of the challenge, the Secret Cove Yacht Club had been created at a marina sixty-five miles north of Vancouver, British Columbia, under the name of one Donald McDonald. This sort of well-intentioned yet groping spadework happened to coincide with a period in Canadian sailing history when the nation had begun to display international stature on the Olympic and major race circuits. Olympic sailors Hans Fogh, David Miller and Terry McLaughlin were but a few world-class sailors in the country and they were strongly tested by their compatriots. The other coincidence was that Bruce Kirby, it would seem, was a Canadian waiting for a 12-Meter to design.

The course of events after the challenge was eventually accepted seldom ran smoothly but ever present in the minds of McDill and his syndicate members was the firm resolve to float the challenge. The path this notion took was Canadian baroque.

In April, 1981, the syndicate was faced with staggering problems. They needed money (it was thought that a total of three million dollars would be sufficient at that time); they needed a designer for the boat, a crew, an operations staff and, of course, a boat. Everything.

One of McDill's first moves was to approach George Cuthbertson, doyen of Canadian yachting and president of C&C Yachts, to commission a design for the new 12-Meter. Cuthbertson declined and recommended Bruce Kirby for the job. It happens that Kirby, a 12-Meter afficionado, has never missed an America's Cup race and has files bulging with his own analyses of all the boats he has seen or read about. 12-Meters have been the private obsession of this designer who is much better known for his Laser design and for his IOR boats such as *Runaway*, the first Canadian boat in the 1981 Admiral's Cup. Despite having lived for many years in Rowayton, Connecticut, Kirby had retained his Canadian citizenship and was an admissible designer under the rules.

Kirby is both pragmatic and intuitive. In the matter of the challenge, he very quickly brought things down to earth. He specified priorites for the boat, for the crew, for training and made it clear that nothing but a rigorous and well-funded campaign would have a chance. In the matter of design, he felt his way. Drawing on his store of observations and, among other things, precise measurements of *Clipper*, he developed two sets of lines for a fairly conservative, all-round boat, somewhat in the *Freedom* and Sparkman & Stephens tradition. He accepted the penalty for a low freeboard and showed an unusually squared-off base to the keel. Keel and hull separation were originally clearly defined but, during the Elimination Series, the turn was softened to advantage. Extremes had been avoided because exuberant experimentation was an unaffordable luxury. He and Steve Killing tank-tested the first model at the National Research Council in Ottawa, one of the best equipped tanks in the world, and the results, along with Killing's computer performance predictions, looked good. A second model, slightly more developed, looked better. The final lines combined features of both boats but were never tank-tested.

After more than a century the Canadian were
back again with a new America's Cup challenge.
They last raced in New York in 1881.

about to begin its ritual dance, a tango in pinstripe and spurs. McDill, still believing that the Western syndicate could manage the whole campaign, was invited to lunch at the Royal Canadian Yacht Club in Toronto — the bastion of the Canadian yachting establishment. As a warm-up speaker before successful America's Cup defender Ted Turner, he presented his plan with boyish optimism, ingenuously admitting his ignorance of sailing. Despite the gaffe, the audience warmed to the call, but only for as long as it took Ted Turner to contemptuously pour cold water over the whole idea. Kirby had never designed a Twelve before; there was no depth to the offshore talent — the chill deepened as RCYC members saw their pool of Olympic sailors being drained away by a futile and misguided effort that was doomed to failure. A short letter to this effect was sent to McDill by former RCYC Commodore Gordon Fisher and, though private, it spoke for many. The Royal Canadian Yacht Club, the only entré to Eastern yachting money, was a closed door.

Committed, yet strapped for funds, McDill flew back to Calgary muttering, rumor has it, "pessimistic Eastern bastards." The Canadian America's Cup challenge would probably have quietly expired had not Calgary oilman Verne Lyons underwritten a one-million dollar loan — the signal to build a new boat, select a crew and go for it. The original name for the boat, happily long forgotten, was *Let's Do It*.

The choreography of the East-West imbroglio is a masterpiece in entente between two incompatible styles, and the complexity of the manoeuvring is something to wonder at. The attempt almost disintegrated under the strain, but one cannot help but wonder if the purging was not a necessary and typical part of the process.

It happens that Paul Phelan, a wealthy Eastern yachtsman, was initially of the pessimistic school as far as the Canadian America's Cup challenge was concerned. It so happened, too, that his cousin, Terry McLaughlin, was the helmsman of choice in the challenge crew, and McLaughlin was not a man to be put off. The 1980 Flying Dutchman world champion, who had seen his chances of a gold medal disappear in the aborted 1980 Olympics, was intensely ambitious to lead the Canadian challenge to victory. The syndicate needed a trial horse and ultimately would need, they then thought, an additional two-and-a-half million dollars. What was Phelan going to do about it? Phelan was cautious about being entangled in syndicate debts; as a personal gesture he would buy *Intrepid*, two-time America's Cup defender, and rent her to the syndicate for a dollar. As if to disclaim *his* indebtedness, McDill clinched a hard-won lease-purchase deal for *Clipper* from her owner, Russell Long, much to the resentment of the New York Yacht Club.

Meanwhile George Wilkins, a yachtsman and journalist from Vancouver, was given the task of selecting a crew. He travelled the country interviewing 130 applicants for 25 positions, while retired admiral of militaris-

If Kirby was the artist, Killing was the scientist. Steve Killing was brought into the design function at an early stage to add his considerable computer expertise to the process. As a brilliant engineer and former C&C designer, Killing had taken his fascination with computers into his own yacht design business near Toronto. His reputation was centred on the design of *Evergreen*, the 1978 Canada's Cup winner, and on a number of successful production boats. Equipped with a small desk-top computer, he had the knack of turning the figures. They made a good pair and the predictions and tank testing indicated a boat with quick turning ability, fast acceleration out of the tack and good upwind performance, especially in moderate to heavy air. A non-sailor, Marvin McDill was in no position to know how sound a design it was; a pity, since his worries at this time were legion.

The date was September, 1981, and the peculiar interaction between East and West — two nebulous but vital nerve centers in Canadian consciousness — was

On the opposite page: Canada 1, *like* France 3, *passed the winter prior to the challenge working out the crew in Florida. Below: Canada's skipper Terry McLaughlin, F.D. World champion. Above: Canada 1 taking some exercise. Because of lack of funds work on* Canada 1 *had to be stopped for three months prior to the challenge. On the right: detail of the two wheels.*

tic outlook, Jeffrey Brock, was put in charge of operations. The crew were young, immensely keen, and not responsive to a disciplinarian approach. Brock, along with other officials, left to leave the crew firmly unified by their desire to win in their way. McLaughlin's guiding hand was more than established at this point and without his resolve and powers of leadership vital crew morale might well have dissolved.

Early encouragement, however, was taken from the quality of the boat under construction. In an unlikely shed north of Toronto, the aluminium hull was being welded together by McConnell's Marine under the brilliant eye of Brian Riley, a New Zealander who had already worked on *France 3* and *Ceramco New Zealand* and who skillfully fashioned aluminium plates to within sixteenth-of-an-inch tolerances. *Canada 1* is, by any reckoning, an extremely well-built boat.

Almost predictably, however, her birthing was a saga in itself. When the hull was virtually complete, the syndicate was desperately short of cash and until this was made available, the boat could not be completed or removed. Fred McConnell, the builder, publicly and prematurely announced that the syndicate was broke. The training camp in Florida was disbanded — the whole campaign again teetering on the brink of collapse. McDill knew that the mortgage of $200,000 he thought he had secured against the boat was not enough to re-float the challenge. The only solution was a transfusion of Eastern money. In August, 1981, McDill was back in Toronto, cap in hand.

This meeting with Paul Phelan and members of a committee that included IYRU member Paul Hender-son, retired trucking magnate R.D. Grant and Bill Cox, brought into the open another element to the negotiations — effective control of the campaign. In return for $400,000 the committee demanded the option to manage the campaign at its discretion. A deal was struck: Phelan assumed a second mortgage on the boat and was made head of the powerful Eastern committee.

It was while these deliberations were dragging on that a turning point was reached in the campaign. The twenty-five man double crew had been disbanded and had returned home — deeply frustrated. They were eager to show their mettle. When Xerox invited all contenders for a shakedown series, skipper McLaughlin lit up, phones rang, and a raggle-taggle bunch of lads drummed up a few dollars and high-tailed it down to Newport. The group in the back of Bob Muru's '76 Chevy van passed muster at customs as sailbags; *Clipper* was appropriated and her patched and baggy sails shaken out for the series.

The Xerox challenge proved beyond doubt that the Canadian team were contenders. In their ability to beat the deeply-funded British boat, *Victory*, on the water and with their consistent tactical and starting skills, the press finally realized that the Canadian challenge meant business. "Canadians aching for new sails!" ran the headline and from that time on public awareness of what was being attempted, increased.

Right from the start, Marvin McDill had envisaged nation-wide popular support. It was part of his dream of bringing a focus to what he saw as Canada's sagging psyche — a bit of good old bloody-minded competition that would stir nationalistic will and pride. "I would rather have a dollar from five million people," he said, "than one million from five people." As we have seen, the money to date had been from the few.

At the Toronto International Boat Show, however, January, 1983, two months after the belated launch of *Canada 1*, the boat was put on public display. Floodlit and glistening, she drew gasps from the thousands of show-goers. Finally, the grass-roots' support had begun to grow. Yacht clubs gave fund-raising dinners, commercial memorabilia were hawked, paintings commissioned and small private donations attracted. Simultaneously, major corporate sponsors, who had been waiting on the sidelines to see how the backroom bargaining was

going to shape up, took heart. Air Canada, Alcan Canada, Coca Cola, Labatt's, Seagram's and Texaco Canada are some of the companies that contributed in cash, kind or services and helped make the campaign financially operable.

Above and beyond the convolutions of getting the campaign financed and organized, there have been the actions of the sailors themselves and their immediate support body. Without question, the lion of the group is Terry McLaughlin, champion sailor, mastermind, gall and gadfly to his crew. As a skipper, he had shown himself one of the world's best match-racing starters and had an uncanny feel for boatspeed. Tactically, he was aided by his long-time friend and sailing partner, Jeff Boyd. The two have an instinctive rapport when it comes to calling the shots and Boyd had been a mainstay of the team from the start. Peter Wilson, the third member of the triumvirate, was the navigator — cool, quiet and accurate. His loyalty and expertise made him an inseparable part of the team.

It is due to the other members of the crew to mention them individually, because one of the most remarkable aspects of the Canadian challenge proved the sustained zeal of its young crew (average age 25). Twenty-five crew members were selected to sail *Canada 1* and the trial horse *Clipper* for proving. They were: Sandy An-

According to Bruce Kirby, below, designer of Canada 1, *his Twelve, seen above, is rather classic both where displacement and shape are concerned.* Clipper, *built for the 1980 challenge, served as sparring partner to* Canada 1. *The boat's strength lay in her very young and aggressive crew.*

drews, Don Campbell, Tom Cumming, Brent Foxall, Philip Gow, Edward Gyles, Paul Hansen, Eric Jesperson, Robert Kidd, Fernando Larrey, Jay McKinnell, Al Megarry, John Millen, Bob Muru, Daniel Palardy, Paul Parsons, Paul Phillips, Fred Schueddekopp, David Shaw, Rob Webb, Evert Bastet, Robin Wynne-Edwards and Robert Vaughan-Jones. Ever present, too, was head mechanic, Bob Whitehouse.

The Canadian America's Cup challenge, the first in over a century, is significant from both a yachting and a cultural point of view. It is a symbolic coming-of-age for Canadian yachting.

Having made its mark in recent years in Olympic and international racing, the pursuit of the America's Cup underscores Canada's sailing stature. Culturally, the original aims of mounting a challenge supported by the enthusiasm of the nation at large have, in a circuitous way, been met. With *Canada 1* as a benchmark 12-Meter to hand, the door is wide open.

Italy

When the Italian challenge through the Costa Smeralda Yacht Club arrived at the New York Yacht Club, on April 1, 1981, someone may well have considered it the usual April Fool trick. All told, the Italians are more well-known in the United States for their spaghetti and Cosa Nostra than for sailing, despite being a seafaring nation as Columbus, Verrazzano and others recall in no mean way.

Even though the Italian team had shown up well in a few Admiral's Cup races, but with American "advisers" on board as malicious tongues hastened to add, and despite having done well enough both in level class and Olympic Class racing, Italian victories in international yachting have always appeared as somewhat sporadic episodes, due more to the talent of one individual or of a small group of people than to the combined effort of a number of people. It would have seemed far more likely to expect a challenge from Germany, New Zealand or Japan; nothing would have led one to have dreamt that the Italians were on the point of embarking upon what is considered the most complex and costly venture in the world of sailing.

In fact, not even those who had made the challenge were at the time completely sure of carrying it through: there was not even the design for the boat; there was only the support of a few key personalities, the first in the history of Italian yachting who had succeeded in drawing the interest of the nation away from soccer and toward a simple sailing boat. One must not overlook, however, the fact that Italy, the home of Ferrari, is the country in which hyperbole is the order of the day and so it is not so difficult to understand how *Azzurra* became a reality. The Italians always tend to extremes, especially where sport and beauty are concerned, and the America's Cup, an aesthetic and philosophical phenomenon more than a real sporting event, has for some time fascinated the Italians for this very reason.

Interest in the America's Cup had, in fact, begun in Italy back in the early Sixties, in a particularly happy moment for national competitive sailing. Those were the times of the Olympic Gold medal of Straulino and sailors of the caliber of Capio, Cosentino and Sorrentino. "Agnelli is the only person who can afford such a venture" was repeated over and over again in the Yacht Clubs and in moments of boredom on board racing

yachts caught in the Mediterranean calms. In fact, *l'Avvocato*, (this is the nickname of Fiat owner, Gianni Agnelli) had already been considering the matter. He was a very keen sailor and also owner of a splendid old 12-Meter, *Tomahawk*, built by Camper and Nicholson in 1939, which he later gave to the Naples Yacht Club since the Italian Yacht Club could not accept her due to its rules. In the summer of 1962 he went to Newport, along with Beppe Croce who was at home with 12-Meters like no-one else in Italy, and unofficially proposed his own nomination as a challenger. At this point the versions differ; some give the American reply as being: "With you we can do business but the America's Cup is out of the question", whereas a more than reliable witness, Croce himself, says that the American willingly accepted the idea but for 1969, not before. Agnelli, who was interested in a challenge within the span of a couple of years, dropped the project.

However, the time was not yet right. Italy, despite its eight thousand kilometers of coastline and its seafaring traditions, was not yet up to such an ambitious undertaking. The idea of an Italian challenge therefore remained a mere dream, which left a trace of bitterness with those who felt it was already possible to enter into the Olympus of sailing. Twenty years have gone by since then and Italy has undoubtedly matured from the sailing point of view and the challenge has become reality. It is interesting to point out, however, that alongside the new generation of Italian sailors there is still Agnelli as the key man behind the project.

As often happens on similar occasions, the idea of an Italian challenge for the America's Cup in 1983 did not come from just one person. While Riccardo Bonadeo, a Milanese businessman, a keen and expert racer and member of the Costa Smeralda Yacht Club, made the first moves on behalf of a group of industrialists in the North, at the same time farther South, in Rome to be exact, the naval design studio of Andrea Vallicelli and Pasquale Landolfi, another businessman with a long sailing curriculum, also showed interest.

Fortunately, typical Italian individualism on such an

Azzurra, the Italian Twelve, challenged on behalf of the Costa Smeralda Yacht Club, based in Porto Cervo on the Northern coast of the island of Sardinia.

occasion gave way to a joint effort instead of each forming his own syndicate in a country where not even one sailor had a reasonable experience of 12-Meters. Not without hitches and a certain ill-feeling, the Italian syndicate for the America's Cup challenge thus came into being, with Commander Gianfranco Alberini as Chairman and Riccardo Bonadeo as Vice-Chairman. It was immediately clear that what would not be lacking as regards *Azzurra* were the funds. Prince Aga Khan, Chairman of the challenging yacht club, had promised a billion liras, while the support of the Fiat Group drew further sponsors like the proverbial flies round a honeypot. "If Agnelli phones and asks you for three hundred million liras over a three year period you need not even ask why he needs it", said one of the fortunate sponsors, "just remember that each year either directly or indirectly he gives a few billions' worth of business to your company and then, the next time you meet up, he may even thank you". Therefore, if credit for the initiative must undoubtedly go to the Costa Smeralda Yacht Club, one of the newest Italian sailing associations that the Aga Khan founded for the benefit of yachtsmen visiting his Costa Smeralda, from the financial point of view Agnelli's support proved decisive. This was forthcoming when he himself was convinced that the undertaking was being entrusted to solid reliable people who intended to treat the matter seriously; he was not the only one to wish to avoid going to America to lose face. Luca di Montezemolo was chosen to deal with the financial problems, understandably considering his past at Ferrari and his being related to Agnelli.

It was decided that each member would subscribe a share of 300 million liras with some members of the syndicate undertaking further financial responsibilities. The Fiat group immediately agreed to three shares for three companies under their control, Cinzano, Florio and Iveco. Before long, other companies were at logger-

Above: Andrea Vallicelli, designer of Azzurra, *and, on his right, Riccardo Bonadeo, a member of the Italian syndicate. Below: detail of* Azzurra *while being built by Yacht Officine in Pesaro.*

Azzurra, top right, *was launched on July 19, 1982. The Aga Kahn,* above, *is Chairman of the Italian syndicate. Below: Gianni Agnelli, Chairman of Fiat, one of the leading members of the syndicate, seen, center, during the launching ceremony.*

heads trying to become part of the "élite" behind *Azzurra*: all in all seventeen sponsors. For some it meant an excellent opportunity for advertising, for others a simple matter of prestige.

Once the finances had been secured, it remained to find the boat. The first step taken by the syndicate was that of buying *Enterprise* from the Americans for $250,000. This was the Sparkman & Stephens boat with which Lowell North, the sailmaker, had tried in vain to qualify for the finals in 1977 and was later bought by the Dennis Conner syndicate to act as sparring partner for *Freedom* in the 1980 challenge. Following two years of trials, *Enterprise* proved almost as fast as her more recently built companion.

Enterprise was thus an excellent yardstick both for the designer who had to project the shape of the new Italian 12-Meter and for *Azzurra*'s trial races. The choice as to who was to put his name to the project fell somewhat naturally on Andrea Vallicelli, the 32 year-old head of

the Roman studio of the same name, who had, amongst other things, designed *Filo da Torcere,* winner of the Naples One Ton Cup World championships in 1980. At a certain stage there was talk of bringing in Mario Tarabocchia, an Italian who had been working for years at the studio of Sparkman & Stephens in close collaboration with numerous 12-Meter projects. There were unofficial negotiations, but in the end nothing came of it perhaps because the offer was not sufficiently inviting or because Tarabocchia was loth to leave New York. *Enterprise* arrived on a cargo vessel in the port of Genoa in the autumn of 1981. While Vallicelli was completing the design of *Azzurra,* the ex-American 12-Meter became a floating test center for scores of sailors who aspired to have the privilege of the challenge. The first trial runs were held at Porto Cervo, the capital of the Costa Smeralda, on the northern coast of Sardinia. Cino Ricci was chosen to supervise the crew formations for *Azzurra* and *Enterprise,* not so much due to a long curriculum of

179

The Italian crew in front of Salve Regina College, the residence of Azzurra's crew while in Newport. Center is Cino Ricci, the skipper and, on his left, Laurent Cordelle, a Frenchman naturalized Italian, who has been alongside Ricci in innumerable races. Below: a crewmember climbs on the spinnaker pole of Azzurra.

victories but rather because of his time-honoured experience of IOR races and his fame for being able to mediate between the different personalities of a heterogeneous crew and of perfectly understanding the role of each member. Born around fifty years ago in Rimini on the Adriatic, Ricci, with his well-trimmed beard, has never denied anyone the chance to aspire at being included in *Azzurra*'s crew.

"In America there are at least three thousand people with 12-Meter experience, in Australia and England around three hundred, while here there is nobody and we must start from square one; everybody must be given a fair chance." This was the leitmotif that Ricci loved and still loves to repeat.

Azzurra was launched at the beginning of the summer of 1982 at the Yacht Officine in Pesaro on the Adriatic, well-known for having built some IOR boats in aluminium which took part honourably in the Admiral's Cup. The event was naturally celebrated with all due pomp: helicopters landing and taking off amidst a crowd of spectators, carabinieri, Ministers, the Bishop and the Mayor of Pesaro, Agnelli, the Aga Khan and a host of beautiful ladies.

After the launching, *Azzurra* and *Enterprise* carried out some trial runs for a while on the Adriatic and were later transferred to Formia on the Tyrrhenian Sea between Rome and Naples where the weather conditions were more similar to those of Newport. The two boats spent the winter here on the Italian "West Coast" with the crews who could use the conveniences of the local Olympic center. Slowly but surely Vallicelli's boat succeeded in proving herself faster than *Enterprise* which had purposely been made lighter. "She's faster than *Enterprise* on almost all goings and in almost all conditions" was Vallicelli's satisfied comment after almost a year of trial runs at Formia on the occasion of the official "presentation" to the public. It was in fact a demonstration race between the two boats followed by a large gathering of the public crowded along the quays, by hundreds of journalists on board a ferry-boat and by the authorities from the decks of a destroyer of the Italian Navy. It was a tribute to *Azzurra* before her departure for the United States, without her sparring partner *Enterprise*. Cino Ricci had in fact reached an agreement with Bruno Troublé, skipper of *France 3*, to tune the boats together.

On April 11, 1983, little more than two years after the New York Yacht Club had received the Italian challenge, *Azzurra* was blessed by the Naval Chaplain in the square at the port of Naples and taken aboard the vessel *Costa Ligure* to be shipped to New York and then Newport, Rhode Island. Here, the pleasant surprises began immediately; in the early tuning races the Italian boat was able to rival the other 12-Meters. Being particularly fast downwind, with excellent sails thanks to Guido Cavalazzi, the young sailmaker with a wealth of experience gained at North U.S.A., *Azzurra*'s crew began to believe in her potential.

Azzurra racing in Formia, Italy, against Enterprise, *built in 1977 and bought from the* Freedom *syndicate in 1981 to serve as sparring partner to the Italian Twelve.*

The choice of helmsman was made, however, at a later stage, at least a month after *Azzurra* had begun to cleave the waves of Newport. Until the last moment the choice was between Flavio Scala, Italian Star class champion, and Mauro Pelaschier, twice Olympic helmsman for Italy in the Finn class, who had passed to IOR classes four years ago. Since Ricci failed to decide, Scala preferred to leave the Italian scene. Ricci, who had the role of navigator on board *Azzurra*, had no other choice than to name Pelaschier official helmsman reserving, however, the right to reconsider. The alternative helmsman was Stefano Roberti, the mainsail trimmer, formerly skipper of the winner of the 1980 One Ton Cup. The afterguard, the ''intelligentsia'' on board, also included Tiziano Nava, 25, who was the tactician. Nava boasts a world title to his credit in Minitonners and has won the Italian championship in both Laser and J-Classes.

However, beyond all shadow of doubt, the most expert as regards 12-Meters in the Italian team was a Frenchman: Laurent Cordelle. He is a close friend of Ricci and has worked alongside him in innumerable races, only recently being naturalized Italian. Cordelle lives in Ravenna working as a naval architect and was involved on a number of occasions in Baron Bich's attempts to bring the America's Cup to France. His time-honoured experience, along with his close ties with Ricci, led the team manager to demand he be included as the first condition when drawing up the campaign with the Syndicate.

In Italy, after the World Cup victory in the 1982 soccer season, any achievement by now seems possible, even a victory in the America's Cup. Cino Ricci had always been far more realistic and had always felt that one could but hope to get to the semi-finals. ''We have come to learn, to build up our experience for next time'', he said quite openly. He knew full well that in Italy it would be enough if *Azzurra* beat the French. Should she do more, then all the better.

The Elimination Trials

The elimination trials for the 1983 America's Cup were complex beyond all expectations. Newport's weather was spotty and too many races were inconclusive, though official nonetheless; protests abounded; bitterness flourished on the racecourse and ashore as the pressure of competition affected wisdom and judgment on all sides. Still, no one who observed this summer's passionate events could feel cheated of drama, expectation and the historic moment.

The complexity began with the challenger eliminations. The computer-designed race series was the best the International Jury could come up with, but it wasted a great deal of racing time, as strong contenders had to race too often with boats lacking even a slim chance of success: thus, *Australia II*, which showed her all-around speed and tactical superiority from the start, raced *Advance* and *France 3* through each series, though their elimination could have been predicted by early summer. Still, the races had to be fair, and the jury arranged the following system.

Three Round-Robin race series were run. Series "A" was a double Round-Robin; race winners were awarded one point and 20 per cent of each yacht's points carried over to the "B" series (also a double) from which 40 per cent of the points were carried over. The "C" series was a triple Round-Robin carrying a 40 per cent weight. During that series, however, the Twelves whose point total made it mathematically impossible for them to win were systematically eliminated. The semi-finals, a triple Round-Robin among the remaining four Twelves, eliminated two, leaving two to sail a best-of-seven final series on the full America's Cup course.

The New York Yacht Club Selection Committee, on the other hand, continued its long tradition of subjective selection of the defender. Its less formal trials — Preliminary, Observation and Final — were a search for the yacht with momentum. How "momentum" is defined is always a vague question, but political urgencies often lurk in the background and influence the Committe's thinking. In the 1983 case, one such urgency was the age of *Courageous*; it is difficult to select a 10-year-old boat unless she is unbeatable. Another was the fact that *Liberty*, with the unpublicized sanction of the NYYC, could legally sail under any one of three rating certificates (for light, medium and heavy air).

This clearly strengthened *Liberty*'s case on the racecourse and in the meeting rooms ashore, and would become one of the many sources of controversy and acrimony to haunt the NYYC in the 1983 season.

This friction, and the secret "superkeel" of Ben Lexcen's *Australia II*, enlivened matters before the world's knowledgeable sailors, yachting journalists and the largely uninformed general press, to produce a media barrage beyond the hopes of any public relations firm.

One of the themes the media latched onto early was the in-fighting among syndicates and their personalities. Two Aussie syndicates — *Australia II* and *Challenge 12* — allied to the exclusion of the third (*Advance*). And the Blackaller/Conner feud heated up to the point of silliness. Beyond that, the media also noted that nearly all the Twelves needed modification during the long campaign — more lead and aluminum were shifted in 1983 than ever before.

Both the defense and challenger eliminations began on June 18, in disappointingly light air. The entire summer, in fact, was plagued by softer and shiftier breezes than in a normal Newport summer. In the challenger's "A" series *Australia II* stepped out as the yacht to beat by winning eleven of her twelve races; her only loss was to her stablemate, *Challenge 12*. This prompted the ever-vociferous Alan Bond to lament the lack of competition for his favorite Twelve. It also inspired challengers and defenders alike to consider adding "winglets" to their Twelves, even though no-one was certain just what those winglets looked like.

The other challengers, besides *Challenge 12*, put in mediocre performances; and her 10-2 record in the "A" series demonstrated that Ben Lexcen could put a fast boat together without resorting to wings. *Victory '83* continued to suffer from organizational confusion — after Harold Cudmore's resignation as helmsman, Phil Crebbin, Rodney Pattisson and Lawrie Smith rotated at the wheel and their crew was constantly changed. The French continued to have money and sail problems — their inventory of both was minimal. *Canada 1* also suffered cash deficiences, and lost her prime mast early in

On the opposite page:
Liberty, with Dennis Conner at the helm, during one of the innumerable elimination trial races.

the summer. *Azzurra*, the wonderful dark horse of 1983, managed a level of momentum and dignity that should make all Italians proud. *Advance* simply demonstrated that a radical Twelve, designed for Newport's anticipated light air, is a risk; she lost most of her races in gentle breezes.

The defense Preliminary Trials, unlike the challengers', were far from conclusive. Traditionally considered a tune-up opportunity, the races were used by the three American entries to test sails and get a measure of the others' strengths and weaknesses. Visited by fog and light winds, the races were split almost evenly: *Courageous* 6-5, *Defender* 5-6, and *Liberty* 5-5. *Courageous*, however, surprised her opponents with good light-air speed, which seemed to strengthen the Blackaller/Kolius team's intention to eliminate Dennis Conner early. Though *Liberty* emerged with good momentum — she won four of her last five races — Conner willingly admitted his fear of *Courageous*'s speed. And Kolius publicly expressed concern over his crew's weak performance. Following the Preliminaries, *Defender* (which had raced with too little sail area) was hauled for major surgery. She was found to be sagging at the ends, and a thin wedge was cut from her midships sections and welded to lift her bow and stern. *Courageous* received a much-needed rudder bearing. *Liberty* and her sparring partner, *Freedom*, were each lightened to leave Conner the option of reverting to the older boat

in the July trials, should she have proven faster.

She did not. The defense Observation trials began on July 16, and Conner sailed *Liberty* again. This series showed some chinks in the *Courageous* armor: she won only two of her fifteen races, but she showed that her afterguard could outsmart Conner and beat him at his game, particularly in starting. In *Liberty*'s only loss to *Courageous*, the two Twelves exchanged leads several times and never rounded a mark more than twelve seconds apart. In a match race of brilliant intensity, Conner showed that the ultimate weakness in his historic, and unsuccessful defense was not *Liberty*'s speed but his afterguard's failure to sail the boat to the right places with consistency.

The challengers' "B" series, begun July 2, heightened the suspense of the selection, but only with respect to which boat would be second to *Australia II*. The Twelve with the mystery keel dominated the racing again, winning ten of her twelve races, while the best her opponents could do was an unimpressive 7-5 record.

However, by the time the series ended, the major story of the 1983 America's Cup, long simmering on the back burners of propriety, boiled over from the heat of accusation. For all the time she had been in Newport, *Australia II*'s keel had been shrouded under green polyethylene and hidden behind a plywood structure. No outsider knew with certainty what its shape was, but enough information — right and wrong — had leaked for a grotesque description of it to circulate among the knowing: it was small and upside down; it had a large bulb and two fins. The case would have rested there, but for *Australia II*'s awesome speed — her record of twenty-one wins and three losses terrified defenders and challengers alike. The Americans naturally did not want to lose the Cup; the foreigners each wanted to be the ones to take it. (So fearsome was *Australia II* that a rumor circulated that Bertrand cocked her trim tab occasionally to slow her down to conceal her speed).

As the street-corner description of the superkeel waxed clearer, it became apparent that *Australia II* gained draft as she heeled because her leeward wing would swing down; she gained lateral surface as well. This was a cause for concern, as the additional draft was not included in her measurement. On July 24, the chairman of the America's Cup Committee, Robert W. McCullough, wrote a forceful letter to Mark Vinbury, the American member of the three-man measuring team. He quoted two documents: the International 12-Meter Rules (Rule 27) and the Measurement Instructions (Instruction 7).

Rule 27 states that a 12-Meter's measurement "shall be deemed incomplete" if "from any peculiarity in the build of the yacht... the measurer shall be of the opinion that the rule will not rate the yacht fairly, or that in any respect she does not comply with the requirements of these rules..." Measurement Rule 7 states that if such "peculiarities" place the measurer "in doubt as to the application of the rules or instructions, or the calculation of the rating," the rating shall similarly be "deemed incomplete." War was declared.

Vinbury, who had measured *Australia II* at least three times without objection, wrote to his counterpart on the measurement team, Tony Watts, of the International Yacht Racing Union. Vinbury said there was "no question that our committee measured *Australia II*'s keel according to the rule." He felt, however, that "the

Australia II, circling with France 3, *which, along with* Advance, *was the first to be eliminated. Below:* Challenge 12 *and* Canada 1. *On the previous page: the Newport harbour.*

rule as it is currently written is not able to assess the unusual shape'' of the keel. He also chided Ben Lexcen, the designer, whom, he said, ''should have informed the measurer of the theoretical advantages of this keel... not being assessed by the rule.'' He requested a ruling from the IYRU, which administers the 12-Meter Rule.

At the same time, Halsey Herreshoff, *Liberty*'s navigator, went public with a declaration that *Australia II* was likely to win the Cup if allowed to race as she was rated. He called for the keel's unveiling and re-measurement. He suggested that the challengers and defenders file a formal protest and that *Australia II*'s syndicate be given the choice of withdrawing, removing the fins or being penalized for the additional draft.

The world was stunned. So late in the game the NYYC was again trying to change the rules to retain the Cup. But that was not necessarily the case. The mistake the New Yorkers made was in waiting so long to raise a fuss. *Australia II* had by now won twenty-one out of twenty-five races and the NYYC's excuse that the keel had been kept secret from it did not convince the press; the NYYC was made to look as though it was again violating the precepts of good sportsmanship. To make matters more embarrassing, the NYYC asked the remaining challengers to file a protest, and they refused.

Trapped, on August 3 the NYYC appealed directly to George Andreadis, chairman of the IYRU Keelboat Technical Committee (KTC). With drawings and back-up statements by noted designers Bill Luders and Britton Chance, the yacht club's James Michael reiterated the claim that the keel was unfairly measured and that *Australia II* ''rates at least somewhere between 12.5 and 12.8 meters.'' Michael asked that the IYRU instruct the measurers to re-rate the boat. On August 10 — *Australia II* had now won thirty-six out of forty races — the NYYC supplemented its request to the IYRU, repeating the Vinbury comment on the keel's doubtful

The four challenging semi-finalists. Above: Australia II *at the start with bowman forward and* Canada 1*'s sails approaching. Below:*Azzurra *and* Victory *in a neck-and-neck struggle to get through to the finals. On the opposite page:* Victory *is ahead of* Azzurra *while the spinnakers are being lowered to prepare the boats for the last windward leg.*

The final race between Australia II *and* Victory. *The outcome was almost certain and the Australians won 4-1.*

rating. And Thomas F. Ehman Jr., executive director of the USYRU, also requested an interpretation of the applicable rules. Ehman reminded the IYRU that the Australian measurers had also expressed some doubt about the keel's measurement and had asked the Australian Yachting Federation to query the IYRU and ask Ben Lexcen to do the same; neither Lexcen nor the AYF took any action (Lexcen because of his desire for continued secrecy).

Nigel Hacking, the IYRU secretary-general, responded with a different interpretation: that the measurers' view should stand and that it was not up to the IYRU to "intervene in this challenge event" in view of the America's Cup conditions which require the measurers to initiate the request and of the fact that the NYYC was not a member of the IYRU. Tony Watts and John Savage voted, as a majority of the Measurement Committee, to reaffirm that "the keel of *Australia II* is legal," thus closing the door further on the NYYC.

The near final blow, protracted as it was, came from the Australian camp in mid-August. Warren Jones, the *Australia II* syndicate manager, had written a long, detailed letter to Beppe Croce, IYRU President. In the letter he countered all of the NYYC's arguments. He claimed that *Australia II* was designed and measured according to the Conditions of the America's Cup, and that the NYYC was trying to change those rules (which cannot be done less than eighteen months before a Cup series). He repeated the yacht's measurement history, and Vinbury's statement about his measurement "according to the rule." He accused the NYYC of a "self-serving" argument that the more races *Australia II* won, the more the NYYC deemed her "rated unfairly." Jones also specified the Race Agreement rule which provides that the Measurement Committee's decisions as to ratings shall be final, and that the Committee had reaffirmed the legality of the keel. But all that was prelude;

	ROUND ROBIN A			ROUND ROBIN B			ROUND ROBIN C			
	races	won	points (20%)	races	won	points (40%)	races	won	points (100%)	order
Australia II	12	11	2.2	12	10	4.8	16	15	19.8	1
Challenge 12	12	10	2.0	12	7	3.6	16	7	10.6	5
Victory	12	8	1.6	12	7	3.4	16	10	13.4	2
Azzurra	12	5	1.0	12	7	3.2	16	9	12.2	3
Canada	12	4	0.8	12	6	2.7	16	9	11.7	4
France	12	4	0.8	12	2	1.1	—	—		
Advance	12	0	0.0	12	2	0.8	—	—		

	SEMIFINALS				tot. elim. trials		FINALS	
races won	Australia II	Victory	Azzurra	Canada I	won	lost	Australia II	Victory
Australia II	X	2	3	3	44	5	X	4
Victory	1	X	2	3	31	18	1	X
Azzurra	0	1	X	3	25	24	—	—
Canada I	0	0	0	X	19	30	—	—

Above: John Kolius, at the helm of Courageous, *came from behind to beat stablemate* Defender. *Below: Tom Blackaller receives members of the selection committee following his elimination.*

the real blow came when Jones revealed that his syndicate had caught the Americans red-handed in trying to "purchase a non-American, Australian keel design, in clear violation of the 1980 Resolution of the Board of Trustees of the NYYC."

When the smoke cleared, this was apparently the story. Quite by accident, it appears, the *Liberty* camp learned that a Dutch engineer with the Netherlands Aerospace Laboratory — J.W. Slooff — had participated in the keel's design in Holland. In an effort to determine whether that work had indeed been done in violation of the requirement for wholly domestic design and construction of Cup contenders, Ed du Moulin, the *Liberty* syndicate manager, sent a telex to Dr. Peter van Oossanen, head of Design Research at the Netherlands Ship Model Basin, in Wageningen. This read, in part: "Understand that you and your team are responsible for development and design of special keel for *Australia II*. We are fully convinced of her potential and would therefore like to build the same design under one of our boats..." Whether the wording was chosen to elicit a confession by the NSMB that it was guilty of violating the 1980 Resolution, or was a naive way to get a keel designed, it gave Warren Jones all the ammunition he needed to counter-accuse the Americans of trying to use an Australian design on one of its Twelves. The chain reaction exploded.

The NSMB answered that it was under contract to Alan Bond until the completion of the 1983 Cup series, and that it could do no 12-Meter work for others. The NSMB informed the Bond syndicate of the du Moulin request and the Australians, no surprise, refused permission. Not satisfied, the Americans sent a delegation to NSMB — Wil Valentijn, an uncle of Johan Valentijn, and Tony van Rijn. On August 8 they first went to the Dutch patent office and found that Ben Lexcen had applied for a patent on the keel. On August 9 they met with Slooff, who, though reluctant to discuss the keel,

Courageous, modified and very well-handled, had excellent results, but in the end Liberty *pulled it off, to the great disappointment of the numerous admirers of John Kolius.*

was surprised to learn of the Lexcen patent application. Next day Valentijn and van Rijn had several meetings, ending with a discussion with van Oossanen from which they concluded "that the yachts *Australia II* and *Challenge 12* were actually designed in Holland with technical input by eight highly trained Dutch engineers, along with one Australian yacht designer (Lexcen), using the most sophisticated and up-to-date Dutch technology, leaving us in no doubt that the 12-Meters are actually Dutch."

This conclusion came despite van Oossanen's insisting that Lexcen was the group leader; that he had provided initial sketches for his keel design; that he had worked in Holland four months. But, the Dutch engineer admitted that his group had computer-tested several designs, then tank-tested full-size models of the best. They then used their computers to develop the best associated hull shape, draw the lines for the Twelve and even the templates for her lofting — the result was

Australia II. NSMB also designed computer systems and programs for *Australia II*'s performance analysis.

On August 24 van Oossanen again played host to the NYYC — this time Richard Latham was accompanied by Valentijn. The discussion became heated as Latham tried to press the Dutch into spelling out the extent of their work on *Australia II*, even to asking van Oossanen to sign an affidavit concerning the discussions of the first meeting. He refused, and the standoff continued. But Latham learned that the Dutch engineers were not aware of the national restrictions on design of America's Cup contenders. Warren Jones's revelation that the NYYC's Victor Romagna had approved their use of the Netherlands facility, embarrassing as it was to the NYYC, did not quite close the case. What did close it was the NYYC's announced withdrawal of all objections to the keel on August 26 because it had learned that the IYRU's Keelboat Technical Committee had already approved "winglets" more than one year earlier. A request for such approval had been submitted by Ian Howlett, designer of *Victory '83*, and the approval that followed specified that it would apply to the 1983 America's Cup. The British had apparently kept the approval secret in a game of one-upmanship while they (gleefully?) played with their own winglets; the IYRU kept it secret, and Tony Watts in particular, because of a confidentiality standard on these matters (though in this case it was carried to an absurd extreme).

With the keel question out of the way, it would seem that the racing could resume untainted. But yet another controversy arose, this one among the Americans, but which further embarrassed the NYYC. Unknown to the *Defender/Courageous* group, *Liberty* had been sailing the July trials under the aforementioned multiple rating certificates: one each for light, medium and heavy conditions. The system had the blessing of the NYYC. When the *Defender/Courageous* people learned of the tacit approval, they were furious, and not a little envious. After all, the system was not illegal; they had simply not thought of it, though both their Twelves had two certificates each.

The racing did resume. During the "C" challenger series, *Challenge 12* fell suddenly behind her pace, and *Canada 1* and *Azzurra* squeezed in ahead of her into the semifinals. *France 3* and *Advance*, with their abysmal records, were also mathematically eliminated.

In the semi-finals, *Canada 1* lost all nine of her races; *Azzurra* acquitted herself admirably as an underdog by winning four out of nine. The finals, which were the anticlimax of the long summer, were delayed three days for lack of wind. *Victory '83* surprised everybody by winning the first race against *Australia II* by thirteen seconds in winds ranging between 7 and 15 knots. Her win prompted the dockside joke that *Australia II* was "sandbagging" to make her keel seem less threatening to the Americans (Conner publicly confessed his fear of the keel). But *Australia II* did not "sandbag" the next

Liberty and stablemate Freedom *sailing back into harbour after one of the many exercise races. Even in the final against* Australia II *Conner wanted to have his sparring partner on hand for last minute fine-tuning.*

four races, which she won easily to become the clearly favored challenger.

In the defense Final trials, *Courageous* made her move. With a new inventory of sails — delayed because of a shortage of Kevlar sailcloth — she showed a new burst of speed. *Defender*, on the other hand, took a drubbing from both her opponent and stablemate and was excused from racing on August 27 with a dismal 1-9 record.

In the eight races that followed *Defender*'s elimination, all but two were abandoned before being finished, to allow for more races each day, and to permit the syndicates to continue learning from experiments with winglets on *Defender* and *Freedom*. *Liberty* won both races and was ahead in four of the abandoned ones. The NYYC Selection Committee, wishing to give the defender ample time to tune and to make a decision on winglets, excused *Courageous* on Friday, September 2.

Immediately, the competitive spirit between the finalists was turned toward winning the Cup; the *Courageous* camp offered all the help it could give including its new carbon fiber boom, and the final week before the challenge became the Americans' last opportunity to prepare for the defense with vigor and dignity, leaving scandal far behind.

By the eve of the Cup series, *Freedom*'s winglets — level, as opposed to the canted ones on *Australia II* — had proven little (as had winglets on *Defender, Victory '83* and her sparring partner *Australia*). These desperate trials proved that Lexcen's design of *hull and keel* gave *Australia II* her speed and manoeuvrability, and that add-ons would serve no useful purpose.

With all the failed Twelves retired and the two selected yachts inspected and prepared for the first race, their crews retired for a last, long night's rest. Elsewhere in Newport, pre-race parties blared late into the night; then, in the pre-dawn darkness the great constellation of Orion, the hunter, rose silently over sleepy Newport.

The 1983 Challenge

After all the effort and after the long summer British-born Australian multi-millionaire Alan Bond and his crew of jolly swagmen have carried off America's most coveted yachting trophy. *Australia II*'s skipper John Bertrand has done what many Americans thought would be impossible and never believed would ever happen. America is in a state of shock. Half a world away, Bond's countrymen sat through eight hours of nail-biting televised hell and then drank their way through a sea of alcohol to celebrate the victory. Prime Minister Hawke was the first to open a floodgate of well-wishers' accolades on the one-time signwriter who had made and lost a million at twenty-six and swore he would one day bring home the "Auld Mug".

It was also the first time in the history of the event that the finals had stretched to the full seven races. Earlier, most observers had predicted that following Conner's first win with *Liberty* over the Australian challenger, the finals would go to four races, an easy win for the man considered to be probably the world's top match racing skipper. Neither they nor the American camp had allowed for mistakes which would be made by Conner as well as Bertrand over the next six races.

On September 5, Australian syndicate manager, Warren Jones, told a press conference after *Victory '83* had been eliminated in the challenger trials, that he thought the final America's Cup races would go to all seven for the first time in the event's 132 year history. Few believed he would be proved right, except those who knew better.

Evidence that the long hot summer of '83 was almost over for sailors and residents of Newport came in a chilly northeaster gusting to over 20 knots on September 14 after a postponement due to shifty winds the previous day. The wind blew and kicked up a nasty short chop in the Sound, conditions to which Dennis Conner's defender was ideally suited and which resulted in probably the closest fought race since the series between Australia's *Gretel* and the American yacht *Weatherly*.

At the start, promptly at 12.10 local time, *Liberty* had the edge, but Conner was not so far to weather of the challenger as he would have liked and Bertrand, with the aid of the magic keel, was able to pinch and pinch, forcing Conner to tack away and allowing *Australia II* through to leeward after some eight minutes of racing.

For the next four miles, only seconds separated the two yachts. At the first mark, *Liberty* tailed the challenger by eight seconds, about two boat lengths, and by the end of the first reach to the second mark, the lead had increased only by a mere two seconds. Conner was playing a waiting game watching for the mistake which could provide a gate. It came soon enough. Bertrand sailed too low, allowing *Liberty* to sail over the Australians' wash and take the wind. At the leeward mark, the defending yacht had effectively notched up an advantage of twenty-six seconds to be ahead by sixteen at the mark. In retrospect, it is possible that the Australians could have regained the lead, for on the square run the challenger had once more moved up into a threatening position only a boat's length from *Liberty*. It looked as if they were all set to blow past. At that instant, a steering cable sheave failed as she tried to nudge under *Liberty*'s stern and gain the advantage of the inside track. The rudder gone, it was all Bertrand could do to keep the boat under control with the trim tab. She luffed sharply and then crept uncertainly around the leeward mark. It was enough to give Conner back a half minute lead. At the finish, the American boat was up 1'10''. One down and three to go.

Promptly at 12.10 the following day, in conditions similar to the first day's racing, the two yachts began a tacking duel that ushered in another exciting contest. After an aggressive pre-start run-around, the Australian boat on starboard crossed at the committee boat end of the line, well up to weather and only a few seconds behind Conner's *Liberty*. But Bertrand was already in trouble. The mainsail headboard had torn away from its boltrope in the 17 knot winds. While the main flogged, the Australian skipper managed to keep the yacht pointing high enough and, moving faster than the defender, at the first mark Conner was lagging. The wind was dying as both boats hunted the shifts, *Liberty* falling further astern as *Australia II*'s mainsheet trimmer Colin Beashel was hoisted aloft to effect repairs on the headboard. At the jibe mark, Conner had gained fourteen seconds on his rival and got some more when Bertrand,

On the preceding page: at last, Australia II *and* Liberty *are face-to-face for the twenty-fifth America's Cup challenge, which turned out to be the race of the century.*

still not happy with the way the main was setting, hoisted his repair man to the truck for a second time.

Conner played the shifts and, on the second weather leg after a series of some eighteen tacks in a still dying breeze, squeezed under the Australians' bow so close on starboard that the challenger later filed a protest under Rule 41. Bertrand had made the fatal mistake earlier in the leg of not covering his opponent, opting while ahead, to stay on a long starboard tack to gain from a series of lifts. So the positions were now almost exactly reversed as Conner increased the lead from zero to thirty-one seconds as *Liberty* went into the final leg of the course. The wind had died to around 10 knots. Holes pock-marked the course and while there could have been one or two close encounters, Conner pushed *Liberty* to a convincing 1'33" win at the line.

It was beginning to look as if the Warren Jones' prediction might turn sour. The protest concerning *Liberty*'s manoeuvres under the bow of the challenger had been overruled by the special five-man jury at a hearing which lasted almost $6^1/_2$ hours.

On September 17, racing commenced once more. Spectators lined the course in their thousands, in anticipation perhaps of something big. But it was not to be. What they got was a drifting match in two to three knot puffs, the last of which finally expired at 17.25 local time when *Australia II* was ahead of *Liberty* by an incredible 5'57" — almost 6 minutes! Conner's neck had been saved by the time limit.

The following day, with high hopes of a repeat performance within the time limit, the Australian challenger crossed the start line on starboard to leeward of *Liberty*, which although credited with an eight second advantage was so far over the committee boat end of the line she was forced to luff around *Black Knight*'s anchor. It cost Conner the race.

At the first mark, the challenger was 1'14" ahead,

It is now Liberty's *turn to suffer damage: just before the fifth race two men were hoisted to repair a broken jumper strut. Below:* Liberty *being cheered after one of her wins.*

having sailed that leg in thirteen tacks, one fewer than *Liberty*. On the two reaching legs, Dennis Conner was able to retrieve some of the ground he had lost. However, by the time the race was over, John Bertrand had managed to build a margin of 3'14", the biggest margin for a win by a challenging yacht in cup history. A deafening roar of sirens blasted across the sunset waters of Rhode Island Sound. Street parties erupted in Newport as the news and the noise filtered through.

After the Australian win, the Americans called a lay day, using it no doubt to reflect upon the words of Alan Bond at the outset of the series, "the one who makes the least mistakes will be the winner."

Thus armed, Conner and his crew went forth with but one intent. To show Australia and the world that all was not lost. For once the wind had steadied more or less southwesterly and at the start was up to over 10 knots with a good possibility of a steady increase. Having cleared the challenger's bow by a mere fifteen feet. On port tack, *Liberty* held on, covering Bertrand's every move while refusing to be drawn into a duel. Slowly but surely Conner increased the lead to six lengths by the first mark. On the reaching legs, the margins stayed roughly the same but Bertrand was forcing Conner to work hard to maintain that lead. Twice the challenger came hard on Conner's heels only to be forced under the defender's stern. And while *Australia II* may have gained an inch or two on the square run and even seemed to be level with *Liberty* at one point on the last upwind leg, it was Conner's day. The score was 3-1.

Psychologically, the defeat at that stage of the game would have been enough for most to give in. *Liberty* needed only one more win and the "Auld Mug" would stay firmly bolted to its pedestal in the trophy room of the New York Yacht Club.

In a gusting 18-22 knots southwesterly, challenger and defender both had serious problems for the fourth race. *Liberty*, which had started the day with *Freedom* in practice, broke a port jumper-strut an hour before the official start. The essential strut hydraulically controlled upper mast tension. The VHF airwaves fairly buzzed with clipped military back-and-forths as a frantic search for spare parts got underway. Crew members Tom Rich and Scott Vogel were sent aloft to cut off the offending strut and effect repairs. Not the easiest of tasks under the prevailing conditions, but they managed it, with two minutes to spare before *Black Knight* hoisted the warning signal for a race. As she swung into the starting area, *Liberty*'s jib appeared to have ripped down the luff tape as it was being hoisted in the last minute panic. Another was set, but by now *Australia II* was practically sitting on top of the defender, flying a protest flag. Five minutes before the off Bertrand had been squeezed off to leeward, and crossed the line early to be recalled. It gave Conner a 37" edge which on any other day in moderate conditions would probably have given the Americans the race.

On the average, Conner proved to be a better helmsman than Bertrand at the starts. In the fifth race he did, in fact, force his opponent into starting ahead of time.

However, the defender was crippled as Conner later conceded. Four minutes into the race and the same jumper-strut broke again and while *Australia II* inched up to close the gap, still some forty odd seconds astern, Conner opted for a nineteen minutes port tack. After nearly half an hour, the two yachts were almost level and at the first mark *Australia II* had regained her lost time plus another 23".

Liberty seemed to be coping well on starboard, but each time she came over to port the mast slot and the main hung like a limp sheet.

Try as he might, Conner could not catch the challenger and in weather that by rights should have given him the race. Had it not been for the defective strut things might have been different. *Australia II*, now on the final leg, added seconds with each new tack. At the line the margin was 1'47" — a decisive and much needed victory for the Australians.

The next day a galloping 20 knot northwesterly sent

A historic moment: on the square leg of the last race Australia II *made up fifty-seven seconds and passed* Liberty: *it is here that the America's Cup changed hands.*

Flying her battle standard, a kangaroo with boxing gloves, Australia II *is given a hearty welcome after her well-deserved victory, which broke the longest winning streak in sporting history.*

the opponents into battle for the sixth time, only the third occasion in the history of the event that such a race had been necessary. Wearing moderate weather mainsails and no. 4 genoas the two yachts played the shifts. It was Bertrand who got the best of it and Conner who failed once more to cover. *Australia II* came from behind twenty-eight minutes into the race to take the lead. At the first mark the difference was 2'29''. Conner held on and clipped one second off *Australia II*'s lead at the jibe mark, by which time the wind had risen again.

There was nothing Conner or *Liberty* seemed to be able to do except nibble a few seconds here and there. *Australia II* was revelling in the wind shifts and the fiercer breeze. If earlier indications had been that *Australia II* was a light weather boat, here was proof indeed that she could romp away in conditions most would have said only favored the defender. Barring further gear failures, *Australia II* looked set to shake up the records. At the second weather mark she led *Liberty* by 3'22''. The

wind was still increasing but the American skipper could only watch and Bertrand coaxed every ounce of speed from his yacht. There would be no ''blowing by'' this time for *Liberty*. At the final weather mark, *Australia II* had opened up the gap to a staggering 4'8'' and although she lost some ground to the defender on that last lap, the result was a 3'25'' lead at the finish.

Even-stevens. For the first time in 113 years of challenges the long tradition of unbroken defenses looked seriously threatened. Never before in the history of the event had seven races been necessary to decide the winner. Only twice before, in 1920 and 1934, had the event gone to six races.

The question now on everyone's lips was simply: ''Can Bertrand pull it off?''

However, this was all a matter for conjecture until the final race was won. The grand finale had been scheduled for Saturday, but too shifty and too fickle a wind forced a cancellation. Seizing the opportunity to carry out fur-

ther fine-tuning on the defender, the Americans immediately called for, and were granted, a lay day.

It was at this point in the proceedings that Mr. Alan Bond revealed the attempt by a frogman to sabotage *Australia II*'s keel by stringing a line to which were attached a number of plastic bags across the entrance to their dock. The anonymous swimmer was seen clambering ashore on a pontoon some half-mile away when the booby trap was discovered prior to Saturday's scheduled departure from the dock.

September 26, 1983, dawned clear and fine, with a crisp snap signalling the end of summer and the beginning of a fine New England fall.

A 6 knot breeze had steadied by 11.50 hrs. when course signals were hoisted above *Black Knight*. Up went the sails as the respective crews made decisions on which to use for the pre-start manoeuvres. But then, 2¹/₂ minutes before the scheduled off, up went the postponement flag, the wind had shifted or lulled, or both. No one was sure which. You could have cut the air with a knife, the tension around the course was electrifying. Both yachts had broken manoeuvres and jilled around waiting for the next preparatory signal. It came at 12.45 for a 13.05 start.

Then they were off. Conner led by eight seconds, but the Australian boat was better placed at the pin end of the line. Bertrand eased ahead in the shifting breeze to get on top of the defender by four boat lengths after some twenty minutes of racing. While Conner gradually eased across the course to get under *Australia II*, Bertrand let the American go. A fatal mistake, for when the two next came together *Liberty* crossed ahead. The defender built on the lead until, at the first mark, she was 28'' ahead. The wind had increased very slightly as *Liberty* went into the first reach and slowly began to pull ahead. Around the jibe mark and back down to the America's Cup buoy *Australia II* gained some so that, by an hour and forty minutes into the race, *Liberty*'s

Above: surrounded by hundreds of boats, Australia II *is about to be hoisted. Below:* Australia II*'s keel with the bulb and side fins painted blue to make it invisible through the water.*

197

Alan Bond (right) and John Bertrand with the Cup.
Below: Dennis Conner, with tears in his eyes, gives the bitter
account of the last race. On the opposite page: Australia II.

lead had, in fact, been cut to a mere 23 seconds.

Now the wind freshened and shifted as *Black Knight* approached to indicate a new course. Some twenty minutes later, Bertrand took *Australia II* to the port hand side of the course and, once again, Conner failed to cover his opponent. It seems he was intent on hunting the wind shifts. He was lucky, and by the second weather mark he had increased the lead to 57''.

Bleary-eyed Australians glued to their silver screens back home as satellites beamed in the live pictures must have watched in horror as *Liberty* seemed to edge away. Conner must have been well-pleased with his strategy and decided that was the option to go for even if it meant slackening what little cover he was already giving to *Australia II*. As *Liberty* went into the fifth leg with nearly a minute's lead, the wind shifted again making the best run down the course on port jibe. Bertrand followed, but instead of sticking to Conner's wake he shot off to an area of darker water to the right. By the time Conner and his crew had realised that Bertrand had got *Australia II* moving again, it was too late. The American tried desperately to cross, hoping that *Australia II* would sail into the defender's wind shadow. *Australia II* sailed by and into a historic 21'' lead at the mark. From that point on there was no stopping and Bertrand made sure that he covered each of the forty-seven tacks it took to reach the finish line. 41'' was all Australia needed to end the longest winning streak in the history of any sport.

At a short and quietly dignified ceremony in one of Newport's famous mansions, the Vanderbilt's Marble House, the grand prize of yachting, together with the four-foot-long bolt which had held it in place in the New York Yacht Club for more than a century, was handed over to Alan Bond. The recipient's only regret was that he had not been given the chance to unbolt the Victorian silver ewer from its pedestal with a solid gold wrench he had had specially made.

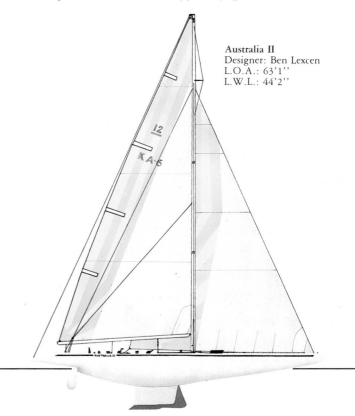

Australia II
Designer: Ben Lexcen
L.O.A.: 63'1''
L.W.L.: 44'2''

	date	wind (mph)	start	finish
Liberty	9/14	18	h. 12.10.08	h. 15.35.50
Australia II			h. 12.10.05	h. 15.37.00
Liberty	9/15	17/13	h. 12.10.08	h. 15.58.14
Australia II			h. 12.10.13	h. 15.59.47
Australia II	9/18	7/10	h. 14.00.10	h. 17.50.34
Liberty			h. 14.00.02	h. 17.53.48
Liberty	9/20	10/15	h. 12.10.07	h. 15.39.24
Australia II			h. 12.10.13	h. 15.40.07
Australia II	9/21	18/16	h. 12.10.43	h. 15.39.56
Liberty			h. 12.10.06	h. 15.41.43
Australia II	9/22	12/19	h. 12.10.21	h. 15.41.36
Liberty			h. 12.10.14	h. 15.45.01
Australia II	9/26	8	h. 13.05.16	h. 17.20.45
Liberty			h. 13.05.08	h. 17.21.26

BIBLIOGRAPHY

The sources for this history of the Cup are many and varied, ranging from *The Diary of Philip Hone*, which provides a clear picture of New York social life when John Cox Stevens was one of its leading figures, to Don Russell's biography of the Earl of Dunraven's hunting guide, Buffalo Bill Cody, to those historian's stand-bys, *The Dictionary of National Biography* and *The Dictionary of American Biography*. The scrapbooks in the library of the New York Yacht Club (assembled by Mr. Sohei Hohri and his equally distinguished predecessors) contain just about every word ever published in the leading English language newspapers about the Cup. In addition to consulting those clippings and many general books, I used quite a few yachting histories on the shelves of the yacht club's magnificent library, some of which were unexpected mines of rich information. For example, Charles H.W. Foster's privately published history of the Eastern Yacht Club, *The Eastern Yacht Club Ditty Box*, is the source of the accounts of Charles J. Paine's sly tactics and assiduous attention to detail, and a brief history of the Royal Sydney Yacht Squadron's nineteenth-century flirtation with the Cup can be found in P.R. Stephenson's *Sydney Sails*.

Several books about the Cup and sailing were especially helpful and should be mentioned and commented upon. *The Yacht America* (Boston, 1925) is the definitive history of that great yacht written by Winfield M. Thompson, William P. Stephens, and William U. Swan. Thompson also wrote the historical sections of *The Lawson History of The America's Cup* (Boston, 1902), which covers the early matches in patient detail. John Parkinson Jr.'s two-volume *History of the New York Yacht Club* (New York, 1975) describes the main actors in the Cup's history — and not always with blind praise. In *The America's Cup: An Informal History* (London and New York, 1980), the English yachting historian Ian Dear offers some interesting new information about the challengers over the years. *The America's Cup Races*, by the editors of *Yachting* magazine, (New York, 1970) is the longest history, and the most fair as well. John Leather's *The Big Class Racing Yachts* (London, 1982) and Ian Dear's *Enterprise to Endeavour: The J-Class Yachts* (London and New York, 1977) offer considerable fascinating detail about the big yachts that sailed in the early twentieth century. Harold S. Vanderbilt wrote two brilliant (and at times poetic) books about his successful defenses in the 1930's: *Enterprise* (New York, 1931) and *On the Wind's Highway* (New York, 1939). Even more revealing about how a Cup campaign evolves is an assemblage of first-person accounts of *Intrepid*'s triumphal year in 1967, *Defending the America's Cup*, edited by Robert W. Carrick and Stanley Z. Rosenfeld (New York, 1969). Of the many books that have been written about the 12-Meter matches, Bob Bavier's *America's Cup Fever* (New York, 1981) offers the best view of the people, boats, and controversies involved on all sides. Bavier describes the design parameters in language that any sailor can understand. For a more analytical look at yacht design — as well as pages and pages of well-informed observation — see the best of all yachting histories, William P. Stephens' *Traditions and Memories of American Yachting*. First published as a long series of articles in *Motor Boating* magazine between 1939 and 1946, it is now available in one volume published by International Marine Publishing, Co., Camden, Maine.

PHOTO CREDITS

Allain Frederic: p. 11.
Beken of Cowes: pp. 13, 16 (bottom), 26, 42 (top), 42 (bottom), 46 (top), 49, 51, 52, 61 (bottom), 74 (top), 77, 78, 81, 82, 84 (top), 89, 93, 95, 103 (bottom), 109, 117.
Besana Davide: p. 1, sail plans and burgees.
Black Alastair: pp. 126 (top), 126 (bottom), 133, 134 (top), 134 (middle), 138 (right), 159.
Borlenghi Carlo: pp. 186 (bottom), 187.
Bottini Margherita: Cover photo, pp. 148 (bottom), 149 (top), 150 (bottom), 154 (top), 155 (left), 155 (top and right), 160 (top and bottom), 161 (top and right), 162 (top and bottom), 167 (bottom), 173 (bottom), 174 (top), 175 (bottom), 177, 178 (top), 180 (bottom), 182, 186 (top).
Cavalli Angelo: pp. 179 (left), 180 (top).
Dreyer Lois: backflap.
Ferrari Renato: pp. 15, 28 and plates hors text.
Forster Daniel: pp. 120, 134 (bottom), 139 (right), 140 (left), 140 (right), 151 (top), 166 (top), 171, 173 (top), 178 (middle), 184.
Grace Arthur: p. 190
Hopf/Gallimard: p. 96.
From *The Lawson History of the America's Cup*, Boston, 1902: pp. 9, 14, 16 (top), 17, 20, 27, 29, 34.
Levick Collection, Courtesy of the Mariner's Museum, Newport News, Virginia, U.S.A.: pp. 46 (bottom), 54, 60, 61 (top), 68, 69, 70 (top), 74 (bottom), 76, 80, 84 (bottom), 86, 87, 88.
The Thomas Lipton Collection, the Mitchell Library, Glasgow,
Scotland: pp. 64, 65 (top and bottom), 70 (bottom), 72, 75.
Lipton Export Library: p. 58.
Mystic Seaport Museum, Mystic, Connecticut, U.S.A.: pp. 19 (top), 19 (bottom), 21, 25, 47, 57, 59, 66, 67, 71, 73.
The National Maritime Museum, London, Great Britain: pp. 23, 24, 30.
Nerney Dan: pp. 105, 111, 122 (right), 125, 128, 130, 135, 136, 138 (left), 139 (left), 143, 146 (top), 147 (bottom), 148 (top), 149 (left), 150 (left), 150 (right), 151 (bottom), 154 (bottom), 156, 157 (bottom).
New York Yacht Club Collection: p. 43.
From the *Paine Burgess Testimonial*, Boston, City Council, 1887: pp. 3, 37, 38, 40, 41, 45.
Pyle Barbara: pp. 185 (top and bottom), 188, 189 (top) 191, 192, 194 (bottom), 195, 196 (left and right), 196 (right), 197 (top and bottom), 199.
Rannou Thierry: pp. 165, 166 (bottom), 167 (top), 168 (left), 168 (right), 169, 172 (top), 172 (bottom).
Ratti Fabio: p. 163
Richard François: pp. 145, 149 (right), 153, 157.
Rosenfeld Stanley: pp. 48, 53, 56, 63, 91, 94 (left and right), 97, 98, 99, 100, 101, 103 (top), 108 (bottom), 110, 112, 118.
Ross Bob: p. 161 (left).
Schweikardt Eric: pp. 107, 108 (top), 113, 114, 115, 123, 131.
Tenin Barry: pp. 141, 189 (bottom).
Villarosa Riccardo: pp. 12, 62, 121 (left), 127 (top and bottom), 179 (top), 179 (right), 181, 194 (top), 198 (top and bottom).